BLACK SUBJECTS

BLACK SUBJECTS

Identity Formation in the Contemporary Narrative of Slavery

ARLENE R. KEIZER

Cornell University Press

Ithaca and London

Portions of *Black Subjects* have been previously published as follows:
An earlier version of chapter 1 appeared in *African American Review* 33.1:105–23.
A portion of chapter 5 appeared in *American Literature* 72.2:387–416.
Segments of the conclusion appeared in *Michigan Quarterly Reivew* 40.2:431–36.

First published 2004 by Cornell University Press
First printing, Cornell Paperbacks, 2004

Printed in the United States of America

Design by Scott Levine

Library of Congress Cataloging-in-Publication Data

Keizer, Arlene R.
Black subjects : identity formation in the contemporary narrative of slavery / Arlene R. Keizer.
p. cm.
Includes bibliographical references and index.
ISBN 0-8014-4095-5 (cloth : alk. paper) — ISBN 0-8014-8904-0 (pbk. : alk. paper)
1. American fiction—20th century—History and criticism. 2. Slavery in literature. 3. Caribbean literature (English)—History and criticism. 4. Walcott, Derek. Dream on Monkey Mountain. 5. Identity (Psychology) in literature. 6. African Americans in literature. 7. Slave trade in literature. 8. Blacks in literature. I. Title.
PS374.S58K45 2004
813'.5093552—dc22

2004001133

Cornell University Press strives to use environmentally responsible suppliers and materials to the fullest extent possible in the publishing of its books. Such materials include vegetable-based, low-VOC inks and acid-free papers that are recycled, totally chlorine-free, or partly composed of nonwood fibers. For further information, visit our website at www.cornellpress.cornell.edu.

Cloth printing   10 9 8 7 6 5 4 3 2 1
Paperback printing   10 9 8 7 6 5 4 3 2 1

This book is dedicated to my beloved mother
Annette R. Keizer
and to my beloved mentor and friend
Barbara T. Christian
(1943–2000)

Oh, we have paid for our children's place in the world
again, and again . . .

Dessa Rose, SHERLEY ANNE WILLIAMS

So it is important to undo whatever words obscure the fact that slave law was at least as fragmenting and fragmented as the bourgeois world view—and in a way that has persisted to this day, cutting across all ideological boundaries. As "pure will" signifies the whole bourgeois personality in the latter, so wisdom, control, and aesthetic beauty signify the whole white personality in the former. The slave-master and the burgermeister are not so very different, when expressed in those terms. The reconciling difference is that in slave law the emphasis is really on the inverse rationale: that irrationality, lack of control, and ugliness signify the whole slave personality. . . . In my search for roots I must assume, not just as history but as an ongoing psychological force, that irrationality, lack of control, and ugliness signify not just the whole slave personality, not just the whole black personality, but me . . .

To look is . . . to make myself vulnerable; yet not to look is to neutralize the part of myself that is vulnerable. I look in order to see, and so I must look. Without that directness of vision, I am afraid I shall will my own blindness, disinherit my own creativity, and sterilize my own perspective of its embattled, passionate insight.

PATRICIA J. WILLIAMS, *The Alchemy of Race and Rights*

The themes, then, that I wish to pursue here are centered on the relation between the writing of history as prediction and as retrospection. The history that will be is, after all, as much how we recount what happened as how we project a future; the history that will be is, inevitably, a history of the present, that divided site that must look both ways at once.

JONATHAN GOLDBERG, "The History That Will Be"

Contents

ACKNOWLEDGMENTS

Many people and institutions deserve thanks for their contributions to the development of this book. My gratitude first goes to the project's initial readers: VèVè Clark, David Lloyd, and especially Barbara Christian, who was my adviser, guide, and advocate through every stage of my graduate education. I am also grateful to the friends and colleagues, now dispersed, who constituted my intellectual community at the University of California, Berkeley: Gloria Bowles, Isabel Bradburn, Anne Cheng, M. Giulia Fabi, Peter Lurie, Barry Maxwell, Alberto Perez, Caroline Streeter, Theresa Tensuan, and Shelley Wong. They offered extensive comments on chapters as well as warm and humorous companionship. Eithne Luibheid has always been an especially generous and careful reader and an excellent sounding board. In addition to providing an insightful analysis of my manuscript, Simon Gikandi shared his expertise in theory, strategy, and tactics with me. I appreciate the emotional support Alan Wald offered me during a critical stage in the life of this project.

A remarkable group of feminist writers and scholars at the University of Michigan read and commented on my work and created a "female world of love and ritual" for me: Carol Bardenstein, Frieda Ekotto, Jacqueline Francis, Sandra Gunning, Anita Norich, Ifeoma Nwankwo, Eileen Pollack, Yopie Prins, Suzanne Raitt, Valerie Traub, and Patricia Yaeger. Carroll Smith-Rosenberg's intellect, wit, elegance, and generosity have helped to sustain me and continue to serve as a profound source of inspiration. (Quotation is the sincerest form of flattery.) Lorna Goodison helped to keep the spirit of poetry alive in me when it was failing. She is a light. I also thank Carol Hollenshead, feminist administrator extraordinaire. I'm just glad she's on *my* side! The grit and mother wit of the women of WOCAP (The Women of Color in the Academy Project) have enabled me to see academia "through my lens," a critical skill. Marianetta Porter's art works and our rich conversations gave me a new window into this project in its late stages, and I express my gratitude to her for allowing "Many Thousands Gone" to appear on the cover. The photographs of enslaved men and women featured in "Many Thousands Gone" were taken by the nineteenth-century photographer C. T. Zealy, and they are reproduced here by permission of the Peabody Museum at Harvard University, where they now reside. This book owes an enormous intellectual and spiritual debt to the work of Hortense Spillers and Sylvia Wynter. If they had not so fabulously invented themselves, we would have had to invent them.

I thank Tobin and Jill Siebers for hosting the wonderful First Draft forum, where I presented a version of chapter 5. I hope I haven't forgotten anyone who provided me information along the way, including Mieke Bal, Matt Biro, K. Ian Grandison, Martha Jones, Mervyn M. Keizer, Jr., Mervyn M. Keizer, Sr., Jack Kerkering, Elaine Kim, Fernando Lara, and Katrin Pahl. I also thank Madhu Dubey, Farah Griffin, Carla Peterson, and Valerie Smith for their support of my work. I learned an enormous amount through teaching this material, and, in discussions with the energetic and engaged graduate students in my Winter 2000 seminar, "History, Memory, and Subjectivity in Contemporary African American and Caribbean Literature," I discovered many of the nuances of my argument. Conversations with three graduate advisees and research assistants in particular—Clare Counihan, Shani Mott, and Shawan Wade—have enriched and complicated my ways of thinking about these literary texts and critical theories.

Support from a variety of funding sources also facilitated the completion of this work. An American Fellowship from the American Association of University Women (AAUW) supported me during the 1995–1996 academic year at Berkeley. A Michigan Faculty Fellowship (2000–2001) from the Institute for the Humanities at the University of Michigan gave me time away from teaching to complete the book manuscript. A Spring/Summer Research Grant from the Rackham School of Graduate Studies and a Career Development Award from the College of Literature, Science, and the Arts, both at Michigan, allowed me to employ the graduate student researchers I came to refer to as my research angels: R. Scott Heath, Lydia Middleton, LaTissia Mitchell, Jocelyn Stitt, and Kelly Williams.

Cornell University Press and especially my editors Catherine Rice and Teresa Jesionowski deserve thanks for their meticulous work and accommodating style. I also appreciate and have responded to the comments offered by the two anonymous readers of my manuscript.

Special thanks:
Kimberlyn Leary knows all my secrets and has promised not to tell. I would not have finished this book without her help. The late Lemuel Johnson,

my beloved colleague, applied his capacious and incisive intellect to my manuscript-in-progress, and it is a better book as a result. May perpetual light shine on him. Marlon Ross knew where I was going with this book before I did and helped me to get closer to my ideal. For more than twenty years, Valentina Vavasis has been the best, most supportive friend I can imagine, and I look forward to at least forty more years of ridiculously long telephone conversations. I carry my family with me always; they will find my love for them hidden in these pages.

ARLENE R. KEIZER

Ann Arbor, Michigan

BLACK SUBJECTS

INTRODUCTION

"THE MIDDLE PASSAGE NEVER GUESSED ITS END"

New World Slavery in Contemporary Literature

Slavery haunts contemporary African American and Afro-Caribbean literature. As we begin the new millennium, as U.S. and Caribbean slavery recedes further into the past, it seems to loom larger in the black literary imagination. Yet the history of slavery is not merely a nightmare from which contemporary, New World black writers are trying to awaken; instead, the "peculiar institution" serves as a catalyst and site for theories about the nature and formation of black subjectivity. In an interview published in 1993, Toni Morrison noted,

> Slavery wasn't in the literature at all. Part of that, I think, is because, on moving from bondage to freedom which has been our goal, we got away from slavery and also from the slaves[;] there's a difference. We have to re-inhabit those people. ("Living Memory" 179)

Morrison's contention that "slavery wasn't in the literature at all" is not technically true, but not until the last third of the twentieth century did a large body of African American and Caribbean literature seek to consider the conditions for identity formation under slavery and to examine closely the identities thus created.

Black Subjects argues that contemporary black writers in the United States and the Anglophone Caribbean are intervening in a theoretical debate about identity in the African diaspora through representations of slavery. Rather than viewing contemporary literary works solely as texts to which established theories can be applied, I contend that these literary works themselves theorize about the nature and formation of black subjects, under the slave system and in the present, by utilizing slave characters and the condition of slavery as focal points. In each chapter, a theory derived from fictional works is examined in light of more established theories of subject formation, such as psychoanalysis, Althusserian interpellation, performance theory in relation to identity, and theories, such as Fredric Jameson's, about the formation of postmodern subjects under late capitalism. Black writers' theories of identity formation, which arise from the particularity and variety of black experience, re-imagined in fiction, force us to reconsider the conceptual bases of established theories of subjectivity. Called upon to take into account the subject coming into being on the margins, European and Euro-American theories of subjectivity can and must be transformed. My analysis of African American and Caribbean critical/theoretical formulations reveals the variety of ways in which theory can be articulated and demonstrates how theories from New World black cultures dovetail with, critique, or diverge from mainstream theories of subjectivity.

The Contemporary Narrative of Slavery

A wide variety of works belong to the group I have designated "contemporary narratives of slavery"; these texts fall into three major categories: (1) the historical novel of slavery (*Beloved, Cambridge, Oxherding Tale*); (2) works set in the present which explicitly connect African American/Afro-Caribbean life in the present with U.S./Caribbean slavery (*The Chosen Place, The Timeless People, Corregidora, Dream on Monkey Mountain*); and (3) hybrid works in which scenes from the past are juxtaposed with scenes set in the present (*An Echo in the Bone, Thereafter Johnnie*). Numerous critics have commented on the fact that "novels about slavery have appeared at an unstoppable rate" (McDowell 144) from the late 1960s to the 1990s, yet the critical literature has not kept pace with this outpouring of fiction. In *The Afro-American Novel and Its Tradition* (1987), Bernard Bell coins the term "neoslave narratives" to refer to these fictions, which he defines as "residually oral, modern narratives of escape from bondage to freedom" (Bell 289); he devotes a short section of his literary history to analyzing and establishing a genealogy of these works. *Slavery and the Literary Imagination*, a ground-breaking collection of essays edited by Deborah McDowell and Arnold Rampersad (1989), analyzes both slave narratives and twentieth-century novels of slavery. A more recent anthology, *Black Imagination and the Middle Passage*, edited by Henry Louis Gates Jr., Maria Diedrich, and Carl Pedersen (1999), contains critical essays that deal specifically with the legacy of the trans-Atlantic slave trade in nineteenth- and twentieth-century African American literature. Ashraf Rushdy's *Neo-*

Slave Narratives: Studies in the Social Logic of a Literary Form (1999) was the first full-length study of a group of contemporary narratives referencing slavery. Rushdy defines "Neo-slave narratives" as "contemporary novels that assume the form, adopt the conventions, and take on the first-person voice of the antebellum slave narrative" (Rushdy 3). He analyzes these contemporary versions of the first-person slave narrative form, registering the ways in which these novels revise the classic slave narratives in light of the social and cultural changes wrought by the Black Power and Black Arts Movements.

In contrast to Bell and Rushdy, I refer to these works as "contemporary narratives of slavery" to cast a wider interpretive net than either of these critics do with their nearly identical neologisms. (Rushdy is, of course, borrowing and refurbishing Bell's term.) The influence of U.S. and Caribbean slavery upon contemporary black literature is much greater than Bell and Rushdy acknowledge. Though Bell's definition is more inclusive than Rushdy's, it nevertheless limits the scope of these works because of its focus on the movement from enslavement to freedom, the trajectory of the traditional slave narrative. Rushdy focuses even more narrowly on the influence of the antebellum slave narrative, analyzing only those contemporary novels that clearly and explicitly reference nineteenth-century, first-person, literate slave testimony. Though a number of writers are directly addressing the slave narrative, others simply take the form for granted as a precursor to a twentieth-century discourse on slavery. Contemporary writers' views of slavery are certainly informed by slave narratives and their speaking silences, yet many writers move so far beyond the traditional narratives that their works are not bound by that frame of reference. It is striking, for example, how few contemporary narratives of slavery are written in the first person.[1]

As I was completing this book, two other critical books addressing contemporary narratives of slavery by African American women writers appeared: Elizabeth Beaulieu's *Black Women Writers and the American Neo-Slave Narrative* (1999), and Angelyn Mitchell's *The Freedom to Remember* (2002). Beaulieu's analysis focuses on the authors' creation of strong female characters for whom motherhood is a source and site of resistance to the slaveocracy. She argues that the female-authored "slave narrative of the late twentieth century is the inevitable literary outgrowth of both the civil rights movement and the feminist movement" (Beaulieu 4). Mitchell coins the term "liberatory narratives" (4) to refer to those works whose goal is, in her words, "to engender a liberatory effect on the reader" (6). Her contention is that these late-twentieth-century narratives go beyond their nineteenth-century forerunners by analyzing the concept, nature,

and problems of freedom. One of her most resonant points is that intertextuality in the liberatory narrative is a method of encoding memory
(17). She reads Harriet Jacobs's *Incidents in the Life of a Slave Girl* as an in-
tertext for all of the female-authored contemporary narratives she analyzes (as well as reading the contemporary narratives as intertexts for one
another). While both of these works contribute important insights to the
growing discourse on the contemporary narrative of slavery, their insis-
tence on focusing solely on narratives by women is a significant drawback.[2]
While the approaches of contemporary black male and female writers to
the subject of slavery may differ markedly—and my study details a number of those differences—I contend that these works belong to the same,
still-developing subgenre. Mitchell's definition of the liberatory is constructed in such a way that it excludes male-authored narratives, though
many (including authors like Ishmael Reed and Charles Johnson themselves) would argue that their novels are very much intended to liberate
the reader. In addition, there are a number of female-authored narratives,
such as *Corregidora* and *Thereafter Johnnie,* that would not qualify as liberatory, either for their characters or their readers. Beaulieu sees black wom-
en's narratives as being explicitly opposed to male-dominated civil-rights
and black-nationalist discourse (as well as white-feminist discourse), and,
while I concur in many respects, it remains clear that, in their return to
slavery, contemporary black novelists and dramatists are participating in
a literary movement that crosses gender lines. In *Black Subjects,* I have constructed the category of contemporary narratives of slavery as inclusively
as possible, while indicating a variety of ways in which this rubric is internally divided.

Furthermore, these conceptualizations of the neoslave / Neo-slave / liberatory narrative have failed to take into account the diasporic reach of
this literary form.[3] Caribbean and Black British writers have also turned
back toward slavery as a touchstone for present-day meditations on the formation of black subjectivity. For practical reasons, this study deals only with
contemporary narratives of slavery from the United States and the Anglophone Caribbean, but it is necessary to recognize that these narratives have
emerged from every site in the diaspora where people of African descent
are present in significant numbers. Despite the very different sociopoliti-
cal geographies of the United States and the former English colonies in
the Caribbean, contemporary narratives of slavery from both locations are
participating in the discovery and production of counterhistories to destabilize the official history imposed by colonial and neocolonial powers.
Throughout the chapters, I have noted the important differences between
U.S. and Caribbean narratives, but it is this search for and construction of

counterhistories that informs their overwhelming similarities. As Edouard Glissant asserts in *Caribbean Discourse,*

> One of the most disturbing consequences of colonization could well be this notion of a single History, and therefore of power, which has been imposed on others by the West. . . . We begin to realize that as much as the stages of the class struggle or the growth of nations, the profound transformation of mentalities in this regard creates the possibility of changing the world order.
>
> The struggle against a single History for the cross-fertilization of histories means repossessing both a true sense of one's time and identity: proposing in an unprecedented way a revaluation of power. (93)

Like Afro-Caribbean history, African American history was submerged under the totalizing narrative of Western history until very recently. Part of the argument of *Black Subjects* is that the contemporary narrative of slavery is a literary form through which writers of African descent in the Americas are attempting to reclaim a "true sense of [the] time and identity" of the black diasporic subject.

In *Cultural Trauma: Slavery and the Formation of African American Identity,* Ron Eyerman argues:

> Without the means to influence public memory, blacks were left to form and maintain their own collective memory, with slavery as an ever-shifting, re-constructed reference point. Slavery has meant different things for different generations of black Americans, but it was always there as a referent. It was not until the 1950s, even the 60s, that slavery moved outside group memory to challenge the borders, the rituals, and sites of public memory. (18)

This critical insight helps to explain the genesis of the contemporary narrative of slavery. But it is my contention that an even more powerful psychological factor also drove the development of this literary form. The contemporary narrative of slavery began to take shape at precisely the moment that the last of those who had experienced New World slavery first-hand passed away. The questions of who would be a witness to slavery and how it would be remembered became critical at the moment this first-hand experience disappeared from living memory. Two of the earliest contemporary narratives of slavery from the United States, *Jubilee* (1966) and *The Autobiography of Miss Jane Pittman* (1971), are explicitly based on the memories of African American elders. Margaret Walker's memory of her grandmother's stories about slavery is the foundation of the former novel; Ernest Gaines's *Miss Jane Pittman* is structured around the tape-recorded memories of the title character beginning in slavery and continuing up to the Civil Rights Movement. In George Lamming's *In the Castle of My Skin* (1953), the memory of slavery is maintained by the oldest member of the community, Pa, and he recounts the story of his and the community's enslavement on his deathbed. Memory in these texts clearly functions as a counter-history to mainstream U.S. and Caribbean historiography about slavery, which, until the 1960s, had little to say about individuals' experiences of bondage.

The moment at which the last survivors of a cultural trauma die is a critical juncture for the culture in question. Memories of the traumatic event are available in written or tape-recorded form only, and in the "postmemory" of descendants of the survivors. Marianne Hirsch employs the term "postmemory"[4] to refer to the secondary memories of events absorbed by the children of survivors of trauma. (Hirsch's work deals specifically with the Holocaust.) She writes,

> I use the term *postmemory* to describe the relationship of children of survivors of cultural or collective trauma to the experiences of their parents, experiences that they "remember" only as the stories and images with which they grew up, but that are so powerful, so monumental, as to constitute memories in their own right. The term is meant to convey its temporal and qualitative difference from survivor memory, its secondary or second-generation memory quality, its basis in displacement, its belatedness. Postmemory is a powerful form of memory precisely because its connection to its object or source is mediated not through recollection but through projection, investment, and creation. That is not to say that survivor memory itself is unmediated, but that it is more directly connected to the past. Postmemory characterizes the experience of those who grow up dominated by narratives that preceded their birth, whose own belated stories are displaced by the stories of the previous generation, shaped by traumatic events that they can neither understand nor re-create. ("Projected Memory" 8; original emphasis)

African American and Anglophone Caribbean writers, from the mid-1960s on, have been writing from the space of postmemory with regard to slavery. This fact is made explicit in Walker's "How I Wrote *Jubilee*"; in fact, Walker's family stories about slavery were, for Walker herself, third- or fourth-generation memories. Even when these writers were not dealing with memories of slavery in their own families, all of them were grappling with the difficulty of addressing a trauma that was constitutive not only of numerous features of African American and Afro-Caribbean everyday life and thought, but of contemporary economic, social, and political arrangements as well. Individually, African American and Afro-Caribbean subjects were faced with the question of how one constructs a subjectivity in relation to postmemory. If, as Hirsch argues, the children of survivors "can neither understand nor re-create" the experiences that engendered their postmemory, how can the creative artist break through that veil to release herself or himself and the culture from the traumatized "acting out" of responses to violent and dehumanizing acts in the past?[5] The writers whose works are examined in this study have devised a brilliant array of answers to this question.

The twentieth-century literature of slavery has developed in close connection with the new historiography of slavery in the United States and the Caribbean. As Hazel Carby argues in "Ideologies of Black Folk: The Historical Novel of Slavery," Arna Bontemps's *Black Thunder* (1936), a fictionalized account of the Gabriel Prosser revolt, "prefigures Afro-American historiography in the late sixties and seventies, which would focus on the slave through slave testimony" (137). For *Jubilee*—generally acknowledged to be the first contemporary narrative of slavery in the United States— Margaret Walker spent years doing historical research, which she combined with her own grandmother's stories of Walker's great-grandmother's life in slavery. From the mid-sixties on, African American historiography has focused more and more upon the everyday lives of slaves; works like John Blassingame's *The Slave Community* (1972), Angela Davis's essay "Reflections on the Black Woman's Role in the Community of Slaves" (1971), Herbert Aptheker's *American Negro Slave Revolts* (first published in 1943 and re-issued in 1963), and Eugene Genovese's *Roll, Jordan, Roll: The World the Slaves Made* (1974)—as well as sociological works like Orlando Patterson's profoundly influential *Slavery and Social Death* (1982), which placed U.S. and Caribbean slavery in the context of slave societies all over the world—provided new historical methods, information, and analyses, thus facilitating the transformation of the contemporary narrative of slavery into a body of literature focused on the formation of black subjectivity. For example, as historian Nell Irvin Painter argues in "Soul Murder and Slavery: Toward a Fully Loaded Cost Accounting," the application of modern psychological analyses to slave psyches has proven and will prove extremely fruitful, notwithstanding the extensive problems with one of the first attempts in this direction, Stanley Elkins's 1959 history, *Slavery: A Problem in American Institutional and Intellectual Life* (137–8).

A similarly reciprocal interaction between the writing of literature and history has taken place in the Caribbean. In the twentieth-century Caribbean historiography of slavery and resistance, C. L. R. James's remarkable history of the Haitian Revolution, *The Black Jacobins* (1938), set a high early standard, which was taken up in the late sixties and early seventies by works like Patterson's *The Sociology of Slavery* (1967), Edward Kamau Brathwaite's *The Development of Creole Society in Jamaica, 1770–1820* (1971), and historical essays on the Maroons collected in Richard Price's *Maroon Societies* (1973). George Lamming's *The Pleasures of Exile*, a series of literary and cultural critiques published in 1960, drew together James's analysis of the Haitian Revolution with an interpretation of *The Tempest* as a template for the colonial encounter between master and slave, colonizer and colonized. As Rob Nixon argues in "Caribbean and African Appropriations of *The Tempest*," a number of Caribbean writers from the 1950s through the 1970s "seized upon *The Tempest* as a way of amplifying their calls for decolonization within the bounds of the dominant cultures" (Nixon 558). Thus a literary character, revised and appropriated for anti-colonial purposes, became an integral part of the Caribbean discourse of revolution. In both the United States and the Caribbean, the historiography, sociology, and literature of slavery developed together and facilitated one another, and works from the two regions have often responded to one another. As several scholars have noted, history "from the bottom up" helped to create literary works focused on the psychic lives of the enslaved.

The past and the present are also linked in this literature by the necessity of resistance. In response to the physical, social, and psychological forces brought to bear upon them as slaves, Africans and their New World descendants managed to create resistant selves and communities, and it is primarily this spirit of resistance that black writers in the Anglophone Americas, up through the mid-1960s, recorded and re-imagined in their narratives of slavery. The rebel slave came to symbolize black agency within the slave system, and the theme of resistance structured most African American and Anglophone Caribbean literature about slavery. In the United States, this theme was established primarily through the slave narrators and their written narratives, which, in the eyes of many critics, function as the founding documents of African American literature. The oral tradition and the recovery of oral histories of slavery have also been a focus of this literature. In the Anglophone Caribbean, the theme of resistance has been established through the use of Shakespeare's Caliban, through references to the Maroons (the most successful rebel slave communities) and the Haitian Revolution, and through images of the rebel slave in oral and popular culture. As Carby argues in the article cited above, "a narrative of slave rebellion can be read as a figure for the revolutionary change that has not come. [C. L. R.] James, in the context of colonial politics, and [Arna] Bontemps, in the context of American oppression, were representing the collective acts of a black community as signs for future collective acts of rebellion and liberation" (140).

The figure of the rebellious slave is thus particularly important to an investigation of the black subject, because the black slave in rebellion against white domination is the prototype for a black resistant subjectivity, a founding model of African American and Afro-Caribbean subjectivity. As a response to the overvaluation of direct, armed slave resistance or successful escape, the contemporary narrative of slavery demonstrates how fraught with difficulty resistance is and has been. In fact, one of the signal characteristics of these works is their problematization of resistance. These texts never question the need to struggle against a system that has consistently subjugated people of African descent, but the means through which such resistance can be carried out are closely examined and the contradictions inherent in certain modes of resistance are evaluated. For example, in *Oxherding Tale,* Andrew Hawkins's punching of the woman who keeps him in sexual servitude can be read as a parodic revision of Frederick Douglass's famous fight against Edward Covey. *Beloved*'s Paul D attacks the man to whom schoolteacher has sold him, an attack that does not verify his manhood but instead it places him in a much more desperate situation—working on a chain gang—where the threat of sexual abuse from the white guards threatens his manhood even further. In *The Chosen Place, The Timeless People,* the history of slave revolt as a promise of "future collective acts of rebellion and liberation" (Carby 140) is held in suspension; the islanders have been unable to find an effective means of collective revolt in the present. In general, contemporary African American and Caribbean writers have begun to treat resistance as a variety of strategies that come with their own problems, rather than as a straightforward solution. Furthermore, contemporary narratives of slavery consistently question the equation of overt resistance with black subjectivity; that is, they demonstrate that visible acts of resistance are not the sole signs of black agency and encourage us, as contemporary readers, to assume full and complex personhood in the enslaved and recently freed. Morrison's character Sethe performs acts of self-affirmation that could never have been articulated in a slave narrative. Permitted to choose her own sexual partner from amongst the Sweet Home men, both by the Garners' investment in "liberal" slaveholding and the black men's sexual restraint, she decides on Halle. Deprived of a state- or church-sanctioned ceremony and any of the trappings that attend such ceremonies, she crafts a dress for herself from household scraps that must later be returned to their proper places. Her will to feel herself a bride and to create, with Halle and the other slaves, a ceremony that will mark her move from girlhood to womanhood is an assertion of agency too small to have been registered in the political self-representation necessary in the slave-narrative genre. In "The Site of Memory," Morrison discusses her desire to reconstruct the "interior life" of the slave, saying, "My job becomes how to rip that veil drawn over 'proceedings too terrible to relate'" (302). In performing that task, she has also brought to life the acts that were simply too small to relate within the larger goal of the abolitionist movement, but were critical to the self-creation of black individuals and communities. These are fictions that must stand in for what we cannot know but must assume to be true, in order to believe in our own humanity in the present. I will return to this point later.

Most contemporary narratives of slavery also contest progressive visions of African American history as a relatively simple, though hard-fought, movement "up from slavery" to black middle-class life. Alex Haley's *Roots* (1976)—the most widely read (and seen, in the film version) contemporary representation of slavery—was just such a progressive narrative; virtually all African American and Caribbean writers who have addressed slavery in fictional works in the 1970s, '80s, and '90s have written against this progressive line and called attention to the deep social contradictions begotten during slavery and still with us. A case in point is Carolivia Herron's *Thereafter Johnnie*, which, in its apocalyptic nature, goes far beyond most modern and contemporary African American novels in its rejection of a narrative of progress. This novel recalls the fire-and-brimstone vision of David Walker's *Appeal* (1830), where Walker warns of divine retribution for the crimes of slavery and racism. The return to a vision of cataclysmic disaster is almost certainly a product of the current social and economic situation for African Americans, in which legal changes have not brought about equality yet are nevertheless being revoked. A similar situation exists in the Anglophone Caribbean, where the islands are technically no longer colonies but continue to labor within the cultural, social, and economic spheres of colonial powers, old and new. In both locations, the recognition of continuing oppression that has deep roots in history is responsible, in large part, for a resurgence of interest in the ways in which black subjectivities were formed in response to the clear and brutal oppression of slavery.

Theorizing Black Subjectivity

These complex representations of resistance support my contention that, in the wake of the Civil Rights Movement in the United States and anti-colonial movements in the Caribbean, black writers' orientation to slavery has undergone a sea change. Rather than using representations of slavery primarily to protest past and present oppression—this is how slavery had figured in most African American and Caribbean works up through the early 1960s—black writers have begun to represent slavery in order to explore the process of self-creation under extremely oppressive conditions. These writers have begun, in Morrison's words, "to re-inhabit those people," to focus on the interiority of the slaves' experiences. The effects of this major change in the representation of slavery are at least twofold: establishing that black identity in the Americas, from slavery to the present, has never been a fixed essence, either biological or cultural, but instead consistently marked by fragmentation and differentiation; and forcing a rethinking of the unitary black subject that white-supremacist and black-nationalist ideologies find necessary for their mobilization in the present.

The primary argument I make in *Black Subjects* is that contemporary black writers' representations of slavery can be read as theoretical and that one can examine these fictionalized theories (as I call them) alongside established theories of subjectivity. Since 1903, when W. E. B. Du Bois coined the term "double-consciousness" to describe the divided identity currently embodied in the designation "African American," black intellectuals have carried on a public discourse about what we now refer to as black subjectivity. In recent years, literary and cultural studies of African American and Caribbean expressive forms have combined this ongoing theoretical discussion of black identity with critiques of the human subject that question the possibility of a fixed, unitary identity. Critic Paul Gilroy characterizes the opposing perspectives in the current debate as, on the one hand, a group that sees black culture "as the expression of an essential, unchanging, sovereign racial self," and, on the other hand, a group that "affirms blackness as an open signifier and seeks to celebrate complex representations of a black particularity that is *internally* divided: by class, sexuality, gender, age, ethnicity, economics, and political consciousness" (*Black Atlantic* 36, 32). *Black Subjects* shows how a number of contemporary African American and Caribbean writers have charted a middle course between these two extremes—avoiding the complete reification of race on the one hand and its virtual eclipse on the other. Through their representations of slaves, these writers have managed to destabilize blackness as a biological or cultural essence, while maintaining a sense of the integrity of creolized black cultures in the Americas and showing how black subjectivities are produced and contested within these cultures.

As Rushdy convincingly argues in *Neo-slave Narratives,* many of the novels referencing slavery from the vantage point of the 1970s, '80s, and '90s are, at least in part, responses to the politics and aesthetics of the late '60s and early '70s Black Power Movement. Though my genealogy of these works differs from Rushdy's—for instance, I read Styron's *The Confessions of Nat Turner* (1967) as an irruption into a discourse already in formation rather than as a major catalyst—his analysis of these works in the context of the Black Power and Black Arts Movements allows us to see how the writers whose works he analyzes, and a wide range of other black writers, were building upon the gains of these movements, while critiquing the essentialism and the fixed teleology of black identity posited by some of the movement's most vocal representatives. As a more meditative/theoretical discourse on slavery has come to replace a protest-oriented discourse, the idea that one could determine a fixed black identity, in the past, the present, or the future, has been challenged more and more consistently. Yet all of these writers stop short of arguing for the abolition of black identity altogether. African American and Afro-Caribbean literature continues, therefore, to be grounded in a lived experience of blackness, both in terms of cultural formations and figurations by the dominant culture. Cultural integrity without essentialism is figured in the past to guarantee its existence in the present and the future.

My contention that these fictional works theorize black subjectivity and thus participate in a theoretical debate is, admittedly, polemical; as a claim, it is neither self-evident nor unassailable. I have used a variety of means to establish two critical points with regard to each literary work: (1) that the text is explicitly concerned with subjectivity/subject formation, and (2) that the text examines subjectivity/subject formation in a sustained fashion, such that one can argue convincingly that the work has an identifiable approach to identity and the means by which it is achieved. In many cases, I have used authors' statements in interviews and essays to demonstrate how consciously and deliberately they have set out to address black subject formation. But even without these specific articulations of engagement or intent, a focus on the creation of black individual and communal identities is easily discernible in the narratives this study analyzes in depth—prose fiction and drama from the late 1960s to the present.

In *Beloved,* musical improvisation functions as a means of self-fashioning for African Americans emerging from slavery. The dismembering logic of bondage is counteracted through individual and communal composition and performance of work songs, the blues, and secularized sacred music. Charles Johnson's postmodernist fictions of slavery, "The Education of Mingo" and *Oxherding Tale,* theorize the African American male slave as, on the one hand, a Frankenstein-like creature constructed by the white male master, and, on the other hand, an almost infinitely Protean everyman. The Manichean worldview derived from plantation slavery and represented in the Caribbean Anancy tales is critiqued in *Dream on Monkey Mountain;* and the main character, Makak, passes through a Eurocentric stage and an Afrocentric stage to arrive at a self-identification as a "cultural mulatto" (Olaniyan, "Corporeal" 165). Paule Marshall's main characters in *The Chosen Place, The Timeless People,* Merle Kinbona and Vere Walkes, are fragmented, migratory Caribbean subjects constructed through the complex routes of global capitalism. Finally, in *Thereafter Johnnie,* spatial representations are used to demonstrate the construction of black female subjectivities under white and black patriarchy. Incestuous sexual abuse perpetrated by white and black fathers upon their black daughters is represented as a circumstance through which black female identities are created, both in slavery and in the present.

The literary texts themselves suggested the established theories that I analyze alongside their fictionalized theories. Morrison's interpretation of slavery as capitalist and her explicit concern with the mechanisms—both coercive and consensual—that slaveholders used to construct and control black men and women call to mind Louis Althusser's theory of interpellation, articulated in "Ideology and Ideological State Apparatuses." Charles Johnson has written extensively about his engagements with Western and Eastern philosophy; thus, he himself has identified the body of theory with which his fictional work is consistently concerned. Derek Walcott's *Dream on Monkey Mountain* foregrounds the mechanics of drama, like Japanese Noh theater or the plays of Brecht. *Dream*'s fusion of a narrative of identity with performance that calls attention to itself as such prefigures arguments raised in performance theory of the 1980s and '90s. Paule Marshall's astute and direct critique of global capitalism and the ways in which it constructs damaged Caribbean subjects through its labor and education schemes broadens our contemporary understanding of the cultural effects of this stage of capitalism, articulated most notably in Fredric Jameson's *Postmodernism, or The Cultural Logic of Late Capitalism. Thereafter Johnnie*'s spatial obsessions mandate a reading of the novel's geography in tandem with social theories of space and place, and the novel's deployments and rebuttals of psychoanalysis (Western society's most fully elaborated theory of incestuous desire) likewise call for direct critical evaluation.

Clearly, other pairings of fictionalized and established theories are possible. For example, many critics have used the lens of psychoanalysis to examine the souls of *Beloved*'s black folk, especially Sethe; and Charles Johnson's engagement with Eastern, rather than Western, philosophy has been highlighted by several commentators on his work. Two priorities governed my selections. First, I wanted to examine contemporary narratives of slavery from all three of the categories I have identified, and from both the United States and the Caribbean—the sites of the African diaspora with the largest populations of African descent and the oldest and most influential diasporic literatures and cultures. My second aim was to juxtapose the major theories of subject formation circulating in the humanities with the various analyses of subjectivity emerging from contemporary black fiction and drama. In each pairing, I chose one of the least-traveled analytical routes, in order to highlight the literature's focus on subject formation and, more generally, to enlarge the critical conversation about these works.

Thus, my role as literary critic has been to stage direct conversations between fictionalized and established theories where these connections were implicit and to elaborate upon and critique the explicit theoretical debates taking place between creative writers and theorists. In the introduction to *Caliban's Reason: Introducing Afro-Caribbean Philosophy,* Paget Henry, Caribbean sociologist and philosopher, notes that many Afro-Caribbean intellectuals have been asking the question, "Where is our philosophy?" (xi). *Black Subjects* can be read as a response to the question, Where are our theories of subjectivity? Like Henry, in his analysis of the philosophical dimensions of critical and creative texts throughout the African diaspora, I have argued that what he calls "poeticism" (46) can be accorded the status of theory. As numerous feminist and anti-racist critics have pointed out, Western philosophies and theories of subjectivity have proven inadequate to an analysis of the formation of black subjects (especially black female subjects) because of their universalizing tendencies and sexist and racist biases. Yet, because one must begin with the tools one has, these theories have been used as starting points for analyses of subjectivity in African American and Caribbean literature and culture. *Black Subjects* brings African American and Caribbean theories of subjectivity together with European and Euro-American theories of subjectivity in a sustained conversation. My arguments are intended as interventions into a critical discourse that positions African American and Caribbean literary texts as "bodies" that can be illuminated and fixed in place by European and Euro-American theories operating as "minds."

It seems necessary in this context to address polarizing controversy that erupted around Barbara Christian's 1987 essay "The Race for Theory." Christian was a major proponent of the idea that African American fiction theorizes, and her work has had a significant impact on this study. Though "The Race for Theory" was clearly an attempt to expand our understanding of what constitutes theorizing, she was widely understood as dismissing "theory" altogether and pilloried for that ostensible dismissal. Postmodernist and poststructuralist conceptual frameworks—those theories about which Christian was sounding the alarm—have in some cases proved useful for my analyses here; in some cases they have not. While I share Christian's concern about the hegemony of these theoretical perspectives in the academy, I feel strongly that a refusal to engage these theories constitutes a missed opportunity. What I have tried to demonstrate in *Black Subjects* is the sometimes conflictual, sometimes fruitful interaction between theories derived from a variety of social and cultural standpoints.

Where I disagree with Christian most is around her contention that people of African descent theorize in fiction because this medium is a more comfortable or natural one; I find this claim both essentialist (as many have argued) and unnecessary to her larger argument.[6] Any number of black diasporic thinkers, beginning in the nineteenth century, have written theory-as-such, despite the fact that their work has rarely (until recently) been thought of in this way. From the moment African American and Afro-Caribbean cultures developed an economic base and political autonomy sufficient to support formal intellectuals, these intellectuals have produced formal theories. I argue that this fiction is another site of theorizing because of my somewhat old-fashioned belief in imaginative writers (and other artists) as weather vanes of the cultures they inhabit—they tell us which way (and how hard) the social and cultural winds are blowing. Fiction writers, dramatists, and poets, it seems to me, arrive on the scene of cultural transformation first, and those who create traditional theory appear later, examining and commenting upon the primary interpretations produced by witnesses. This pattern has held true in every major phase of African American and Afro-Caribbean history, from (at least) the late nineteenth century to the present. Acknowledging these witnesses, these writers, as critical intellectuals is a first step toward according their fictions the status of theory. Finally, it should be clear that, while these literary works theorize, they are not reducible solely to theoretical constructs; their other properties as art are undiminished.

In the excerpt from "The History That Will Be" quoted as an epigraph to this book, Jonathan Goldberg addresses the critical issues raised by "the relation between the writing of history as prediction and as retrospection" (4–5). African American and Caribbean writers have been considering these issues for the past forty years. The project in which writers of contemporary narratives of slavery are engaged is nothing less than that of representing a new black subject. Just as writers of the Harlem Renaissance registered the existence of a "New Negro" in their works, so these post-Civil-Rights and postcolonial writers are signaling the emergence of a "newer Negro,"[7] a black subject whose range of potential identities is greater than at any other time in U.S. and Caribbean history. That contemporary African American and Anglophone Caribbean writers have returned to the past in their attempts to both recognize and fabricate new black subjectivities may at first seem counterintuitive. Yet this study will demonstrate that the meditation on the past in the contemporary narrative of slavery is also an attempt to theorize and shape the future. For a number of contemporary African American and Afro-Caribbean writers, representing the broadest range of black subject positions under slavery enables the representation of the myriad black subjectivities of the present and the future.

A comparison of these fictional representations of slavery and its legacy with contemporary historical/cultural-studies perspectives further highlights the imaginative work of cultural reconstruction these narratives perform. One such work, Saidiya Hartman's *Scenes of Subjection,* is a compelling analysis of the conditions of possibility for black subjectivity in the antebellum and postbellum eras. Given what we know about the legal and social constraints on black agency in this period, and given the fragmentary (though potent) evidence of everyday practices of resistance, Hartman asserts that we cannot assume slave agency when we examine slave culture. She writes,

> Is it possible to consider . . . the agency of the performative when the black performative is inextricably linked with the specter of contented subjection, the torturous display of the captive body, and the ravishing of the body that is the condition of the other's pleasure? . . . How is it possible to think "agency" when the slave's very condition of being or social existence is defined as a state of determinate negation? In other words, what are the constituents of agency when one's social condition is defined by negation and personhood refigured in the fetishized and fungible terms of object of property? (52)

Given the same conditions, most contemporary black writers assert that we can and, indeed, must assign agency and personhood to those in bondage and those emerging from it. For writers living with slavery as a postmemory, assuming agency on the part of the enslaved appears to be a psychological and textual imperative.

Thus, when considered in light of contemporary narratives of slavery, Hartman's theoretico-historical analysis appears strikingly anomalous. With very few exceptions, contemporary African American and Afro-Caribbean creative writers have chosen to represent enslaved or recently freed subjects who are far more self-possessed and aware of their identities and their immanent power than would seem possible from Hartman's interpretation. Regardless of what it might be realistic to assume was possi-

ble for blacks in the final decades of the nineteenth century, black fiction
writers and dramatists have chosen to represent enslaved and recently
freed blacks as subjects with agency, often basing their works on fragmentary but suggestive historical accounts. As contemporary literary critics,
historians, and creative writers, we can never really know what it felt like to
inhabit an enslaved body; whether or not such complex personhood was
available to slaves is a question that we cannot, in the present, actually answer. Yet these fiction writers seem to be telling us that denying the possibility of such agency to the enslaved and recently freed constrains our own
sense of agency in the late-twentieth and early twenty-first centuries. These
texts seem to be saying that we need to imagine those ancestors as psychically free if we are to imagine ourselves as psychically free. None of these
texts is invested in a realist re-creation of slavery; even Marshall's *Chosen
Place*, which seems to be a realist novel, represents the folk history of slavery as mythic, its signal details repeated in a ritualistic fashion. These narratives are very clearly attempting to re-imagine the past for the benefit of
the present and the future, regardless of the dismal realities that may have
made these fictional identities virtually impossible.

As black writers' fictionalized theories of subjectivity are, necessarily, at-
tentive to race, they are also necessarily gendered; and their gendered nature is a critical aspect of all of my analyses. A number of black feminist
scholars, especially Hortense Spillers and Nell Painter, have laid the
groundwork for my investigation of black subjects, especially black female
subjects, under slavery, using the tools of late-nineteenth- and twentieth-
century critical and psychoanalytic theory and reading them back into the
past. More generally, the ways in which some contemporary feminist theory has been able *both* to insist upon the importance of gender as a category of analysis *and* to insist upon the problems of reifying gender have
provided a model for my thinking about the nature of race in the literary
texts under study.

Influenced by the "vernacular theories" of African American literature
and culture (pioneered by Houston Baker, Jr., and Henry Louis Gates, Jr.),
I use African American and Caribbean expressive forms to develop critical
models for reading the literature as a whole. There are at least two significant differences between my project and theirs, however: first, the theories derived from the literary works examined here cannot be termed
"vernacular"—they are the products of self-conscious intellectuals strug-
gling with the problem of black identity in the Americas; second, many of
the writers whose works are examined in this study are consciously in conversation with established theories of subjectivity.

My method has been both literary-critical and theoretical, offering close readings of fictional works and analyses of the ways in which these works function as and interact with theory-as-such. These literary/theoretical analyses are supplemented by analyses of other African American and Caribbean cultural products and practices, including folktales, the blues, calypso, Carnival, and African-based religions, because both literatures have been influenced so profoundly by the music, folklore, and spiritualities of the cultures from which they have emerged. By addressing Caribbean and African American literary works, *Black Subjects* broadens the scope of the discussion of the contemporary narrative of slavery and makes it clear that the goal of re-imagining black subjectivity through slavery is and has been a diaspora-wide objective.

Each chapter of *Black Subjects* not only investigates a different approach to incorporating slavery into contemporary fictions but also interrogates dominant notions of how subjects in the West have historically been constituted. Chapter 1, "*Beloved:* Ideologies in Conflict, Improvised Subjects," explores this novel's representation of the conflict between European American, white-supremacist, capitalist patriarchy and the broken system of communal West African cultural beliefs and practices under the U.S. slave system and in its immediate aftermath. I contend that, after showing the forces that compete to create the African American subject in the antebellum and Reconstruction periods, Toni Morrison goes beyond influential theories of ideology and interpellation (articulated by Althusser and followers) to demonstrate how black subjects invent themselves out of the conflict between ideologies, using musical improvisation as a means of self-fashioning.

Chapter 2, "Being, Race, and Gender: Black Masculinity and Western Philosophy in Charles Johnson's Works on Slavery," analyzes the importance of slavery to Johnson's critical engagement with philosophers ranging from Hobbes to Merleau-Ponty. Because of his abiding interest in philosophy, and his belief that philosophy and literature are "language in its two analytic forms" (*I Call Myself* 110), Johnson uses slavery as a site for staging a complex series of arguments about the formation of subjectivity in general and black subjectivity in particular. In theorizing the enslaved African American as representative man, Johnson also constructs profoundly negative representations of women, and my argument in this chapter is that these negative images are driven by the Enlightenment and post-Enlightenment philosophies to which he responds in his fiction based on slavery. In order to critique the black-white binary latent (and sometimes blatant) in the philosophical discourse on Being, he returns to a masculine-feminine binary also embedded in these philosophical texts.

In chapter 3, "*The Chosen Place, The Timeless People:* Late Capitalism in the

Black Atlantic," I analyze Marshall's representation of the subject formation of Afro-Caribbean people in the era of multinational capital in light of Fredric Jameson's theories about subjects under late capitalism and the prevalence of "national allegory" in the literature of the "Third World." By constructing a theory of the movement of workers and global capital which places the Caribbean at its center, Marshall disrupts the teleological narrative in which the Third World is simply "behind" the First World in its development. This disruption enables a different reading of Caribbean literature and culture, one that recognizes the variety of modernisms and postmodernisms and the possibility that social forms answering this description may have emerged in the developing world at the same time that they emerged in Europe and the United States.

Derek Walcott's play *Dream on Monkey Mountain* has been read as a narrative that develops beyond a simple inversion plot—in which the colonized vanquishes the colonizer in order to take his place—into a narrative that offers the possibility of radical social transformation. In Chapter 4, "Performance, Identity, and 'Mulatto Aesthetics,'" I contend that Walcott, in calling attention to the ways in which Eurocentric, Afrocentric, and creolized identities are performed, anticipates aspects of contemporary performance theory as it relates to subjectivity. Yet, the gender dynamics of *Dream* limit the extent to which this work is able to envision a radically different society, one in which creolized aesthetics prevail over hegemonic Eurocentric or insurgent Afrocentric aesthetics. While Walcott deconstructs and reconstructs black male identity in the Caribbean, his representations of black female identity are static and reinforce the black woman's placement at the bottom of the hierarchy established by Western Europe.

Finally, chapter 5, "The Geography of the Apocalypse: Incest, Mythology, and the Fall of Washington City in Carolivia Herron's *Thereafter Johnnie*," analyzes geography and incestuous sexual abuse as means by which black female sexuality is constructed. Herron's novel, focused on the incestuous relationship between a middle-class black father and daughter in the present, also reaches back to the past to connect the twentieth-century incident of incest to a history of white slave owners sexually abusing the daughters they fathered with enslaved women. I contend that the main characters' formation as female subjects of patriarchy is inscribed in and through geography, specifically the geography of the nation's capital, and that Herron both invokes and critiques the psychoanalytic discourse on incest, using feminist psychotherapy to destabilize the Freudian view of incest as phantasmatic.

Mikhail Bakhtin has argued that "the most intense and productive life of culture takes place on the boundaries of its individual areas and not in places where these areas have become enclosed in their own specificity" (Bakhtin 2). *Black Subjects* maintains that literary representations of the figure of the slave—a figure positioned always on the boundaries of New World culture through both condition of servitude and race—provide especially fruitful sites for examining the multiple and often contradictory processes through which human beings in the modern and postmodern worlds come to identify themselves. If Atlantic slavery was indeed constitutive of modernity, as a number of critics argue, then African and African-descended slaves in the Americas were some of the first modern subjects. Understanding the construction and reconstruction of such subjects thus becomes critical not only for the study of black diasporic identities, past and present, but for the study of modern subjectivities in general.

BELOVED

Ideologies in Conflict, Improvised Subjects

My father, by his nature, as well as by the habit of transacting business as a skilful [*sic*] mechanic, had more of the feelings of a freeman than is common among slaves. My brother was a spirited boy; and being brought up under such influences, he early detested the name of master and mistress. One day, when his father and his mistress happened to call him at the same time, he hesitated between the two; being perplexed to know which had the strongest claim upon his obedience. He finally concluded to go to his mistress. When my father reproved him for it, he said, "You both called me, and I didn't know which I ought to go to first."

"You are *my* child," replied our father, "and when I call you, you should come immediately, if you have to pass through fire and water."

HARRIET A. JACOBS, *Incidents in the Life of a Slave Girl*

This excerpt from Harriet Jacobs's narrative is a striking depiction of dual interpellation in the U.S. slave system. Under North American and Caribbean slavery, slaves were being "called" by at least two competing systems: European American, white-supremacist, capitalist patriarchy and the broken system of communal West African cultural beliefs and practices.[1] Slave traders and slave masters were attempting to re-interpellate as slaves the already interpellated subjects of West African social, political, and religious systems; in other words, they were attempting to transform subjects into slaves. At the same time, they were attempting to interpellate from birth those of African descent born into slavery. In both cases, West African cultural mores and practices also were in operation, fostering a culture of resistance within the black community. By reading the conflict of interpellating systems in Toni Morrison's *Beloved,* I demonstrate how the novel intervenes in current debates about black subjectivity, helping to define a position for the black subject between essentialism and postmodern fragmentation.

Some critics may question my use of Louis Althusser's concept of interpellation—the process by which subjects are constructed by ideology—in the context of slavery. I recognize that invoking Althusser's theories of ideology and interpellation in the analysis of representations of a system more coercive and less consensual than modern, Western, industrial capitalism is controversial. However, it is my intention to highlight the capitalist aspects of the U.S. slave system, as Morrison does, and to note the operation of ideological state apparatuses in concert with consistent physical violence. The work of Orlando Patterson and other contemporary commentators on slave systems is a critical part of my analysis. In *Slavery and Social Death,* Patterson delineates the ideological means that all slave systems used to interpellate either captives or those born into the system. Patterson writes, "The arrogance of power knows no bounds, for the master desired too that the slave recognize his authority, as well as his right to dominate him. To the extent that he did, to that degree was he able to walk fearlessly into the desert with his slave. And the truth is that many masters succeeded" (36). This extra-coercive authority was secured through ideology, and Morrison's *Beloved* details this process as well as the slaves' resistance to it.[2]

In a number of interviews, Morrison has called attention to the fact that twentieth-century African Americans lost contact with the memory of slavery. In a conversation with Ntozake Shange, she says, "somebody forgot to tell somebody something,"[3] speaking of the ways in which African American parents and grandparents, especially in the post-World War II era, often refused to tell their descendants about the horrors of slavery, thus making it difficult for these children to imagine the lives their ancestors had lived. Furthermore, in the interview with Paul Gilroy quoted in my introduction, Morrison notes,

> Slavery wasn't in the literature at all. Part of that, I think, is because, on moving from bondage into freedom which has been our goal, we got away from slavery and also from the slaves[;] there's a difference. We have to re-inhabit those people. ("Living Memory" 179)

Beloved is obviously an attempt to "re-inhabit those people," to examine the identities of the enslaved as they moved "from bondage into freedom." Because Morrison is explicitly concerned with the formation of black subjectivity, both individual and communal, it is appropriate to compare her fictional representation of this process to contemporary theoretical writings about subject formation.

While numerous critics have used psychoanalytic theories as rubrics for analyzing *Beloved,* I have chosen a different approach. While I draw upon several of these psychoanalytic readings,[4] their focus upon Sethe's individual psyche and its recovery from trauma fails to address the novel's systematic analysis of U.S. slavery and communal, as well as individual, responses to it. Althusser's Marxist interpretation of the process of subject formation dovetails, in many respects, with Morrison's representation of the process by which slaves were positioned as such. Because slaves were intended to be marginal subjects, their hailing by ideology was often indirect, a critical point I will elaborate upon later. If in this context one examines *Beloved*'s representation of subjectivity-in-process, it is clear that the novel also challenges two significant assumptions that underlie Althusser's theory: the assumption of cultural homogeneity and the belief in most subjects' tacit consent to ideology's demands. Morrison's representation of slave/black subjectivity-in-process shines a light through the cracks that appear in Althusser's theory as soon as it is applied to an actual social formation.

As critics have noted, in *Beloved,* the capitalist, racial-caste system of American slavery operates by dismembering, both figuratively and literally, the body and spirit of the slave. The subjugated system of West African beliefs and practices—in which family members who have died are kept alive in memory through ritual observances and in which nature is an aspect of the Divine[5]—continues in its claim upon kidnapped Africans and also reaches out to their enslaved descendants. The sites at which these two systems come into conflict are the sites in which black identities are formed, maintained, and transformed.

It is through improvisation—a common element of West African verbal and musical styles infused into black New World culture by African captives and their descendants[6]—that the characters in *Beloved* psychically integrate themselves in the face of the white-supremacist, capitalist system that threatens to pull them apart. Morrison invokes the practices of verbal and musical improvisation as signs and expressions of African American selfhood and agency. Thus, after showing the forces that compete to create the African American subject in the antebellum and postbellum years, Morrison goes beyond canonical theories of ideology and interpellation to show how these subjects invent themselves out of the conflict between ideologies, using improvisation as a form of self-fashioning. Artistic expression allows African Americans to re-create and maintain their identities, in ways that their forced labor does not. In *The Black Atlantic,* Paul Gilroy writes,

> [I]n the critical thought of blacks in the West, social self-creation through labour is not the centre-piece of emancipatory hopes. For the descendants of slaves, work signifies only servitude, misery, and subordination. Artistic expression, expanded beyond recognition from the grudging gifts offered by the masters as a token substitute for freedom from bondage, therefore becomes the means towards both individual self-fashioning and communal liberation. Poiesis and poetics begin to coexist in novel forms—autobiographical writing, special and uniquely creative ways of manipulating spoken language, and, above all, the music. (40)

Gilroy clearly articulates the importance of artistic creation as self-creation in the African Diaspora. In *The Signifying Monkey,* Henry Louis Gates, Jr., comments on one of Frederick Douglass's descriptions of the slave songs and notes that the slave singers "were literally defining themselves in language, just as did Douglass and hundreds of other slave narrators" (Gates 67). Sethe, Paul D, Baby Suggs, and the black community of Cincinnati are the literary descendants of these self-defining slave singers (more than they are the descendants of Douglass and the other slave narrators). Their creations, though rarely acknowledged as art (or even artful) by nineteenth-century white mainstream society, were nevertheless artistic. As Morrison herself has said, "Black Americans were sustained and healed and nurtured by the translation of their experience into art, above all in the music" ("Living Memory" 181). In *Beloved,* the active discipline and play of improvisation, in verbal and musical expression (and in household arts), is what "re-members" the ex-slaves and allows them to live as free people, though still oppressed by intolerable memories of bondage and consistently dehumanizing treatment. Morrison's representations of slave and ex-slave characters creating and performing African American music, from field hollers to early blues, registers the profound importance of improvisational musical practices to the lives of those enslaved and those emerging from the trauma of bondage. By representing the unmaking and remaking of enslaved and newly freed individuals (and a community) through the practice of improvisation, Morrison provides an alternative model of interpellation, one that recognizes the variety of interpellating systems bringing their power to bear upon black subjects in the antebellum and Reconstruction eras and the responses through which these subjects construct themselves.

1. Divided Subjects

As *Beloved* begins, the former slaves Sethe and Paul D meet again after eighteen years of nominal freedom, time in which they have attempted to bury their memories of enslavement and its attendant violations. The "moments of being" by which the subjectivities of these once-enslaved characters have been formed are told in "rememory," the active process by which a memory "[c]omes back whether we want it to or not" (*Beloved* 14). For Sethe and Paul D, trying to survive in the present, the past is a dangerous undertow which threatens to drown them. Yet they must incorporate their past experience into their present lives in order to truly claim their freedom. Theirs is the struggle of the nominally free slave to remake her-/himself into an ontologically free subject. They have cut off the positive as well as the negative aspects of their histories; the knowledge that might sustain them spiritually is consigned to the same forbidden area as the knowledge that might destroy them. One of the major psychological imperatives for the free former slaves is to fill in the absences created by slavery—to reconnect with their ancestral pasts, their dead and living relatives and friends, and their own "conscious community of memory" (Patterson 5).

Schoolteacher's "Call"

In *Beloved,* schoolteacher is the primary representative and agent of white-supremacist, capitalist patriarchy in the era of slavery. His interpellations of Sethe, Paul D, Sixo, and Halle lead to rebellion, madness, and death. Schoolteacher's system operates by dismemberment, dividing the bodies and minds of the slaves into separate parts and evaluating them using "scientific" techniques. Dismemberment is both literal and metaphorical, and either way it produces an effect on the physical bodies of the slaves. Sethe first comes to understand her place in the slave system when she hears schoolteacher ask one of the nephews, "Which one are you doing?" and the boy answers "Sethe" in response. She stops to listen to what is being said about her and finds that schoolteacher is supervising his nephews as they catalog the "human" and "animal" characteristics of the slaves at Sweet Home. As Sethe recalls the event (mentally narrating it to Beloved), she describes her response:

> I commenced to walk backward, didn't even look behind me to find out where I was headed. I just kept lifting my feet and pushing back. When I

bumped up against a tree my scalp was prickly. . . . My head itched like the
devil. Like somebody was sticking fine needles in my scalp. (193)

This is a peculiar scene of interpellation, a case of the subject being called,
literally and figuratively, but also indirectly, by the voice of the master/
state.[7] Sethe's response is one of complete negation. She immediately begins walking in the opposite direction from the "call," without even taking
the time to turn around. Her body responds in the negative before her
mind has completely grasped the implications of schoolteacher's classifi-
cations.[8] Her scalp is still tingling when she asks Mrs. Garner about the
meaning of "characteristics" and fully comprehends schoolteacher's project.[9] Sethe's mental image of "somebody . . . sticking fine needles in my
scalp" registers her unconscious recognition of the experiments that
schoolteacher would, no doubt, like to perform on her.

While imposing his metaphorically dismembering ideologies upon the
Sweet Home slaves, schoolteacher also brings the repressive state apparatuses to bear with a vengeance. The inscription of the master produces a
physical effect on the body of the slave, and indeed, the "writing" of Sethe
is a prelude to the violent milking of her breasts and the beating in which
a "tree" is imprinted on her back. These vicious acts of inscription are articulations of the "American grammar" that Hortense Spillers identifies in
the article "Mama's Baby, Papa's Maybe": "the originating metaphors of
captivity and mutilation" which form a palimpsest over which the history
of African American life and cultural production is written (68). The
nephew "does" Sethe on paper before he "does" her in the barn, and she
is undone, dismembered, by both of these acts. This dismemberment is difficult to counteract. At the end of the novel, when Sethe has been ground
down by her memory's relentless re-enactments of her intolerable past and
by the demands of the vengeful, needy presence of the daughter she killed,
she is not sure that she can hold herself together. She wonders, "Will he
do it [will Paul D bathe her] in sections? First her face, then her hands, her
thighs, her feet, her back? Ending with her exhausted breasts? And if he
bathes her in sections, will the parts hold?" (272).

At other points in *Beloved,* it is clear that Sethe lacks a sense of herself as
a separate, distinct being. When she tells Denver the story of Denver's
birth, she refers to herself in the third person, calling herself "her children's mother" (30). Later in the story of Denver, Sethe repeats her exact
words to herself: "I believe this baby's ma'am is gonna die in wild onions
on the bloody side of the Ohio River" (31). At these crucial moments—
moments when she believes she is going to die—she consistently envisions
herself only as her children's mother, eschewing any identification of her-

self *for* herself. She also identifies her children as "parts" of herself—the only parts she wants to claim, parts that have not been "dirtied" by the violations perpetrated by the slave system and its agents. Sethe's murder of her daughter is an abbreviated suicide; she has to kill her children before she kills herself, to be sure that they will not live to be brutalized as she has been. This view of her children's lives as coterminous with her own demonstrates her lack of a bounded sense of her own identity. She is both shrunk down to nothing, finding it hard to say "I," and magnified, spread out across the lives of her four children.

Paul D is also dismembered by the new master's interpellations. After schoolteacher and the patrollers have lynched Sixo, they lead Paul D back to Sweet Home, discussing the fact that he must be sold.

> Shackled, walking through the perfumed things honeybees love, Paul D hears the men talking and for the first time learns his worth. He has always known, or believed he did, his value—as a hand, a laborer who could make profit on a farm—but now he discovers his worth, which is to say he learns his price. The dollar value of *his weight, his strength, his heart, his brain, his penis, and his future.* (226, my emphasis)

$900 is the price schoolteacher attaches to Paul D's parts; under this blatantly capitalist interpellation, indirect as in Sethe's case, Paul D cannot envision himself as whole. In order to keep himself sane through the events that follow his sale by schoolteacher, he maintains a compartmentalized self.

> After Alfred he had shut down a generous portion of his head, operating on the part that helped him walk, eat, sleep, *sing*. If he could do those things—with a little work and a little sex thrown in—he asked for no more. . . . (41, my emphasis)

He seals away the painful, significant events of his past in a metaphorical tobacco tin that takes the place of his heart. The tobacco-tin metaphor is a striking one, making it clear that Paul D sees his ruined heart as a product of slavery, as much as tobacco itself was. His life is circumscribed by commerce and it invades his body as well; he cannot imagine himself as whole with the symbol of his degradation lodged inside him. This passage also illuminates the critical place that musical expression plays in Paul D's constrained life. Both work and sex are less important to his survival than self-generated music.

Though it is certainly schoolteacher's "corrections" which are the im-

mediate catalyst for Paul D's psychic disintegration and loss of manhood,
Paul D later comes to realize that Garner's form of slavery was not entirely
different from that of his brother-in-law.

> For years Paul D believed schoolteacher broke into children what Garner
> had raised into men. And it was that that made them run off. Now, plagued
> by the contents of his tobacco tin, he wondered how much difference there
> really was between before schoolteacher and after. Garner *called* and an-
> nounced them men—but only on Sweet Home, and by his leave. (220, my
> emphasis)

At the distance created by eighteen years and a constant struggle to retain
his manhood, Paul D can recognize the tenuous nature of the identity his
master created for him and realize that Garner, like schoolteacher, was
playing God, indulging in a form of social experimentation by "mak[ing]
and call[ing] his own niggers men" (11). One of Althusser's critical points
is that every ideology postulates "a Unique and central . . . Subject"
(178) through which individual subjects are interpellated; in religious ideology, this Subject is God. In slave systems, masters establish themselves as
the supreme Subject of their own slaveholding ideology. Patterson quotes
a saying from the Kel Gress group of the Ahaggar Tuaregs of the Sahara:
"All persons are created by God, the slave is created by the Tuareg" (4).
Through Garner's construction of Sweet Home as the rational plantation—the logically regulated factory in the field—Morrison represents a
slaveholder's self-positioning as the supreme Subject of white-supremacist,
capitalist patriarchy.[10] Paul D understands how the masculine identity con-
ferred by Garner falls apart upon Garner's death and reflects upon it in an
economical, vernacular rendering of Patterson's concept of "social death":
"Without his life each of theirs fell to pieces. Now ain't that slavery or what
is it?" (220).

Mrs. Garner participates in the slaves' ideological formation as well. In
her casual refusal of Sethe's request for a wedding, a request partly inspired
by the mistress's description of her own elaborate nuptials, Mrs. Garner
attempts to enforce Sethe's positioning as a marginal subject. Sethe's response—improvising a wedding dress out of everyday scraps of material—
marks the slave's aspiration to full subjectivity, her rejection of the master
and mistress's interpellation.

In general, the Garners represent a milder (but in some ways more subtle and insidious) form of ideological domination of African Americans
than one generally assumes of slaveholders. Their abolitionist friends, Mr.
and Miss Bodwin, share negative views of African Americans with slave-

holders, despite their belief that "human life is holy, all of it" (260). The statue that Denver sees at the Bodwins' house is a representation of black dismemberment in the service of the needs of whites:

> His head was thrown back farther than a head could go ... Bulging like moons, two eyes were all the face he had above the gaping red mouth. His hair was a cluster of raised, widely spaced dots made of nail heads. And he was on his knees. His mouth, wide as a cup, held the coins needed to pay for a delivery or some other small service, but could just as well have held buttons, pins or crab-apple jelly. Painted across the pedestal he knelt on were the words "At Yo Service." (255)

This American grotesque is missing a nose and has a head whose angle, in a real human being, could only be accounted for by a broken neck. Nails have been hammered into his head as a substitute for hair. His mouth is a receptacle for anything the owner wants to put into it. The statue embodies nineteenth-century white Americans' hatred of and fetishistic attachment to the black body, and this symbolic dismemberment is an analogue to the physical, mental, and spiritual onslaught perpetrated by white-supremacist ideology.[11]

Though some critics have questioned my focus on wholeness, especially in view of contemporary representations and celebrations of identity as fragmented, I am adhering to the novel's concerns here. *Beloved* both recognizes and problematizes the fragmentation of identity. In another context, Morrison has argued that

> black women had to deal with "post-modern" problems in the nineteenth century and earlier. These things had to be addressed by black people a long time ago. Certain kinds of dissolution, the loss of and the need to reconstruct certain kinds of stability. Certain kinds of madness, deliberately going mad in order, as one of the characters says in the book [*Beloved*], "in order not to lose your mind." These strategies for survival made the truly modern person. They're a response to predatory Western phenomena. ("Living Memory" 178)

Morrison is pointing to the fact that the stability of imagining oneself as whole—as an autonomous liberal subject—was available to white male and some white female subjects in the era of U.S. slavery; it was one of the prerogatives of whiteness made possible by the subjugation of blacks. Enslaved and free blacks were rarely, if ever, able to attain such a sense of self; the constant humiliations visited upon them by the dominant cul-

ture in the era of slavery (and for decades afterward) made this virtually
impossible.

In *Beloved,* black individuals and the African American community try
to construct and maintain a sense of selfhood under the pressure of at-
omizing injunctions from those in power. They use many different strategies to heal and hold themselves together; some of these strategies are
drawn from philosophies and rituals of the West African past, transformed
through the Middle Passage and plantation life.[12]

"Called" by the Antelope

Subjugated by the patriarchal plantation system of American slavery, Africans and their African American descendants were socially nonpersons. As
Patterson argues,

> Slaves differed from other human beings in that they were not allowed freely
> to integrate the experience of their ancestors into their lives, to inform their
> understanding of social reality with the inherited meanings of their natural
> forebears, or to anchor the living present in any conscious community of
> memory. That they reached back for the past, as they reached out for the re-
> lated living, there can be no doubt. Unlike other persons, doing so meant
> struggling with and penetrating the iron curtain of the master, his commu-
> nity, his laws, his policemen or patrollers, and his heritage. (5)

For slaves then, the formation of normal human relations, both imaginative and material, with both ancestors and descendants, and with other
members of an ethnic community, became by definition acts of resistance
within the slave system. Social ties that the slaves formed "were never recognized as legitimate or binding" (Patterson 6), and this fact had deep and
lasting consequences for slave families and communities. If we examine
this in light of Althusser's theory of interpellation, it is evident that subjugated groups relate to social institutions in ways that Althusser did not consider.

In "Ideology and Ideological State Apparatuses," Althusser identifies
the primary agents of interpellation of individuals in capitalist society: the
religious, educational, familial, legal, political, and cultural ideological
state apparatuses (ISAs). In Morrison's representation of slave society and
its immediate aftermath, these ideological state apparatuses are certainly
operating, for white slaveholders primarily, but also for black slaves. Althusser wants to distinguish between capitalist social formations, operating
primarily through consent, and slaveholding or feudal societies, operating

primarily through coercion. These systems are operating simultaneously at Sweet Home, and, as noted above, Morrison highlights the workings of ideology in the subjugation of the enslaved. If we focus on Althusser's indictment of the "church-family couple" and the "school-family couple" as the most intense sites of ideological formation of individuals, we can see that these sites performed their work differently in the free, white, slave-holding communities and the enslaved black communities represented in Morrison's novel. In the case of the Garners and schoolteacher and his nephews, these ideological structures operate in a relatively straightforward fashion. The interaction between schoolteacher and his nephews serves as a signal example of the family and the (informal) educational system as places where white-supremacist and capitalist ideologies are purveyed. The nephews learn from their uncle how to be white men in a slaveholding society: both the excessive privileges and the limited restraints, especially in relation to black women. The slaves' consistent designation of Garner's brother-in-law as "schoolteacher" calls attention to his function and links it to the damage wrought by a racist educational system more generally. Paul D is barely able to contain a warning to Denver when he learns that the young woman is being schooled by one of the Bodwins. He thinks, but doesn't say, "'Watch out. Watch out. Nothing in the world more dangerous than a white schoolteacher'" (266).

For the slaves, education and familial connections support the slaves' valuation of themselves as human and capable of the full range of human abilities and desires. Enslaved characters in *Beloved* are represented as repositories of knowledge—practical, historical, and spiritual. Sethe tells Paul D how Sixo doctored Howard's thumb when one of the cows injured it, saying "Taught me a lot, Sixo" (161). When Baby Suggs is asked how she learned to be a cobbler, she says, "Was a slave taught me," (145) referring to her husband. While she is living and even after her death, Baby Suggs offers Sethe advice and spiritual comfort. This chapter's epigraph, from Harriet Jacobs's slave narrative, is a dramatic instance of the slave family's attempt to make binding claims upon its members, claims that thwart those of the master and mistress. John Blassingame, Angela Davis, Eugene Genovese, and other historians of slavery have brought awareness of the resistance cultivated in slave families and slave communities into the late-twentieth-century discourse on slavery. Morrison brings that knowledge to life, demonstrating the way slave families and informal educational and religious practices worked to undermine the dictates of the state and the master, producing not simply "bad subjects" but subjects whose resistance was a product of allegiance to another interpellating system. One of the novel's most significant achievements is representing the ways in which resistant individual subjects are formed through the encounter between dominant and subjugated cultures.

What has often been overlooked in assessments of slavery's toll on the enslaved is the specificity of the worldviews of these subjugated cultures. The inability to "integrate the experience of their ancestors into their lives, to inform their understanding of social reality with the inherited meanings of their natural forebears, or to anchor the living present in any conscious community of memory" (Patterson 5) would have been a heavy burden for any group of human beings. For the West and Central Africans kidnapped and enslaved in the New World, this particular prohibition was a cultural catastrophe.

As Barbara Christian argues in "Fixing Methodologies: *Beloved*," "In not being able to remember, name, and feed those who passed on in the Middle Passage, those who survived *had* to abandon their living dead to the worst possible fate that could befall a West African: complete annihilation" (13). Citing John Mbiti's *African Religions and Philosophy*, Christian writes,

> Mbiti warns us that in traditional West African societies, Africans do not worship their ancestors. Rather, they believe that when a person passes (and this phrase is important, as it is still consistently used by African Americans), that is, "dies," in the Western sense, they do not disappear as long as someone remembers them, their name, their character. . . . The acts of feeding the dead and pouring libations are meant as symbols, active symbols of communion, fellowship, and renewal. Thus continuity, not only of genes but also of active remembering, is critical to a West African's sense of her or his own personal being and, beyond that, of the beingness of the group.
>
> Mbiti also points out that the ancestors are associated with their land, the piece of Nature they inhabit. The people are the land, the land is the people. He tells us: "To remove Africans by force from their land is an act of such great injustice that no foreigner can fathom it." (11–12)

By calling our attention to the African belief systems that were violently disrupted by the slave trade and the North American and Caribbean system of forced labor, Christian illuminates the cultural conflict at work in slavery and represented by Morrison in *Beloved*. The African cultural referents in *Beloved* have indeed been ignored by most critics, probably because of the dearth of knowledge in the West about the actual religious practices and philosophical traditions of African peoples. Despite a growing body of literary, historical, anthropological, and theological work produced in the past thirty to forty years, Africa still remains a "dark continent" to many, if not most, Western readers; few expect to find respectful evocations of African philosophy and spirituality in a book that is being touted as a new classic in American literature. Too often, slaves are still seen as Western subjects manqué, whose sense of themselves was constructed primarily in terms of Eurocentric or Anglocentric concepts of self.[13] Morrison's inclusion of African characters, belief systems, and practices in *Beloved* illuminates the hidden lives of the slaves, the mental attitudes and rituals that allowed some slaves to survive and to resist their bondage.[14]

Thus, despite the power of the master's interpellations, Sethe and Paul D are also being claimed by this broken but not entirely erased world of West African cultural and spiritual practices. This alternative worldview is represented in the novel by Nan (the woman who took care of the young Sethe), Sethe's mother, and Sixo. These three are African by birth, survivors of the Middle Passage. They continue in the observance of cultural and spiritual practices from their homelands, as far as their enslaved condition allows. Nan and Sethe's mother are among the slaves on the plantation where Sethe was born who dance "the antelope" and other dances of African origin, as well as speaking to one another in their native tongue. Sixo dances among the trees at night "to keep his bloodlines open," (25) and maintains his connection to his native language (though he seems to have no one with whom to speak it—it is not clear if the Thirty-Mile Woman is from his ethnic group, or even African by birth). For Nan, Sethe's mother, and Sixo, observances that were once part of a hegemonic interpellating system in their native countries have become, in the land of their exile and enslavement, subversive. These African characters are engaged in resistance to the dismembering logic of the white capitalist patriarchal system of domination. Their resistance is produced, not as a mere effect of the relation of domination, but as a result of the subjugation of one ideology by another incompatible ideology.

The Africans teach the New World children both by example and through direct instruction, and both Sethe and Paul D reach for the meaning of their own lives in connection with the lives of their ancestors. The first-generation, New World children seek, in Patterson's words, "to anchor the living present in [a] conscious community of memory"; and the Africans they encounter, whether actual relatives or fictive kin, transmit to them elements of a West African worldview and call them into the community of their ancestors.

For Sethe, the remnants of African cultural practices are an ambivalent legacy, because they are tied up with her own motherlessness. Sethe has rarely ever seen her mother; she learns to recognize her by her cloth hat amid a sea of straw hats and by the circled cross branded under her breast, which her mother goes out of her way to show her. Nan, her surrogate mother,[15] tells Sethe more of her mother's story.

> What Nan told her she had forgotten, along with the language she told it in. The same language her ma'am spoke, and which would never come back. But the message—that was and had been there all along. Holding the damp white sheets against her chest, she [Sethe] was picking meaning out of a code she no longer understood. Nighttime. Nan holding her with her good arm, waving the stump of the other in the air. "Telling you. I am telling you, small girl Sethe," and she did that. She told Sethe that her mother and Nan were together from the sea. Both were taken up many times by the crew. "She threw them all away but you. The one from the crew she threw away on the island. The others from more whites she also threw away. Without names, she threw them. You she gave the name of the black man. She put her arms around him. The others she did not put her arms around. Never. Never. Telling you. I am telling you, small girl Sethe." (62)

As this memory returns to Sethe, she must translate Nan's words from the African language in which they were spoken into English. She has forgotten both the language and the story told in that language; as she remembers the "message," she feels unfocused anger. On the one hand, she is able to recover the knowledge that she was chosen by her mother. On the other hand, she recognizes that she has been robbed of mothering and her first language—in short, her birthright. This knowledge has not just drifted away; it has been taken from her by the slave system. As she remembers a moment of her interpellation as the chosen child of an African mother, she yearns for Baby Suggs, the only true mother she has known.[16] Sethe's birth mother was clearly rebellious; she was probably caught running away and hanged for this attempt. Sethe does not want to believe that her mother attempted to escape, because it would mean that she left her daughter behind. Her mother's abandonment of her and the fact that Sethe never got enough milk when she was being nursed are the tragedies at the very base of Sethe's life, and she tries to compensate for her own motherlessness by being a supermother to her children.

Other faint memories connect Sethe to African culture. As she is escaping Sweet Home, she thinks of her unborn child as "the little antelope." She wonders why "antelope" occurs to her, since she's never seen one; then she remembers the African songs and dances on the plantation before Sweet Home:

> Oh but when they sang. And oh but when they danced and sometimes they
> danced the antelope. The men as well as the ma'ams, one of whom was cer-
> tainly her own. They shifted shapes and became something other. Some un-
> chained, demanding other whose feet knew her pulse better than she did.
> Just like this one in her stomach. (31)

For its practitioners, the dance is a moment of plenitude, of genuine be-
ingness, and Sethe remembers it as such. Somehow her own being is registered in the dance and, later, in the life of her unborn daughter. The
dance and Sethe's memory of it are fragments of a system in which those
who are now slaves were valued as human beings. The dancers imitate the
antelope, the principal qualities of which are speed and free movement,
and in so doing, they reverse, at least temporarily, their conditions of physical constraint. The freedom of the dance, the way the dancers "shifted
shapes and became . . . [s]ome unchained, demanding other" contrasts
sharply with the day's numbing, coerced work routine. Through this movement, they are able to reconnect body and spirit; in the remembering and
re-enactment of this African practice, they are able to "re-member" themselves to some degree.[17]

From Sixo's example, Paul D understands what it means to be a man by
African standards, though he is not at all sure that he measures up to Sixo's
definition: "When he looks at himself through Garner's eyes, he sees one
thing. Through Sixo's, another. One makes him feel righteous. One
makes him feel ashamed" (267). He more than meets the criteria established for manhood by the standards of the slaveholding patriarchy; however, by Sixo's standards his behavior (especially in leaving Sethe) is
disappointing. Here again, as in the case of Sethe, the African legacy produces ambivalence. Sixo's thirty-mile trips to see his woman fill Paul D and
the other Sweet Home men with deep admiration, but they are mostly
amused by and somewhat fearful of Sixo's dancing amidst the trees at
night. Although Paul D loves Sixo "better than his brothers" (126), and
although Sixo embodies the integrity of African manhood, Paul D cannot
simply adopt this model, just as he cannot simply adopt Garner's. Paul D
is, must be, a different kind of man from either Sixo or Garner, as Sethe
must be a different woman from her African and Euro-American models—her mother, Nan, and Mrs. Garner (who is childless). The challenge
for those coming out of slavery was how to exercise their choices in becoming new people, African Americans—how to create themselves from
the conflict of two cultures, one of them dedicated to denying the existence of the other.

Healing Song for the Inner Ear: Improvisation and Community

It is improvisation, the creative re-arrangement of traditional verbal and musical structures to suit the expressive needs of the present moment, that allows the African American characters to survive and to re-create themselves. The African practices in themselves are not enough; they must be transformed and incorporated into new circumstances in such a way that they make sense both to the individual and the community. When Sixo stops speaking English "because there [is] no future in it," (25) it is clear that he is not and will not become an African American. Painful as this knowledge may seem in the context of slavery, the future for African Americans *is* in English. The songs that Sethe and Paul D create and sing are hybrids, with both African and Anglo/European elements. These songs are on the cusp between work song and blues, sung in what we now call Black English. As LeRoi Jones (Amiri Baraka) writes in *Blues People*,

> I cite the beginning of blues as one beginning of American Negroes. Or, let me say, the reaction and subsequent relation of the Negro's experience in this country in *his* English is one beginning of the Negro's *conscious* appearance on the American scene. (xii)

Sethe and Paul D are not only at the point of beginning their free lives as individuals; they are also at the beginning of the African American community's experience of free life, at the beginning of blues, at what Jones calls "one beginning of the Negro's *conscious* appearance on the American scene." Verbal and musical improvisation, both individual and communal, is one means through which the ex-slaves, both singly and as a group, re-affirm their humanity and create themselves as a new people, African Americans.

The life of Baby Suggs most clearly represents the transition from dismemberment to "re-memberment" through improvisatory self-creation. Before she is freed she answers to the "bill-of-sale name" Jenny Whitlow and doesn't call herself anything (142). In the narrator's/Baby Suggs's description of the effects of slavery upon her, we see again the metaphor of dismemberment: she decides to preach "because slave life had 'busted her legs, back, head, eyes, hands, kidneys, womb and tongue'" (87). Freed by her son's labor, she discovers her heart (initially, in the physical and then in the metaphorical sense) and renames herself, coining and claiming the name Baby Suggs to register the love and desire her slave husband felt for her and to help him find her if he should be in a position to look. Manumission is a resurrection from a living death in which she knows little about the children she has borne (all but one of whom has been sold away from her) and even less about herself. Baby Suggs claims her freedom by claiming her body and her own unique qualities. Denver's name for her, "Grandma Baby" (37), embodies the contradictory miracle of an old woman reborn in freedom.

Though not African by birth, Baby Suggs creates her own syncretic folk religious practice, based on both West African and Christian spiritual traditions. The ceremony in the Clearing reveals the power of individual and communal improvisation to reassemble broken bodies and broken psyches. Baby Suggs issues her "Call" to men, women, and children; their response is laughter, dancing, tears, and "[l]ong notes held until the four-part harmony was perfect enough for their deeply loved flesh" (89).[18] In structure, the ceremony resembles a jazz performance; it begins with three basic elements: children's laughter, men's dancing and women's weeping, and the congregation plays these elements out in every possible combination, in the jazz ideal of group improvisation. Then Baby Suggs comes in with her solo, her improvised sermon about the need to love the body and the soul. Her spoken-word solo segues into a dance and the community provides the music to accompany her. This ritual has the same effect as the antelope dance; it provides a moment of plenitude in which the people can experience themselves, re-member themselves, as whole and free, in an individual and communal way. However, Baby Suggs's creation is a New World ritual, a proto-jazz Black English blues spiritual "healing song for the inner ear."[19] Jazz musician Sidney Bechet's comments on the spirituals and the blues shed light on Baby Suggs's ritual performance:

> One [the spiritual] was praying to God and the other [the blues] was praying to what's human. It's like one was saying, "Oh, God, let me go," and the other was saying, "Oh, Mister, let me be." And they were both the same thing in a way; they were both my people's way of praying to be themselves, praying to be let alone so they could be human. (Bechet 212–13)

With Baby Suggs leading, the community prays with voices, hearts, and bodies to be allowed to be human.

Improvisation works for Sethe and Paul D as well, as a way for them to express and reflect upon their experience and as a sign of their unique selves. Sethe composes and sings her own song to her children; when Beloved hums this song, Sethe knows for certain that the girl is the daughter she killed. While the only sure sign by which Sethe knew her own mother was the circled cross branded under her breast, a physical mark of her oppression, Sethe has been able to pass on something different to her

children, a verbal and musical mark of the self that is undeniably and ir-
revocably her own. At the end of the novel, we know that there is hope for
her return from madness because she is singing her song to herself when
Paul D visits her in the keeping room.

Musical improvisation is a practice that saves Paul D from madness and
death. In Alfred, Georgia, while he is forced to work and live like an animal, he and the other slaves with whom he works help each other through
the ordeal by singing.

> They sang it out and beat it up, garbling the words so they could not be un-
> derstood; tricking the words so their syllables yielded up other meanings.
> They sang the women they knew; the children they had been; the animals
> they had tamed themselves or seen others tame. They sang of bosses and mas-
> ters and misses; of mules and dogs and the shamelessness of life. They sang
> lovingly of graveyards and sisters long gone. Of pork in the woods; meal in
> the pan . . . cane, rain and rocking chairs. . . . Singing love songs to Mr.
> Death, they smashed his head. (108–9)

In Alfred, Georgia, the shout and the work song are called upon daily to
get the men through. They not only sing songs they know; they transform
those songs and create new ones. They are able to preserve their manhood
and their humanity through communal improvisation.

Because they cannot speak to one another, the shout and the song must
carry all of the expressive needs of the moment. The song changes when the
expressive needs change. At 124, "The songs [Paul D] knew from Georgia
were flat-headed nails for pounding and pounding and pounding. . . . They
were too loud, had too much power for the little house chores he was engaged in" (40). Instead, he takes a melody he knows and improvises lyrics
about himself and Sethe; his composing and singing allow him to meditate
on and express his experience, without being overwhelmed by it. When Sethe
asks Paul D if he wants to talk about having been forced to wear the bit, he
replies, "'I don't know. I never have talked about it. Not to a soul. *Sang it sometimes,* but I never told a soul" (71, my emphasis). Singing his grief has allowed
him to live with it and prepared him to speak of it. As considerations of his
own life history, the songs he creates are thus signs of his individual self. Here
again it is useful to refer to Jones's *Blues People,* where, in discussing the movement from field holler to work song to blues in African American culture, the
author notes the identification of particular "shouts" with individuals.

> Each man had his own voice and his own way of shouting—his own life to
> sing about. The tenders of those thousands of small farms became almost

identified by their individual shouts. "That's George Jones, down in Harts-
ville, shoutin' like that." (61)

Hi Man, the leader of the chain gang in Alfred, Georgia, is named for his
shout; through details like these, Morrison traces not only the trajectory
of the characters' lives, but also the evolution of the music, in which the
importance of vocal style as individual signature persisted. Paul D's "Bare
feet and chamomile sap,/Took off my shoes; took off my hat" are an expression of the individual, reflective self in relation, both to the tradition
out of which he's singing and to Sethe and his own history. The full text of
Paul D's improvised song begins the penultimate chapter of the novel, and
by that point in the narrative, the song has become a factual and emotional
record of the recent history of his relationship with Sethe and his encounters with Beloved, told through a combination of original lines and
standard work song/blues lines. The rhymed resolution of this piece—
"Love that woman till you go stone blind.//Stone blind; stone blind./
Sweet Home gal make you lose your mind" (263)—reflects both Paul D's
deep feelings for Sethe and his regret at having been unable, for a time, to
see her and her dilemma clearly.

Thus for Baby Suggs, Sethe, and Paul D, improvisation functions as an
integrative device, a form of self-fashioning. It is also clear from their stories that part of the importance of improvisation, whether in ritual or in
song, is relational. Baby Suggs and the black community of Cincinnati,
Sethe and her children, Paul D and Sethe—the song sung in the presence
of others helps to heal and integrate the individual and the community.
Many critics have noted the emphasis on community throughout Morrison's work. Valerie Smith, in *Self-Discovery and Authority in Afro-American
Narrative,* argues persuasively that

> Morrison does not provide her people with the option of living under-
> ground, in isolation, beyond community. Her characters achieve autonomy
> and a sense of identity only to the extent that they can understand and name
> themselves in relation to a social unit, be it family, neighborhood, or town.
> (123)

Thus Paul D's mental and emotional compartmentalization can only be
undone through his connection to Sethe and, ironically, Beloved.[20] When
Paul D returns to Sethe, he remembers Sixo's comments about the Thirty-
Mile Woman, and they signify to him both the pain of fragmentation and
the way in which loving, human connection can create an integrated image of the self: "She is a friend of my mind. She gather me, man. The pieces

I am, she gather them and give them back to me in all the right order. It's good, you know, when you got a woman who is a friend of your mind" (272–73).

The importance of the collective is also illustrated by the disaster that occurs when community falls apart—when the neighbors become envious of Baby Suggs and her family and fail to warn them of schoolteacher's approach. After schoolteacher and his henchmen come into Baby Suggs's yard, her big heart begins to give out and she takes to her bed to study color. Her ability to respond to "the Misery" by meditating on something harmless is a testament to the strength of her life-force; it takes three years of thinking about colors to wear out Baby Suggs's heart completely. This slow death is also an improvisation of a kind. Meditating on color[21] is a response that says a great deal about Baby Suggs's life philosophy; though she has been harmed over and over again, she doesn't think about revenge, even in her most bitter moments, when she concludes that there is "no bad luck in the world but whitepeople" (104).[22] Instead, she "declare[s] peace" (177). This final improvisation of Baby Suggs's is a solitary one, however, and while it has the power to soothe her mind, it doesn't reach beyond her to the community in the way that her Call in the Clearing did. Schoolteacher's actions have, to her mind, invalidated her Call, and the community has stepped back as a rebuke to what they see as her hubris.[23] Thus the failure of community, the fact that no one warns them of schoolteacher's approach, is a significant element in Baby Suggs's slow demise; she is left to improvise with only her daughter-in-law and her remaining grandchildren for company. For Sethe, isolation from the community is almost fatal, but finally she is rescued from Beloved by the improvised song of thirty neighborhood women, in a ceremony reminiscent of Baby Suggs's in the Clearing.

The women's ceremony is the most dramatic example of the power of communal musical improvisation. Many psychoanalytic readings would have us believe that Sethe's recovery is brought about primarily or solely through her rememory of her traumatic past and her retelling of it in a healing context. This is true to a certain degree, but, as Denver recognizes, Sethe and Beloved reach a point where the endless retelling of the past, the attempt to justify past action, goes nowhere. Sethe feeds her life to Beloved; Beloved swallows it and asks for more. She will never be satisfied. Ella, one of the black community's organic intellectuals, says, of this encounter between mother and murdered daughter, "What's fair ain't necessarily right" (256), a profound statement about the nature of justice. Ella recognizes that the past cannot be allowed to rule the present and foreclose the future. Unlike Sethe, but like Sethe's mother and many other enslaved women, Ella has given birth to a child whom she refused to nurture because it was the product of rape. "The idea of that pup coming back to whip her too set her jaw working, and then Ella hollered" (259), issuing her call to the other women to begin their exorcism.[24] In one of her most explicit revisions of biblical language, Morrison represents the ceremony thus:

> In the beginning there were no words. In the beginning was the sound, and they all knew what that sound sounded like. . . . For Sethe it was as though the Clearing had come to her with all its heat and simmering leaves, where the voices of women searched for the right combination, the key, the code, the sound that broke the back of words. Building voice upon voice until they found it, and when they did it was a wave of sound wide enough to sound deep water and knock the pods off chestnut trees. It broke over Sethe and she trembled like the baptized in its wash. (259, 261)

The "sound" that existed "in the beginning," "the sound that broke the back of words," is the deep structure of African music, an inheritance that survived because it was immanent within the captives and thus could not be expropriated. Morrison has expressed interest in imagining what African culture would have been like "if they had left that continent un-tampered with" ("Living Memory" 178); the "sound" she references here is, I argue, the sound of the culture before that "tampering" began. Though the music has been transformed through slavery and its after-math, the women can use it to make their way back, momentarily, to a feel-ing of cultural harmony and integrity. In the presence of this sound, Sethe can redirect her action toward the (now imagined) master, rather than at-tempting to kill her children and herself as a way out. Improvisation and communal values are linked; sometimes separately and sometimes in tan-dem they help to re-member the ex-slaves in the novel's Reconstruction-era Cincinnati community.

If we accept improvisation as a sign of human agency, we can begin to see how theories of domination fall short in their accounts of the creation of subaltern selves. African American culture is one arena that indicates that the oppressed individual does not simply accept the dominant ideol-ogy; other ideologies provide conflicting interpretations of experience and conflicting expectations. The self, with the help of the community, re-sponds in a unique way, accepting some aspects of ideology as given and choosing among other available elements in the construction of an indi-vidual subjectivity. Morrison's representations of black subjectivity-in-process thus enable us to assess the ways in which Althusser's influential account of ideology and interpellation might be refashioned to apply to

African American lives during and after slavery and, more generally, to the lives of the dominated in societies marked by profound racial and ethnic stratification.

2. Ideologies in Conflict

In "Ideology and Ideological State Apparatuses," two assumptions about social formations undergird the theoretical framework and render it problematic in a bicultural or multicultural context like American slavery. The first assumption is that the culture under study is homogeneous and that the repressive state apparatuses (RSAs) and the ideological state apparatuses (ISAs) consistently produce docile, conforming citizens. Resistance under social formations such as these is created as an effect of ideology, in a dialectical manner. Althusser writes,

> This concert [of the ISAs acting in tandem] is dominated by a single score, occasionally disturbed by contradictions (those of the remnants of former ruling classes, those of the proletarians and their organizations): the score of the Ideology of the current ruling class.(154)[25]

In Althusser's analysis, the homogeneity of society is disrupted only by those who were formerly in power and those whose resistance is produced by the repressiveness of the system. Other commentators on Althusser's work have revised this aspect of his theory.[26] For example, Paul Smith, in *Discerning the Subject,* summarizes ideology's production of dissent thus:

> [T]he interpellation of the "subject" into oppressed positions is not complete and monolithic; rather, interpellation also produces contradiction and negativity. The necessary existence of various and different subject-positions in the interpellated "subject" produces resistance to the logic of domination while still being in a sense part of, or a by-product of, that logic. (152)

While this statement includes refinements of Althusser's theory (subject-positions within the "subject"), both Althusser's original articulation and most subsequent refinements have failed to account for resistance that is produced differently, through the conflict between profoundly divergent ideologies, one subjected to the other. American slavery was just such a system, involving a conflict between ideologies: Eurocentric patriarchal capitalism and African communal systems of subsistence agriculture. In order to comprehend ideology, interpellation, and resistance under a bicultural system such as this, the theories of Althusser and his followers must take into account the processes of ideological conflict—conflict between world-views—within a single socio-economic formation.

Lisa Lowe is one critic who has addressed this task in an essay on Korean American writer Theresa Cha's experimental novel *Dictée*. In this essay, "Unfaithful to the Original: The Subject of *Dictée*," Lowe writes,

> A closer investigation of the instances of subject formation discussed in *Dictée* reveals that Cha episodically focuses on sites of interpellation which are not only multiple, but are also hybrid, unclosed, and uneven. The focus on these instances suggests that resistances to the hegemony reproduced by interpellating structures are not located simply or exclusively in the antagonisms produced by their demands for identity, but that it also may be the non-identity of the irregularly multiple sites to those demands for uniformity which founds the condition of both inadequate interpellation and the subject's resistance to totalization. (56)

That is, resistance is not only produced as a "by-product" of interpellation; the conflict between interpellating systems may also be responsible for what Althusser calls "bad subjects." Lowe goes on to argue that "*Dictée* is more specific [than Althusser's essay] about multiple hailings, particularly about the conflicts and noncorrespondences between hailing apparatuses," and that "within this multiplicity, one site of interpellation may provide the means or instruments with which to disrupt another apparatus" (56). This reading of *Dictée* is extremely instructive for my own reading of *Beloved,* because similar claims can be made for Morrison's novel. My argument differs from Lowe's in two significant particulars. First, Lowe is primarily concerned with the ways in which the overlapping contradictions produced by various systems of domination—capitalism, colonialism, patriarchy—can be played against one another, how the "bad subject" of all three systems can mobilize her contradictory identity in one to confound her interpellation by another. My chief concern is with how subjects choose among the conflicting interpellations of capitalism, white supremacy, and patriarchy, on the one hand, and African belief systems and practices on the other, and from this cacophony create and maintain some sense of harmony and wholeness. Second, Lowe affirms the value of the textual strategies of "discontinuity" and "fragmentation" in her discussion of Cha's "aesthetic of infidelity,"

> [which] not only prompts the revelation of differences beneath the claim to verisimilitude, but in disturbing the function of representation as reconcili-

ation, it returns us, as readers, to the material contradictions of lived political life. (62)

Though Morrison deploys some similar textual strategies in *Beloved,* her
concern with the pain of fragmentation and discontinuity in African American life and history leads me into a different emphasis in my analysis, an
emphasis on the creation of relatively whole selves and relatively whole
(though internally differentiated) communities. Because intense physical
pain is "world-destroying" (29) in Elaine Scarry's words, and because pain
certainly destroyed the worlds of enslaved Africans and their descendants,
the world had to be made anew by those coming out of slavery. Improvisation remakes the world. Like other acts of creation, it reverses the "structure of unmaking" (Scarry 20) that is torture and helps to re-member the
body in relation to the social whole. I am not attempting here to recuperate an essential African American subject; I am, however, noting that all
fragmented subjects may not feel the same way about their fragmentation.
Enslaved African Americans experienced the process of "[a]ll that is solid
melt[ing] into air" (Marx 338) under particularly intolerable conditions;
there is no reason why they would have celebrated a shattered body or a
shattered consciousness, even when they were able to create something
sustaining from it.

These references to the pain and torture enforced upon black bodies
under slavery lead me into my second major critique of "Ideology and Ideological State Apparatuses." Another problematic assumption underlying
Althusser's theory is that capitalist social formations operate primarily by
consent, with the threat of coercion. North American and Caribbean slavery, though exhibiting significant capitalist features by the early nineteenth century, operated primarily by physical and psychological coercion;
to the slaves, the system only rarely disguised its nature with benevolence
(to the outside world, of course, the system presented itself as a benevolent patriarchy). In Marx's view, slavery was "direct forced labour" whereas
wage labour was "indirect forced labour" (Marx, quoted in Patterson, 2).
Much has been made of the distinction between these two forms; in this
context, it is important to emphasize the similarities between them. Accepting that direct coercion was fundamental to American slavery, one
must then consider how constant physical violence changes the operation
of the ideological state apparatuses, and how the oppressed group responds. While it is not possible here to discuss direct coercion and ideology at length, it is important to note that capitalism and consistent physical
coercion are not mutually exclusive or even particularly incompatible. It is
too easy to think of slavery or conditions similar to slavery as anomalies in

the modern or postmodern world. If one accepts the idea that North American and Caribbean slavery was, in its late stages, a capitalist socio-economic formation in many respects, it is then necessary to refigure theories about subject formation under capitalism to include the effects of consistent physical abuse as a factor in interpellation.[27] Doing so will not only illuminate the past; it will also illuminate the present working conditions of many factory and prison workers in the developing and the overdeveloped world.

3. Improvisation as a Model for Human Agency-in-Resistance

In its transformation from African to African American cultural practice, improvisation has undergone a sea change. Under oppressive conditions, it has become a sign of resistance to interpellation by the dominant culture, a refusal of that culture's norms, not by outright rejection but by reinterpretation and integration with African and other cultural influences. In the words of critic Houston Baker, "The song is a sign of an Afro-American discourse that strikingly refigures life on American shores" (Baker 16). Especially in the context of early (and continuing) European and Euro-American views of blacks, improvisation is particularly significant because of its distance from mimicry.[28] Poets from the time of Phillis Wheatley on have been dubbed "mockingbirds" (whether explicitly or implicitly); Black English is often seen as English poorly spoken; and black culture in general is seen as helplessly deviating from the American norm, which it supposedly seeks to reproduce. An understanding of improvisation as a cultural mode in African American life undercuts these hostile and patronizing mainstream readings of black culture. Instead, one is forced to recognize the intentionality behind transformations of European and Euro-American cultural forms in African American culture, the will and intelligence behind black style.

Improvisation is a three-stage process, and in order to name these stages, I borrow terms from the critics Houston Baker and VèVè Clark. In an essay entitled "Developing Diaspora Literacy and *Marasa* Consciousness," Clark briefly describes two major concepts from Baker's work, and transforms them by adding her own third term.

> Representations of African diaspora history and culture have assumed a binary formation—us and the Others—a residual construction surviving from the master/slave heritage. Houston Baker in his *Modernism and the*

Harlem Renaissance (1987) re-examines the binary oppositions existing between the ideologies of Booker T. Washington and W. E. B. Du Bois. From that encounter two intriguing discursive strategies have been identified—mastery of form/deformation of mastery. As I read Baker's work, I was aware that a third principle might well exist beyond the oppositional framework within which we have interpreted new letters. I have termed that third principle *the reformation of form,* a reduplicative narrative posture which assumes and revises Du Bois's double consciousness. In the wider field of contemporary literary criticism, this reformative strategy approximates the deconstruction of mastery. (42)

Clark goes on to note how black music, jazz in particular, "has provided examples of contextual and formal re-presentations by mastering form/deforming mastery and reforming form,"(42) and she cites John Coltrane's arrangement and performance of "My Favorite Things" as an exemplary "text." These three terms—mastery of form, deformation of mastery, and reformation of form—can be used to designate the three formal stages of improvisation, whether in verbal, musical, literary, visual or household arts. The Baker-Clark formulation lends itself particularly well to my analysis, because Baker's work is grounded in the binary opposition of American slavery, as *Beloved* is, and Clark's work moves beyond the binary to a third term, which is the direction in which *Beloved* points. The improviser understands what is expected of her/him and may begin by performing it according to traditional rules (mastery of form). The improviser then deliberately disrupts the traditional form by introducing other elements into it, elements drawn from other contexts, or by using the instrument in a significantly different manner from the way it has been used in the past (deformation of mastery). Finally, the piece composed from both traditional elements[29] and non-traditional, improvised elements is a new whole, with internal integrity (reformation of form). Writer Ralph Ellison, in the essay "The Charlie Christian Story," describes improvisation in jazz in a way that illuminates the points I have made and connects improvisation to the creation of identity.

> For true jazz is an art of individual assertion within and against the group. Each true jazz moment . . . springs from a contest in which the artist challenges all the rest; each solo flight, or improvisation, represents (like the successive canvases of a painter) a definition of his identity: as individual, as member of the collectivity and as a link in the chain of tradition. Thus, because jazz finds its very life in an endless improvisation upon traditional materials, the jazzman must lose his identity even as he finds it. . . . (Ellison 234)

The refigurative properties and collage techniques of improvisation in African American culture make it an apt metaphor for human agency-in-resistance in general. The stages of improvisation can serve as a model of how a resistant human subject comes into being: first by learning what the dominant ideology expects of her/him and performing it "properly"; then by disrupting the expected performance with non-traditional elements (which may come from another culture/interpellating system), and finally by integrating the hegemonic and the non-traditional elements into a new entity with the structure and fluidity of a free jazz composition. This subject is neither seamlessly whole nor completely dispersed into separate subject-positions. Being resistant to ideology does not place this subject outside ideology; she/he must improvise continually to challenge the ideological injunctions of the dominant culture. This is a subject consistently in process, recognizable as a distinct entity both to herself or himself and to others, caught up in compliance and resistance, obedience and contradiction. For this subject and for communities of resistant subjects, artistic creation—"endless improvisation upon traditional materials"—can facilitate effective resistance to hegemonic ideologies.

Toni Morrison's *Beloved* is now regarded as the quintessential contemporary narrative of slavery, perhaps because its representations of trauma and self-recovery are so resonant with our present-day understanding of the psychic work of survival. *Beloved* is not a realist novel, but its representations of slavery are deeply grounded in and faithful to current historical knowledge about the institution (and, of course, Sethe's story is derived from Margaret Garner's very real attempt to save her children from slavery through death). I turn now to a profoundly different body of fiction focused on the experience of bondage. The novelist, essayist, and short-story writer Charles Johnson has crafted several thoroughly anachronistic and playfully postmodernist fictions addressing slavery and black subjectivity; one can hardly imagine a greater contrast between Johnson's works and Morrison's "fixing ceremony" ("Fixing Methodologies" 14) for black bodies and psyches in pain.

BEING, RACE, AND GENDER

Black Masculinity and Western Philosophy in Charles Johnson's Works on Slavery

As the sociologist Orlando Patterson has noted, we should not be surprised that the Enlightenment could accommodate slavery; we should be surprised if it had not. The concept of freedom did not emerge in a vacuum. Nothing highlighted freedom—if it did not in fact create it—like slavery.

TONI MORRISON, *Playing in the Dark*

And whatever else it may be dramatically, each plot—how events happen and why—is also an *argument*.

CHARLES JOHNSON, *Being and Race*

Charles Johnson's literary vision of slavery is as ludic as Toni Morrison's is tragic. In the novels *Oxherding Tale* and *Middle Passage,* and in the short story "The Education of Mingo," Johnson has created representations of slavery cleared of the deep sorrow usually present when the issue is raised in African American literary texts. (Ishmael Reed is the only other contemporary African American writer mining slavery for its comic possibilities.) Because of his abiding interest in philosophy, and his belief that philosophy and literature are "language in its two analytic forms" (*I Call Myself* 110), Johnson uses slavery as a site for staging a complex series of arguments about the formation of subjectivity in general and black subjectivity in particular. The epigraph to Johnson's 1988 critical book on African American fiction, *Being and Race,* is from the novelist Prosper Mérimée, and Johnson himself has clearly taken these words to heart: "In fiction there must be a theoretical basis to the most minute details. Even a single glove must have its theory" (*Being and Race* v). Deeply influenced by a range of Continental philosophers, especially the French phenomenologist Maurice Merleau-Ponty, Johnson applies the phenomenological technique of epoché—"'bracketing' of all presuppositions in order to seize a fresh, original vision" (*Being and Race* 5)—to create his fictional universe.

This chapter explores the development of Johnson's fictional world and the importance of slavery and Western philosophy to his inquiries into the nature of Being in two of his first works on slavery, "The Education of Mingo" and *Oxherding Tale*. My focus on the importance of Western theory in a novel like *Oxherding Tale* may appear anomalous, especially since Johnson himself and a number of critics have emphasized the influence of Buddhist and Hindu philosophy in the novel. Yet the persistence of Western concepts of individuality and subjectivity throughout Johnson's works on slavery is one of their most salient features.

The question of why Johnson uses American slavery as the site of his philosophical meditations on blackness is an appropriate one to ask of a writer whose use of anachronism reveals his strong interest in black ontology in the present. In *Playing in the Dark*, Toni Morrison argues that, in the eighteenth and nineteenth centuries, "The slave population, it could be and was assumed, offered itself up as surrogate selves for meditation on problems of human freedom, its lure and its elusiveness" (37). However, the use of the slave population in this manner was not a fully conscious mechanism; enslaved blacks served as an invisible or shadowy negative second term, albeit a necessary one, in the equation of freedom. Charles Johnson, in a fully self-conscious way, is reconsidering the slave population in the same light. Enlightenment philosophy initiated an indirect meditation on the unfree. Johnson returns to this meditation and approaches it frontally, mining the existential condition of the slave for the insights it can yield about subjectivity and freedom, not just for African Americans, but for Americans more generally. The fact that slavery was already embedded in Enlightenment and post-Enlightenment discourse on Being, will, and rationality (often as a hidden topic) is another reason that it serves Johnson's literary project so well. He is the writer who is most clearly trying to link black subjectivity, during slavery and in the present, with traditional philosophical discourses on the subject.

My contention is that Johnson returns to slavery as often as he does for two major reasons. First, like many other contemporary African American writers, Johnson has identified U.S. slavery as ground zero for African American identity formation. Yet, unlike Morrison, Caryl Phillips, Sherley Anne Williams, and many others who attempt to render the actual conditions of possibility for black selfhood in nineteenth-century slave cultures,

Johnson uses slavery as the site for a philosophical experiment. In other words, the everyday labor, deprivations, humiliations, and pain endemic to American slavery are not the subject of Johnson's inquiry. Rather, slavery's value, for Johnson, lies in its primariness, in the fact that it was the first condition in which Africans found themselves upon their arrival in the Americas. (His decision to investigate the Middle Passage itself in his second full-length work on slavery is a direct outgrowth of his interest in "social death" as the first ontological state of black subjects in the Americas.) Johnson's interest in enslavement as a philosophical problem rather than as a material condition accounts, in large part, for his consistent use of anachronism—his often humorous, even absurd, mounting of late-twentieth-century debates on the stage of nineteenth-century slavery.

In addition, slavery lends gravity to Johnson's theoretical inquiries, a gravity not attained in his novels set in the 1960s and '70s. The life-and-death issues that arose for black people treated as chattel—the ever-present threat of beatings, rape, or separation from loved ones, the possibility of violent or subtle revolt, escape attempts and their uncertain outcomes—create an urgency that Johnson's works both invoke and attempt to defuse or undermine. I will return to this contradiction later.

In his engagement with Western philosophy, and especially with phenomenology, Johnson confronts a fascinating array of problems and opportunities. As the philosopher Lewis Gordon argues in the introduction to *Existence in Black,*

> [I]n spite of biophysical evidence, "world history" . . . questions the humanity of black peoples. As Fanon has so provocatively put it, black defiance to black dehumanization has been historically constituted as *madness* or social deviance. Blackness and, in specific form, *the black* thus function as the breakdown of reason, which situates black existence, ultimately, in a seemingly nonrational category of faith. Blacks live on, as Dostoyevsky might say, in spite of logic. . . . The black stands as an existential enigma. Eyed, almost with suspicion, the subtext is best exemplified by the question: "Why do they go on?" (5)

Given the way in which blackness is posited as a problem in traditional Western philosophy, Johnson is clearly entering a minefield in attempting to fuse narratives about African Americans and slavery with the philosophies of Hegel, Kant, and others who dismissed the humanity of blacks. Yet one can see the allure of phenomenology—with its "radically empirical" way of evaluating experience (Ihde 30)—for such an inquiry. Husserl, Heidegger, Merleau-Ponty and other phenomenologists provide a method of analysis that allows for the disruption or displacement of traditional ways of seeing. This method can be applied to traditional philosophy or to the narrative of African American history—Johnson does both simultaneously in his works on slavery. *Being and Race,* which was published the year after *Oxherding Tale,* explicitly describes the novelist's critical project as one based on Husserl's work. Citing Husserl's "belief that many disciplines and fields of knowing rest on unclarified, naive assumptions that need to be brought forward if these fields are to achieve a securer [*sic*] foundation," Johnson argues that "Black American fiction, indeed the entire area of 'creative writing,' has not seen its basic assumptions subjected to this form of discussion" (ix). Part of my argument is that Johnson began this phenomenological critique earlier, in *Oxherding Tale* itself. I also contend that, in the early short story "The Education of Mingo," the author initiates a critique of traditional Western philosophy (in particular, a critique of Hegel), and that these two critical discourses, one on Western philosophy and one on African American literary history, collide in *Oxherding Tale.*

Johnson's work presents formidable complications for a black feminist critic. His novels and stories about slavery deliberately raise a variety of feminist issues, while his representations of women are profoundly and relentlessly negative. To conclude that Johnson himself is misogynistic—and that his male characters and the violence that befalls women in these novels reflect that attitude—may seem reasonable, but is too simple a critique, especially if one reads his other novels.[1] *Faith and the Good Thing,* his first novel, published in 1974, has a female protagonist, a picaresque heroine who changes her status in life as often as any of Johnson's heroes do in the search for self. Amy, the main female character in his most recent novel *Dreamer,* also escapes caricature, as do at least some of the women in his short stories. The use of U.S. slavery as a temporal and theoretical context seems to determine Johnson's most misogynistic representations of women, and in the analysis that follows, I argue that these negative portrayals are, to a significant degree, driven by the Enlightenment and post-Enlightenment philosophies that the author engages in his works on slavery.

As noted above, anti-racist critics have called attention to the biases against people of color underlying Western philosophy; feminist critics have attacked the sexist assumptions of this tradition. Sylvia Wynter, in "Beyond Miranda's Meanings: Un/silencing the 'Demonic Ground' of Caliban's 'Woman,'" presents an integrated analysis of both sexism and racism in Enlightenment philosophy, arguing that the Enlightenment posited

an ostensible difference in "natural" substance which, for the first time in history was no longer *primarily* encoded in the male/female gender division as it had been hitherto in the symbolic template of all traditional and religiously based human orders. . . . In other words, with the shift to the secular, the primary code of difference now became that between "men" and "natives," with the traditional "male" and "female" distinctions now coming to play a secondary—if none the less powerful—reinforcing role within the system of symbolic representations . . . by means of which, as governing charters of meaning, all human orders are . . . integrated. (Wynter 357–58)

Using *The Tempest* as a symbolic template for the conquest of the Americas and focusing, in particular, on the absence of "Caliban's woman" from that text, Wynter analyzes the positions created for white women and people of color by Western theory and colonial practice. She claims that, with the secularization brought about by Enlightenment theory and empirical science, came the first moment in history when a group of women (in this case, white European and Euro-American women) could dominate a group of men (in this case, men of color). All of Johnson's works on slavery register the trauma of this reversal of traditional gender dynamics for the black man. The negative depictions of women in his works on slavery must be seen in this context. Far from incidental, these representations provide a crucial underpinning to Johnson's theories about slavery and black ontology, as well as highlighting the fundamental questions Johnson's work raises about African American historical novels in the postmodern moment.

1. Functional Misogyny

"This Thing of Darkness I Acknowledge Mine": "The Education of Mingo"

In the 1977 short story "The Education of Mingo," Johnson conducts one of his first philosophical inquiries into the nature of Being in relation to slavery. Moses Green, a small farmer in southern Illinois, buys a slave named Mingo to help him work his property. Green thinks of Mingo as a *tabula rasa* upon which all of Green's own habits, ideas, and morals can be written, and Johnson carries this dangerous notion to its logical (yet fantastical) extreme. Mingo is, of course, not a blank slate at all, but one of the first representatives of the Allmuseri tribe, an invented "tribe of wizards" (4) who appear in all of Johnson's works on slavery and even in his most recent novel, *Dreamer* (which investigates the last few years in the life of the Rev. Martin Luther King, Jr.). Part of Mingo's tribal inheritance is a gift for "intersubjectivity," taking in the qualities of another person so deeply that the idea of a separate, individual self becomes moot; in fact, in Johnson's later articulations of the Allmuseri worldview, he writes, "The failure to experience the unity of Being everywhere was the Allmuseri vision of Hell" (*Middle Passage* 65). The collision of Green's naive pedagogy with Mingo's gift for absorbing other subjectivities leads to a nearly perfect fictional rendering of Hegel's master-slave dialectic, in which the master becomes dependent upon the slave for recognition and the slave eventually recognizes his own power through the work of his hands.

Green takes the task of educating Mingo very seriously, and, because of his fundamental belief in the ignorance of Africans, assumes that he must teach Mingo everything, much as one teaches an infant. After about a year of instructing Mingo in English, table etiquette, the routines of farm work, and even how to laugh properly, Green

> felt, late at night when he looked down at Mingo snoring loudly on his corn-shuck mattress, now like a father, now like an artist fingering something fine and noble from a rude chump of foreign clay. It was like aiming a shotgun at the whole world through the African, blasting away all that Moses, according to his lights, tagged evil, and cultivating the good; like standing, you might say, on the sixth day, feet planted wide, trousers hitched, and remaking the world so it looked more familiar. ("Education" 5–6)

Harriet Bridgewater, the widow Moses Green is ambivalently courting, warns him of the dangers of "playing God and get[ting] too close to that wild African"; she is especially alarmed by Moses's view that "Mingo says just what I says. Feels what I feels" ("Education" 10). She quotes Aristotle and Hume to support her argument against the full humanity of slaves, and Green concedes during the conversation but privately retains his pride in Mingo's mirroring of his own "knowledge, beliefs, and prejudices" (11). That a white woman here becomes the bearer of classical and Enlightenment philosophy is further evidence, humorously rendered, of the transformation in gender relations brought about by slavery and imperialism. In spite of Harriet's warnings, Moses persists in his views about the slave:

> Moses, later on the narrow, root-covered road leading to Isaiah Jenson's cabin, thought Harriet Bridgewater wrong about Mingo and, strange to say, felt closer to the black African than to Harriet. So close, in fact, that when he pulled his rig up to Isaiah's house, he considered giving Mingo his farm when he died. . . . Then again, maybe that was overdoing things. The boy was all Moses wanted him to be, his own emanation, but still, he thought, him-

self. Different enough from Moses so that he could step back and admire him. (11)

That Moses feels "closer to the black African than to Harriet" is telling; it speaks to the changes wrought in the imagination of Being by imperialism and New World slavery. As Wynter argues in a passage quoted above, the primary axis of difference in the West came to be the difference between "men" (white men) and "natives" (men of color). This change created the potential for a shift in the relations between white men and women. "The Education of Mingo" suggests that male slaves may have functioned better than wives as instruments in white men's projects of self-making, especially as white women gained greater access to education and property owner-ship. Green sees himself diminished rather than magnified in the eyes of the learned Harriet; he feels closer to Mingo because he believes he has taught Mingo everything the slave knows, because his own sense of self is dependent upon the presence of the enslaved Other.

In her critique of Willa Cather's novel *Sapphira and the Slave Girl,* Toni Morrison refers to the "sycophancy of white identity" (*Playing* 19) hidden just under the surface of that text. Johnson's short story takes that "syco-phancy" as one of its primary subjects. The construction of white Ameri-can identities through the subjugation of black people—regardless of whether that domination is benevolent, cruel, or somewhere in-between— has been a subject of African American literature since its inception. The slave narratives, both oral and written, often attest to the transformation wrought in the white master or mistress through the exercise of absolute power.[2] In his recent book *Soul by Soul: Life Inside the Antebellum Slave Mar-ket,* historian Walter Johnson uses the diaries and letters of white Southern slaveholders to establish the ways in which these men and women bought and worked slaves for material gain but also to enhance and inflect their sense of themselves. The psychological dynamics of slavery first recognized by Hegel are, in the American slave narratives, early African American nov-els like *Our Nig,* and late-twentieth-century critical works, traced through the peculiar racial and gender dynamics of U.S. slaveholding society. As a writer of philosophical fiction, Johnson crafts a "'fantasy' variation"[3] from these dynamics.

In response to Green's will, but without his express orders, Mingo com-mits two murders and makes it clear to his master that he, the slave, is not responsible for his actions. Mingo's instinctive understanding of the Ro-man concept of *dominium*—the idea that one can have absolute power over a thing and that a slave is just such a thing (Patterson 29–32; Hegel 116)— leads the slave to recognize that the master is actually responsible for the murders since, as Green himself says, "It's like I just shot out another arm and that's Mingo" (10). As Green's human surrogate, Mingo first axes Isaiah Jenson, a neighbor to whom Green had hired Mingo out, and then kills Harriet, Green's almost-intended. (Having had a few drinks from Harriet's liquor cabinet to calm his nerves after he's learned of the first murder, Green emerges from Harriet's house and drunkenly proposes to her, only to realize that she's dead.)

The story's climax is Moses Green's moral battle over how to respond to Mingo's actions. When Green protests that he was friends with Isaiah Jenson, he is brought up short by the realization:

> [W]hat'd [*sic*] he said was a lie. They weren't friends at all. In fact, he thought Isaiah Jenson was a pigheaded fool and only tolerated the little yimp in a neighborly way. . . . He'd even sworn to Harriet, weeks earlier, that Jenson was so troublesome, always borrowing tools and keeping them, he hoped he'd go to Ballyhack on a red-hot rail. . . . [H]e . . . gave a slow look at the African. "Great Peter," he mumbled. "You couldn'ta known that." (14)

Harriet's death undoes Moses emotionally and he tries to raise a similar objection, shouting "I was gonna marry that woman!" Mingo calmly replies, "Naw" and goes on to say, "You say—I'm quoting you now, suh—a man needs a quiet, patient, uncomplaining woman, right?" (21) Mingo's will to act on Green's unspoken intentions, or perhaps more precisely, to carry Green's hostilities to their socially unacceptable conclusions, makes the master realize that he's created a dangerous being he cannot control.[4] He recognizes his moral obligation and prepares to dispatch Mingo with Harriet's flintlock rifle.

What complicates Green's decision and finally stays his hand is, of course, that he, like Hegel's lord/master, has become dependent on his bondsman/slave for recognition. After Jenson's death, he considers manumitting his slave, but then asks himself, "But how in blazes could he disengage himself when Mingo shored up, sustained, *let be* Moses's world with all its sores and blemishes every time he opened his oily black eyes? Thanks to the trouble he took cementing Mingo to his own mind, he could not, by thunder, do without him now" (19–20). Even after the bondsman has killed Harriet Bridgewater, Moses cannot, finally, execute or release Mingo; the two leave the scene of the crime, driving their wagon west toward Missouri.[5]

Johnson's brilliant, amusing engagement with Hegel in "The Education of Mingo" emphasizes the peculiar disjunction between the philosopher's consignment of Africa and Africans to a place outside of history and his valorization of the abstract slave in the master-slave dialectic. In a sense, by staging the master-slave dialectic in the "real" context of U.S. slavery, Johnson pits Hegel against himself, using the aporias in Hegel's thought to deconstruct its racist underpinnings.[6] A number of anti-colonial intellectuals have implicitly done the same by recognizing the liberatory potential for the enslaved/colonized embedded in this dialectic, yet this is not Johnson's primary concern. In this short story, the author is focused upon the master and his inability to extricate himself psychically from the relation of domination. As Paget Henry argues in "African and Afro-Caribbean Existential Philosophies," "Racism . . . becomes a form of existential exploitation as opposed to a form of economic exploitation. . . . The surpluses being extracted by this form of exploitation are ontological—semblances of determined presence, of full positivity, to provide a sense of secure being" (33). Under patriarchy, sexism functions in this way as well, but when women become less available for "existential exploitation," their value for patriarchal culture plummets.

One of the most striking and peculiar aspects of "The Education of Mingo" is the expendability of the woman Mingo refers to as a "[t]alky old hen" (21). Moses Green, who "felt closer to the black African than to Harriet" before the murders, is devastated by her death, but nevertheless chooses the killing machine he has created over surrendering the slave to the authorities or dispatching him himself. It is not at all clear why Harriet's death is necessary to the action that follows; therefore, I want to focus on Johnson's choice to have this character killed by the slave, since it is certainly possible to imagine the plot moving forward without her death. One can imagine a scenario in which Moses flees the town with Mingo after the first killing, choosing his slave over his potential wife but leaving her alive. It is also possible to imagine Moses Green killing the slave when Mingo attacks Harriet, and then feeling inconsolable over his death. Both of these alternative plots, and a host of others, would establish the dependence of the master upon the slave for recognition.

If, just for a moment, we attempt to place "The Education of Mingo" within its actual historical context, it becomes completely clear, if it isn't already, that Johnson's plot is theoretical rather than realistic. The sanctity of white life in relation to black life and the sanctity of white womanhood in relation to black manhood were two of the most strongly held, least-questioned ideologies of U.S. slaveholding society. It is virtually impossible to imagine a white slavemaster failing to kill or surrender to the legal system (or the mob) a black male slave who had killed a white man and woman. Johnson's will to take us into a created space of infinite possibilities within slavery, to use slavery as a staging ground for a philosophical debate or exposition, is evident here. So why does Harriet Bridgewater's death become a symbolic necessity?

Harriet's death, while not necessary to the plot, fulfills an important function in the philosophical-psychological system Johnson establishes in this story and in his novels on slavery. This character dies for two reasons: first, because she has stepped out of her traditional role as a woman, and second, because she can be replaced. The mirroring, magnifying function that the wife performed historically has been satisfied more fully by the male slave. In fact, Harriet Bridgewater is one of an unpleasant cast of female characters who appear, in one form or another, in all of Johnson's works on slavery. She is a highly educated woman (like Isadora Bailey of *Middle Passage* and Peggy Undercliff of *Oxherding Tale*); she's also domineering (like Flo Hatfield, Anna Polkinghorne, and Mattie Hawkins of *Oxherding Tale*) and physically unattractive (like all the female characters listed above, with the exception of Flo Hatfield). In one of the few critical articles to address Johnson's female characters, Elizabeth Muther describes Isadora Bailey as "a type of the predatory female who would bind the male protagonist to bourgeois happy endings" and notes that Rutherford Calhoun, *Middle Passage*'s protagonist, "both loves [Isadora] in theory and finds her intolerable" (Muther 650, 651). One can easily read Harriet Bridgewater as just such a controlling "predatory female," and Moses Green's feelings for her, like Rutherford's for Isadora, are affectionate, though he is incapable of "speak[ing] his mind to [her] unless he'd tied one on" (20). In this particular fictional situation, Sylvia Wynter's claim, quoted above, that "the primary code of difference now became that between 'men' and 'natives,' with the traditional 'male' and 'female' distinctions now coming to play a secondary—if none the less powerful—reinforcing role within the system of symbolic representations" (Wynter 358) is proven correct in the most violent fashion.[7] Not only is Mingo's mimicry superior (from Green's point of view) to Harriet's nagging superciliousness, but Mingo actually carries out the ultimate punishment Green might have fantasized for this woman who is "a composite of misogynistic stereotypes" (Muther 649).[8] Finally, the two men—master and slave, white and black—are bound together over the dead body of a white woman. The historical implausibility of this relationship is all the more reason to pay attention to the message embedded in its complex racial and gender dynamics.

The form of male bonding evident in "The Education of Mingo" is shown over and over again in Johnson's other writing on slavery. Sometimes intraracial and sometimes cross-racial, the links between men in these literary works are often cemented through the discussion, exchange, or demise of black and white women's bodies. The early chapters of *Ox-herding Tale* display numerous examples of this use of the feminine.

Slavery Cleared of Sorrow—*Oxherding Tale*

Oxherding Tale, Johnson's first full novel addressing slavery, depicts the quest for self and freedom undertaken by Andrew Hawkins, a young, mixed-race but phenotypically white slave on a South Carolina plantation humorously named Cripplegate. The novel begins with a drunken instance of the patriarchal exchange of women, an event that brings about, in due time, the birth of the protagonist. Jonathan Polkinghorne, the master of Cripplegate, proposes to his faithful slave butler George Hawkins that the two exchange wives for the night. Both are concerned about how their wives will react to their drunkenness when they go home to bed, so Jonathan convinces George that the two should change places, heading off to the quarters without giving the slave a chance to protest. "[I]n perfect submission to his Master's will" (*Oxherding Tale* 5) (in a twist Justice Ruffin was certainly not imagining when he ruled that "[t]he power of the master must be absolute, to render the submission of the slave perfect" [quoted in Patterson 4]), George makes love to Anna Polkinghorne, fleeing the room to the sound of Anna's screams once she learns that the butler, not her husband, has been her partner in bed (6). Much of the humor in this opening scene comes from the fact that it inverts so many historical facts about slavery and how it was maintained as an institution both legally and socially. The master's right of sexual access to his female slaves, the antebellum South's version of the *droit du seigneur*, is rendered here as an almost equal exchange between men. As is the case with Mingo's murder of Harriet Bridgewater in "The Education of Mingo," the master's bonding with his black male slave at the expense of his wife is historically implausible, given the racial and gendered arrangements of antebellum southern life. Yet, once we get past the humor produced by this anachronism, how do we interpret it? The sexual exchange of female partners between master and slave is a protest against their wives' perceived power. Both men feel that their wives rule the roost and resent their own lack of complete control over their respective domestic spaces. Johnson substitutes the anti-female hostility of late-twentieth-century fraternity brothers for, on the one hand, the sense of sexual entitlement of the nineteenth-century white male slaveholder and, on the other, the black male slave's sense of disempowerment created by his inability to make incontrovertible sexual claims over black or white women. While the reader may recognize that wife-swapping without the wives' consent is, in fact, rape, the story of the exchange is told in such a way that the women's psychological or physical pain is minimized.[9] Anna is represented as having taken enormous pleasure in sex with George, only becoming horrified when she realizes that she's had intercourse with a man who isn't her husband. What happens in the slave quarters, between Master Polkinghorne and Mattie Hawkins, his slave, is not narrated at all. This is another literary choice that draws attention to itself, because it stands in such stark contrast to the history of U.S. slavery. *Oxherding Tale* depicts Mattie as a domineering black woman who throws Jonathan, her master, out of her house in much the same way that Anna, the white mistress, ejects George, the slave. Mattie's sexual violation is not representable within the novel, because to show her almost-total helplessness in the face of the master's sexual demands would invalidate the vision of female domestic dominance and male submission and resistance that the novel establishes over and over again. Paradoxically, gender comes to signify much more than race in this late-twentieth-century narrative of slavery. Re-situating gender as the primary axis of human difference in these works on slavery has enormous, far-reaching consequences; a reading of another example of the centrality of gender will serve as a preface to an analysis of these consequences.

At various points within the novel, both protagonist Andrew, the product of George's rape of Anna, and an omniscient narrator (who sometimes wrests control of the book from its protagonist) meditate upon the general and specific barriers to freedom created by chattel slavery and a world in "where every man is Enemy to every man" (Hobbes 70). At Flo Hatfield's plantation, Leviathan, Andrew comes to an understanding of one of the major transformations in thought wrought by slavery and colonialism:

> the wretchedness of being colonized was not that slavery created feelings of guilt and indebtedness, though I did feel guilt and debt; nor that it created a long, lurid dream of multiplicity and separateness, which it did indeed create, but the fact that men had epidermalized Being. The Negro—one Negro at Leviathan—was needed as a meaning. (*Oxherding Tale* 52)

This insight is one elaborated at length by Andrew's creator in the 1976 essay "A Phenomenology of the Black Body." Borrowing rather heavily from Frantz Fanon's *Black Skin, White Masks,* Johnson examines the phenomenon of epidermalization, the way in which white perceptions of the "black-as-body" collapse the black subject's sense of his (and I use the masculine pronoun deliberately) own subjectivity. Johnson writes,

I am walking down Broadway in Manhattan, platform shoes clicking on the
hot pavement, thinking as I stroll of, say, Boolean expansions. I turn, thirsty,
into a bar. The dimly-lit room, obscured by shadows, is occupied by whites.
Goodbye, Boolean expansions. I am *seen*. But, as a black, seen as stained body,
as physicality, basically opaque to others—a possibility that, of course, whites
themselves have in a room of blacks. Their look, an intending beam focusing my way, suddenly realizes something larval in me. My world is epider-
malized, collapsed like a house of cards into the stained casement of my skin.
My subjectivity is turned inside out like a shirtcuff. "And it is not I who make
a meaning for myself, but it is the meaning that was already there, pre-exist-
ing, waiting for me," [quoting Fanon] much like a mugger at a boardwalk's
end. . . . Epidermalization spreads throughout the body like an odor, like an
echoing sound. This feeling differs little from that of sexuality: a sudden
dizziness and disorientation, an acute awareness of my outside, of its being
for others, a tight swell at my temples. (*I Call Myself* 1 1 5)

This long excerpt from Johnson's essay, written at the same time that he
was drafting *Oxherding Tale,* sheds a great deal of light on Andrew's meditations in the novel and vice versa. "A Phenomenology of the Black Body"
doesn't trace the history of the epidermalization of Being, but the novel
traces it back to New World slavery. The essay raises a variety of issues that
complicate one's reading of the novel. First, there is the fact that Andrew
is not phenotypically black; because of his light skin, Caucasian features,
and elite education, he can very easily pass for white. Thus, his anguished
lament over the epidermalization of Being under slavery is, at least in part,
a lament for his existence in a condition to which he is not permanently
assigned.[10]

Furthermore, one of the historical-philosophical facts that Andrew's
lament obscures is the fact that Being had been fixed in physical difference
before European contact with Africa, in the bodies of women, as Sylvia Wynter (quoted above) and several other feminist critics have established. The
tragedy for which Andrew grieves—the fixing of Being in dark bodies—
was, in Wynter's view, a shift from one essentialism to another, which did
not completely erase the previous essentialism, but merely wrote over it.
The palimpsest of gender essentialism still shows through the new text of
racial essentialism. The connections between these two modes of imagining Being and the elision of gender essentialism from Andrew's account
are crucial for understanding how Johnson's theories of subjectivity in his
works on slavery are constructed.

Immediately after Andrew's meditation on Being, slavery, and blackness, he is seduced by his mistress, Flo Hatfield. Flo is clearly woman as Na-

ture; as Jennifer Hayward argues in "Something to Serve: Constructs of the Feminine in Charles Johnson's *Oxherding Tale*," "Johnson's attitude towards women tends towards a glorification of the Eternal Feminine, an attitude which can (and, in this book, several times does) flip over into the concomitant terror of women as all-encompassing and all-powerful" (690). Andrew, of necessity, places himself entirely at Flo's service sexually and intellectually. He almost completely loses himself in a sex- and drug-induced haze at Leviathan, and his sense of erasure is made even worse by the fact that Flo doesn't really register or recognize him. In their first embrace, when he asks her what she feels when she caresses him, she says, "Me . . . I feel my own pulse. My own sensations." He presses her, asking "That's all you feel?" and she answers in the affirmative (53). After learning that his family and Minty, the woman he wanted to marry, have been killed or sold due to a slave uprising (probably led by his father), Andrew begins to press Flo Hatfield for the "wages" she owes him.

> Then Flo began to rub against me in a raw, hard way. It was, I thought, like using me as a kind of scratching post. What this action said was: What good are you? You have failed to rouse me. Be still while I satisfy myself. And ever she did this the pain was quick, the insult deep, the self-hatred more complete, and I did not, *as she worked toward detumescence,* truly exist. Suddenly, I wanted to hurt her. My fist shot up without telling my brain what it had in mind—these things happen—then smashed five times, straight from the shoulder, into Flo Hatfield's nose, which flattened like soft clay—I watched this all in a daze, distant—and the next thing I knew I was standing across the room, wringing my hands. (73, my emphasis)[11]

Andrew re-asserts his autonomy by establishing his physical dominance over Flo, despite the fact that he's essentially (though not technically) her slave. Andrew's protest is not only against his bondage, but against his bondage to a woman. His fist remembers, though his brain wants to deny, that for a woman to hold such power over a man is profoundly unnatural (in terms of traditional gender roles) and emasculating, an intensification of slavery's generally dehumanizing quality. Though Andrew is ostensibly horrified by his violent act, its excessive quality (he punches her five times before he regains control of himself) points to its ritual necessity. One could read this scene as a parodic revision of Frederick Douglass's fight with Edward Covey, first narrated in *The Narrative of the Life of Frederick Douglass,* which cemented in Douglass's mind the image of his own freedom and manhood.

In spite of Andrew's profuse apologies, Flo Hatfield sends him (with

Reb, the Coffinmaker) to the Yellow Dog Mine; this is how she disposes of most of her black male lovers after they've outlived their usefulness. Andrew passes for white in order to effect his escape and Reb's, but the most telling feature of his first performance as a white man is his bonding with the Chief Engineer at the mine, Noah Walters. Believing that Andrew (now calling himself William Harris) is a white man employed by Flo, Walters says, "to draw [Andrew] out, 'She's good in bed, too.'" (*Oxherding Tale* 96). The Engineer is shocked and delighted to learn that Andrew (William) has slept with Flo as well.

> As it often happens in the world, especially the tiny southern communities of South Carolina, Noah Walters and I had a third person in common: His fifteen year marriage ended, six years before, in Flo Hatfield's bedsheets. He was not free of her yet. Would, I realized as he pumped me for the kind of information only shared by men who have slept in the same places, never be free of her. . . . The Chief Engineer relaxed and let his hair down and looked at me with the preposterous, intimate, slightly embarrassed love of men who have survived—are trying to survive—the same war. (96) [12]

The bonding that occurs between the two men over Flo Hatfield is akin to George Hawkins and Jonathan Polkinghorne's decision to exchange wives for the night. Though the wife exchange has disastrous results for the relationship between master and slave, it began as an agreement between men "trying to survive . . . the same war." Slavery and race prevail over the attachment between George and Jonathan but, because Andrew is phenotypically white, his bonding with Noah Walters ushers the protagonist (now William) out of the "Black World" (97) and into the "White World" (99). Walters provides Andrew/William and Reb with horses and provisions and sends them on their way with an effusive invitation to return and spend the night. [13] Though the connection between them is different in kind from the bonding between Moses Green and Mingo, the fact that it takes place over a woman is significant.

All the Women Are White, All the Blacks Are Men, and None of Us Are Free

Perhaps the most disturbing way in which women are essentialized in *Oxherding Tale* lies in the slave girl Minty's embodiment of slavery. Love for the beautiful, young Minty is what drives Andrew to request his freedom from Jonathan Polkinghorne in the first place, yet Andrew, as a fugitive slave passing for white, is never able to return to Cripplegate or search for

Minty (after she was sold in the wake of the rebellion led by Andrew's father, George). When he finds his lost love on an auction block in Spartanburg, she has suffered from virtually all of the evils that slavery visited upon African American women: back-breaking labor, beatings, sexual abuse, a serious illness left untreated. Sonnet Retman, in her article "'Nothing was Lost in the Masquerade [*sic*]': The Protean Performance of Genre and Identity in Charles Johnson's *Oxherding Tale*," argues persuasively that "[w]hile the novel attempts to dismantle essentialist and individualist constructions of identity, Minty's portrayal unfortunately stands outside of this project—she functions as the explicit female sacrifice in the novel" (431). Yet, after brilliantly analyzing the novel's treatment of Minty, especially the way in which "[h]er death appears to engender the white woman's progeny" and the fact that "Minty's black female body provides Andrew with an embodied site for his highly abstract and metaphysical speculations on being" (432), Retman sets aside this representation of the black woman as an anomaly.

Minty's portrayal, however, does not merely fall outside the boundaries of Johnson's overall project; her sacrifice serves as a guarantee of the success of that project for the now-white and male protagonist. While many critics, Retman included, have argued that *Oxherding Tale* is a liberatory fiction, freeing Andrew/William both from slavery and from fixed notions of identity, one fact that, until recently, has been overlooked or just mentioned in passing is that the protagonist can only find this freedom as a full participant in "The White World," with a white female partner.[14] Though Retman identifies Andrew as "a biracial man" (432), in the antebellum South, even in Johnson's fantastical South Carolina circa 1863, there is no such social identity. Andrew/William's phenotypical whiteness is what allows him both freedom and a life of plenty; were his black ancestry discovered, he would lose everything he has, perhaps even his life. Minty, the African American female, embodies both slavery and blackness, and Andrew/William's love for her is his last tie to those conditions. Once she dies, Andrew is a free man, though he doesn't know it until the Soulcatcher has finished his sadistic game. For the black female, slavery appears to be inevitable in this novel; the text never offers the possibility that Minty will be able to "[milk] the Self's polymorphy to elude" the traps laid by the peculiar institution (*Oxherding Tale* 159). She cannot even escape from the institution in Reb's way, through Allmuseri/Buddhist self-abnegation.

If we return for a moment to Sylvia Wynter's analysis of *The Tempest* as a template for New World race and gender relations in the wake of imperial conquest and slavery, then we can see the wider context for Retman's claim that "[i]n an all too familiar move, the black woman's body becomes the metaphorical grounds upon which Andrew, a biracial man, and Peggy, a white woman, stake out their material being in the form of childbirth" (432). Wynter argues that the "absence of . . . Caliban's Woman, . . . Caliban's physiognomically complementary mate" enshrines Miranda, as a representative of white womanhood, "as the 'rational' object of desire[,] as the potential genitrix of a superior mode of human 'life'" (360). The fact that Caliban does not have a "physiognomically complementary mate" and thus cannot engender little Calibans with whom to people the isle (*The Tempest* 1.2.350) is a dilemma for the prototypical slave. If we examine this template in relation to *Oxherding Tale,* the novel conforms in some ways and escapes in others. Peggy, Andrew/William's white wife, does not serve as an ideal of feminine beauty; Minty, the African American woman, serves that function at the beginning of the novel. Yet by the end of the novel, Minty has literally disintegrated. In Retman's words, "she was begotten out of the African earth, and she melts back into this landscape when she dies" (432). Even more than the black male slave or the white woman, the black female slave represents Nature. As in Wynter's analysis, Peggy, the white woman, has some access to rationality and Culture, yet as several critics have noted, once she marries Andrew/William, and especially after she becomes pregnant, she comes to embody the mystery of Being more and more.

Andrew traverses the distance from black slave to white householder in the course of the novel, and his relationships with women reflect that transformation. Though Minty is his lover and the catalyst for his search for freedom, their romantic and sexual relationship is never represented as it is taking place; from the beginning of Andrew's tale, she is a strangely absent presence. Flo and Andrew have a Miranda-Caliban relationship in which Flo is a hypersexualized Miranda, teaching Andrew not language but sexual and sensual artistry. Finally, in his relationship with Peggy, Andrew/William becomes the white patriarch whose "Wife"[15] serves as one of the mirrors that allows him to complete himself. His former love object, Minty, actually becomes his slave[16] and, in teaching his white wife about his youthful likes and dislikes, she ties his past life to his present and helps to insure his safe and comfortable future. Andrew/William's permanent life in the White World is secured by the disappearance of Minty as an object of desire, a real or potential love object. This underscores Wynter's contention that the absence of "Caliban's woman" is not an incidental omission but a foundational one:

> The absence of Caliban's woman is therefore an ontological absence, that
> is, one central to the new secularizing behaviour-regulatory narrative schema,

or in Clarisse Zimra's term, mode of "story-telling" . . . , by means of which the secular Laity of feudal-Christian Europe displaced the theological spirit/ flesh motivational opposition and replaced it with its own first secularly con- stituted "humanist" motivational opposition in history. (361)

Here, Wynter refers to the opposition between rational (designated as white) natures and sensory (designated as black) natures.

That a writer as inventive as Johnson resorts to a masculine-feminine bi- nary in place of a black-white division in his meditations on subjectivity speaks to the power of this binary in traditional Western philosophy (es- pecially Hegelian philosophy) and the extent to which Johnson's vision is still circumscribed by that philosophy. If male identity is to be fluid, female identity must be fixed; if the possibility of self-transformation and escape from slavery can be granted to men, it must be denied to women.

Since Johnson is indeed theorizing about the formation of black sub- jectivity in his novels and short stories about slavery, what can we conclude from the limits of the "free imaginative variation[s]" (*Being and Race* ix) he's created? Even with the intention of constructing a theory liberating black subjectivity in the past (and, by implication, in the present), Johnson is nevertheless trapped by the binary oppositions embedded in the phi- losophy he is trying to transcend. While he may not share the prejudices against women expressed by his philosophical precursors, he nevertheless repeats some of their sexist rhetorical moves as he employs and critiques their arguments.

In an article entitled "On Hegel, Women, and Irony," Seyla Benhabib argues persuasively that Hegel's conception of women as lacking the po- tential for full rational personhood and his confinement of them to the domestic sphere in his philosophical writings was a consequence of the philosopher's encounters with "a flesh-and-blood example of what moder- nity, the Enlightenment and the French Revolution could mean for women [in the person of Caroline Schlegel Schelling]. And Hegel did not like what he saw" (38). She continues,

The point is that Caroline's life and person provided an example, and a very close one at that, of the kinds of changes that were taking place in women's lives at the time, of the possibilities opening before them and also of the transformation of gender relations. In staunchly defending women's place in the family, and in arguing against women's education except by way of learning the necessary skills to run a household, Hegel was not just 'falling prey to the prejudices of his time.' 'His time' was a revolutionary one, and in the circles closest to Hegel, that of his Romantic friends, he encountered

brilliant, accomplished, and nonconformist women who certainly intimated
to him what true gender equality might mean in the future. Hegel saw the
future, and he did not like it. His eventual critique of Romantic conceptions
of free love is also a critique of the early Romantics' aspirations to gender
equality or maybe some form of androgyny. (Benhabib 38)

In this account, Hegel's response bears a family resemblance to Moses
Green's recoil from Harriet Bridgewater's erudition in "The Education of
Mingo," George Hawkins's violent anger at his wife Mattie's turn to vege-
tarianism, and Jonathan Polkinghorne's complaints about his wife Anna's
domination of the domestic sphere. It appears that Johnson's return to the
moment of slavery is also a return to a moment of resistance in philosophy
to women's emancipation. Rendering Being as a woman reverses, for Andrew and perhaps for Johnson, the debilitating equation of Being with
black manhood, lamented in Andrew's reverie at Leviathan and in Johnson's "A Phenomenology of the Black Body." The conflation of woman
with Being remains intact at the end of *Oxherding Tale* because the most obvious alternatives, the equation of all blacks or black men with Being or
Afrocentrism's reversal of the system (claiming full subjectivity for black
men and partial rationality and support status for black women while rel-
egating whites to the category of Other) are options that Andrew and Johnson are, with good reason, committed to rejecting. Reb the Coffinmaker
indicates Johnson's desire to create an escape hatch from this binary and
reactionary trap, but there are complications inherent in Reb's embodiment of the ideal of freedom which place limits on Johnson's theory of
(black) subjectivity. These will be explored in the next section.

2. The Asceticism of Blackness, The Plenitude of Whiteness

An analysis of Reb's and Andrew/William's respective fates will underscore
my point about the importance of the latter's phenotypical whiteness and
its implications. Though much has been made of the use of Eastern philosophy in *Oxherding Tale*, it is Reb, the Allmuseri Coffinmaker, who ad-
heres to these tenets, not the protagonist. Reb liberates himself from
slavery by denying the self and its desires so thoroughly that Bannon the
Soulcatcher can find no place to settle inside Reb and make the slave desire his own death. As Bannon says, "[Y]o friend didn't want *nothin'*. How
the hell you gonna catch a Negro like that? He can't be caught, he's *already*
free" (173). Reb's asceticism renders him immune to Bannon's methods,

and the Soulcatcher lives up to his commitment to give up bounty-hunting if he should ever "come across a Negro [he] couldn't catch" (174). Thus, like Minty, Reb pays with his sacrifices for Andrew/William's freedom and ability to take up his true "dharma . . . that of the householder" (147). While Reb, visibly black, finds freedom in the denial of all appetites (since the year his wife and daughter died for lack of medical treatment), Andrew/William, visibly white, claims freedom and the life of plenty to which he has access as a white-looking, well-educated slave turned white, bourgeois patriarch.[17]

Critics have produced a range of interpretations of the end of *Oxherding Tale.* Jonathan Little argues that, though Andrew/William has not yet attained "Moksha" (enlightenment, release from the cycle of birth and death), he is on his way toward it: "Andrew has not yet attained this 'anonymous, impersonal, blissful state,' similar to Kaku-an's oxherder's final position. He is, as spiritual apprentice and householder, beginning on the right path toward ultimate moksha, but he is still in the early stages" (Little 101). This reading is supported by at least one other piece of evidence in the text—the sculpture of Andrew that Reb carves. Three sides of the bust represent the circumstances through which Andrew has passed in the course of the novel. There is a "smooth-grained . . . [u]nstained" portrait on one side, representing Andrew's innocence. A second side "portrayed someone else, the knife marks deeper gouges in wood that gave the portraiture a splintered feel, its expression a worldly blend of ecstacy [*sic*] and pain, sickness and satiation" (77); the reader can recognize this as an image of Andrew's experience with Flo Hatfield, though Andrew does not yet understand this. The third side represents the householder and solid community member that Andrew/William is on his way to becoming at the novel's end. The final side is blank, and while Andrew believes that this is where one would mount the object on the wall, the blank side, in Little's reading, actually represents the emptiness of individual identity that the protagonist is on his way toward discovering. Perhaps this is how the author intends the reader to interpret the last view of Andrew provided by the novel.

Ashraf Rushdy is more critical of the novel's end and Andrew/William's final position in the social order and understanding of his own identity. Rushdy writes,

> Andrew clings to two lessons that do not cohere with the beliefs he claims. First, he continues to believe to the end that the world is an essentialized feminine realm. . . . This way of seeing Being, though, "*seeing distinctions,*" leaves him capable of imagining but not fully inhabiting a worldview in which he is

no longer bound to a way of seeing the world in terms of division, as he is
doing here (male person/female Being).

Here also the second problem arises. Andrew does not surrender to Being, cannot in fact, because he still fervently retains a sense of autonomous
selfhood this novel critiques, particularly in its rendition of the Allmuseri
phenomenology. (189–90)

Rushdy goes on to argue that Andrew/William's vow to be "wholly responsible for the shape I gave myself in the future" and his dismissal of his
father's and other blacks' "racial paranoia" represent his true lack of understanding of the nature of slavery, which he defines as merely "a way of
seeing . . . *seeing distinctions*" (Rushdy 190). Critiquing Andrew/William's
short-sightedness and tendency to conceptualize real relations of domination as solely psychological or philosophical constructs, Rushdy contends
that the protagonist's passing is predicated upon his strategic forgetting of
"those violent social forces he had earlier discovered in the workings of an
exploitative society" (197).

Here, Rushdy has uncovered two of the fundamental flaws of *Oxherding
Tale*'s liberatory project. I want to push Rushdy's argument even further.
Andrew/William's limited vision at the end of the novel reveals the extent
to which Western theory has been at odds with Eastern theory throughout,
and finally, the former has prevailed over the latter as the protagonist em-
braces an Enlightenment, humanist vision of freedom and manhood. Mir-
rored by a wife and magnified by property ownership, Andrew/William
inhabits the position of the white male subject of Western philosophy. It is
possible that *Oxherding Tale*'s main character is on his way toward "Moksha"
at the novel's end, but it is more likely that he will remain in the space of
bourgeois contentment.[18] A final touch that reinforces Andrew/William's
emotional choice of whiteness (rather than simply a strategic acceptance
of the privilege assigned him by whites) is his naming of his daughter after the white mother who refused to acknowledge him (rather than naming her after Minty, or Mattie Hawkins, his stepmother, or Reb's daughter,
or anyone whose name might have preserved the legacy of his African
American identity into the future). Andrew/William ends by saying "all is
conserved; all" (*Oxherding Tale* 176), yet virtually nothing memorializing
his life in the "Black World" remains.

It is at this point that the contradictions inherent in Johnson's use of
slavery become most apparent. The primal drama of bondage has provided the reason for the protagonist's actions and the novel's movement,
yet the material effects of slavery are consistently deflected from his body
and displaced onto the bodies of phenotypically black characters (or min-

imized to the point of erasure). In contrast to Rushdy, I contend that it is Johnson who "makes a serious error in reducing the social relation [of slavery] to a philosophical condition" (Rushdy 191). In representing both Reb's transcendence and Andrew's successful escape and passing, Johnson must deny the very danger and pain he has relied upon to establish the novel's stakes. Johnson's phenomenological approach to slavery has enabled this simultaneous exploitation of and escape from the material effects of the "peculiar institution." In his "'bracketing of all presuppositions in order to seize a fresh, original vision" (*Being and Race* 5), Johnson has bracketed the physical suffering and deep psychological scars inflicted by slavery and evident in the slave narratives, both oral and written.

Johnson's implicit and explicit critique of the slave narratives has several curious features. At two moments in *Oxherding Tale*, the authorial persona makes self-conscious intrusions into the narrative; both of these intrusions focus on the slave narrative. The first, "On the Nature of Slave Narratives," provides a taxonomy of the genre that identifies

> three kinds: (1) the twentieth-century interviews, conducted during the Great Depression by the Federal Writer's Work Project, with black citizens born before 1863; (2) the fraudulent "narratives" of runaway slaves commissioned by the Abolitionist Movement as propaganda for Negro manumission; and, finally, (3) authentic narratives written by bondsmen who decided one afternoon to haul hips for the Mason-Dixon line. These last narratives have, as I will demonstrate, a long pedigree that makes philosophical play with the form less outrageous than you might think. (118)

Two difficulties arise immediately when one considers this taxonomy. First, Johnson's authorial persona privileges the written narratives, aligning literacy with the will and ability to escape from slavery successfully (an error Douglass himself makes in his *Narrative of the Life of Frederick Douglass, An American Slave*). Second, the authorial persona omits any reference to a fourth kind of slave narrative: those of illiterate escaped slaves who told their stories to Northern abolitionists prior to the Civil War. These narratives are some of the most problematic, because the intervening, shaping presence of the white interviewer/transcriber weighs on them so heavily. Yet Johnson's omission of these narratives—or, even worse, the possibility that he's subsuming them under his second category, that of fraudulent narratives—is deeply disturbing because it erases a whole category of slave testimony, granting voice only to those escaped slaves (a small minority) who had the ability to read and write.

The second authorial intrusion into the narrative, "The Manumission of First-Person Viewpoint" (152), marks the point at which Johnson's critique of "Positivist science" dovetails with his critique of significant aspects of the African American literary-historical tradition. As Johnson's authorial persona notes,

> By definition, the Slave Narrative requires a first-person report on the Peculiar Institution from one of its victims, and what we value most highly in this viewpoint are precisely the *limitations* imposed upon the narrator-perceiver, who cannot, for example, know what transpires in another mind . . . ; what we lack in authority, we gain in immediacy: a premise (or prejudice) of Positivist science. (152)

The narrator then proceeds to deconstruct the illusion of the "Self," using Hume, Kant, and Heidegger. What this authorial digression acknowledges only by omission is that those who employed the slave-narrative form had virtually no access to the Positivist "I," the gaze or position of the traditional subject. To the extent that some slave narrators were able to lay claim to a bit of that authority, it was through their verbal virtuosity and through the authorizing documents by white men and women that prefaced their work. The tenuous subjectivity writing itself into being in the slave narrative is here subjected to a phenomenological experiment and found to be "like all Subjects . . . forever *outside* itself in others, objects; he is parasitic, if you like, drawing his life from everything he is not, and at precisely the instant he makes possible their appearance" (152). Here we may well ask what purpose, literary or otherwise, is being served by a phenomenological critique of the slave narrative's "first-person viewpoint." I would argue that Johnson's quarrel is not with the narratives themselves but with the authority the narrators' authorial voices have been granted through the social, political, literary, and historiographical changes initiated by the Black Power and Black Arts Movements. The black subject (usually male) in determined and often physical rebellion against white-supremacist oppression is one of the slave narrative's legacies to black identity in the post-Civil Rights era. Johnson's novel appears to be invested in breaking that link, calling into question the rebellious black subject of the past in order to critique the black-nationalist subject in the present.

Virtually every historical novel documents the time in which it is written as much as, if not more than, the time in which it is set. Johnson has exceeded this general rule by composing a historical novel that is hardly about the past at all. *Oxherding Tale* is a fiction about the possibilities for late-twentieth-century American and African American identity wrapped in the cloak of slavery and its exigencies. It variously invokes, endorses, and critiques late-twentieth-century feminism, liberalism, and black national-ism, as well as investigating Marxism, Enlightenment and post-Enlighten-ment Western theory, Zen Buddhism, and Hinduism from the standpoint of twentieth-century knowledge. While critics like Stanley Crouch hail Johnson's experimentation and play with the legacy of slavery as an un-equivocal good which "perforates the lays [*sic*] of canvas-thick clichés that block our access to the human realities of American slavery" ("Free at Last!" 272), I contend that Johnson's major project is to move as far as pos-sible from the "realities of American slavery" while still representing and commenting upon the institution. The message one derives from "The Ed-ucation of Mingo," *Oxherding Tale* and *Middle Passage* is that the legacy of U.S. slavery is primarily to provide a site and a springboard for philosoph-ical inquiry in the present.

I began this chapter by briefly sketching a contrast between Morrison's *Beloved* and Johnson's works on slavery. I want to conclude by returning to this split and addressing it as a conflict between modernism and post-modernism in African American fiction. In *Postmodernism, or The Cultural Logic of Late Capitalism*, Fredric Jameson discusses the historical novel in the postmodern context. He argues:

> Th[e] historical novel can no longer set out to represent the historical past; it can only "represent" our ideas and stereotypes about that past. . . . Cultural production is thereby driven back inside a mental space which is no longer that of the old monadic subject but rather that of some degraded collective "objective spirit": it can no longer gaze directly on some putative real world, at some reconstruction of a past history which was once itself a present; rather, as in Plato's cave, it must trace our mental images of that past upon its confining walls. If there is any realism left here, it is a "realism" that is meant to derive from the shock of grasping that confinement and of slowly becoming aware of a new and original historical situation in which we are condemned to seek History by way of our own pop images and simulacra of that history, which itself remains forever out of reach. (25)

I quote Jameson at length because his description of the postmodernist historical novel illuminates Johnson's literary practice so clearly. Yet what Jameson considers a loss and describes disparagingly (using words like *de-graded, confining,* and *condemned*), Johnson seizes upon as a situation offer-ing the novelist unprecedented opportunities.

In contrast to Johnson, Morrison has composed a modernist portrait of a small group of ex-slaves and their "putative real world." Though she has written at least one novel that could be considered postmodernist (*Jazz*), in *Beloved* the sense of history being re-created as it might have occurred is crucial to the novel's impact. While clearly recognizing the postmodernist moment, Morrison refuses its flattening of affect and insists upon the materiality of the world of slavery and Reconstruction because of the inadequacy of previous representations of blacks in that world. Explicitly viewing her task as one of revealing realities deemed "too terrible to relate" ("The Site of Memory" 301) in the slave narrative, Morrison places her narrative alongside those, attempting to complete the picture for a contemporary audience. Hers is a specifically African American modernism, one that (to quote critic Simon Gikandi's argument from another context) "seeks forms of representing a history of displacement and reversal and valorizes strategies of inscribing and evoking what Maximilien Laroche, the Haitian writer, has called 'the otherness of identity' found in the 'theater of our contradictions'" (Gikandi 9).

Contemporary African American literature, like American literature more generally, cannot avoid existing in and responding to the postmodern moment. But can African American literature and culture afford postmodernist refigurations of history? Can a past that has hardly been valorized at all survive the effects of postmodernist play? Can the postmodernist novel offer an effective social or political critique? Johnson's novels raise critical questions about the uses to which a history fraught with pain and dehumanization can be put, akin to the questions raised about the use of humor in representing the Holocaust. I would like to argue that, as clever, intellectually engaging, and amusing as Johnson's novel undoubtedly is, the ultimate question it poses is a moral one; *Oxherding Tale* runs the risk of allowing the reader to forget the real conditions of slavery, and to view the condition of bondage as primarily an existential problem. Yet this moral argument is unsettled by the novel itself, as well as its cultural context. As Jameson so eloquently argues,

> [I]f postmodernism is a historical phenomenon, then the attempt to conceptualize it in terms of moral or moralizing judgments must finally be identified as a category mistake. All of which becomes more obvious when we interrogate the position of the cultural critic and moralist; the latter, along with all the rest of us, is now so deeply immersed in postmodernist space, so deeply infused and infected by its new cultural categories, that the luxury of the old-fashioned ideological critique, the indignant moral denunciation of the other, becomes unavailable. (*Postmodernism* 46)

The nature of Johnson's novel raises critical questions about the direction of black postmodernism and the African American writer's responsibility to history, questions that will only become more difficult to answer as more black writers produce fiction of this kind. One way of addressing this question is to move backwards in time and situate *Oxherding Tale* in relationship to one of its most important precursors.

Oxherding Tale is not only a revision of the first-person slave narrative and the novel of passing, it is also a comment on a particular novel which also sought to revise the same two literary forms, James Weldon Johnson's 1912 *Autobiography of an Ex-Coloured Man*.[19] J. W. Johnson's novel, published anonymously and accepted initially by many contemporary readers as a true account of passing for white, laid the groundwork for Charles Johnson's novel in a variety of ways. *Autobiography* is the first novel in the African American tradition to comment stylistically upon the slave narrative as a literary predecessor; its narrator, like Andrew Hawkins after him, was born with a foot in both the black and white worlds and phenotypical characteristics that would allow him to pass for white. The ex-coloured man's talents and luck are rendered hyperbolically, as Andrew's are, and both men exhibit a similar kind of naiveté throughout the bulk of their accounts. J. W. Johnson's modernist metafiction passing as autobiography provides a thematic referent for Charles Johnson's novel, but the second Johnson mines the work of the first for specifics as well.

Oxherding Tale's revision of the end of *Ex-Coloured Man* is the most striking feature of the intertextual relationship between the two novels. The ex-coloured man concludes his tale with the lament that, as an "ordinarily successful white man," he feels that he has "sold [his] birthright for a mess of pottage" (*Autobiography* 211). Andrew/William, however, asserts that he, Peggy, and their daughter Anna, have set about the task of "rebuilding . . . the world" (*Oxherding Tale* 176) in the wake of the Civil War. When contrasted with *Autobiography*'s conclusion (in which the ex-coloured man describes his domestic happiness and its diminishment with the death of his wife), Andrew/William's representation of the (visibly) white family as the focal point for rebuilding a society torn apart by slavery and the ideology of white supremacy seems self-deceptive, self-aggrandizing, and absurd. The ex-coloured man recognizes his retreat into money-making and white domestic life as an abdication of the responsibility and potential glory of "making history and a race" (*Autobiography* 211); Andrew/William, on the other hand, believes that the domestic life he's chosen will permit him opportunities to change the social world for the better. While fear and shame at belonging to a race of people who could be lynched and burned to death with impunity drive the ex-coloured man into embracing whiteness, Andrew/William passes for white under even more desperate circumstances: in order to avoid certain death in the Yellow Dog Mine and to escape recapture in Spartanburg. Finally, though, the protagonist's comments on his own accommodation to life in the white world make a mockery of the dangers he had previously feared. He says,

> I had prepared myself for oppression by preliving episodes of disappoint-
> ment, obstacles, and violent death; I felt a shade disappointed the everyone
> in the White World wasn't out to get me. (The truth, brothers, is that it was
> pretty vain to think oneself that important: *hubris,* thinking *I,* one fragile
> thread, made that much difference in the fabric of things.) With no self-
> induced racial paranoia as an excuse for being irresponsible, I turned—and
> Wife turned—to the business of Minty's recovery. (162)

This passage turns the game of anachronism, which is played so humor-ously and skillfully throughout most of the novel, into something vicious and offensive to the history and memory of actual bondage in the Ameri-cas. In his attempt to ridicule late-twentieth-century blacks who hold too tightly to the idea of racial victimization, Johnson ends up making light of the terror blacks legitimately felt when pursued by masters, patrollers, and lynch mobs. However comfortable he becomes, James Weldon Johnson's ex-coloured man is never in any doubt about the very real horrors of racial oppression. The realities of American slavery finally defeat Charles John-son's postmodernist attempt to render its racialized violence and degra-dation as primarily metaphorical.

We must ask, yet again, why Johnson chooses to make his arguments about current problems of black identity formation in the setting of the antebellum U.S. South, especially when this choice of setting makes possi-ble the hollowing out of the meaning of slaves' suffering which appears in the passage quoted above. One might be tempted to interpret this moment as one in which the reader is encouraged to recognize Andrew/William's shortcomings and view his dismissive comments about "self-induced racial paranoia" as a part of his hubris. Yet Andrew/William's opinions on this point are very close to those his creator has expressed; as Ashraf Rushdy notes, one of Johnson's main targets in this novel is the black nationalism of the 1960s and its excesses. In this novel, and in *Middle Passage,* Johnson raises fundamental questions about the black writer's responsibility to African American history, especially the history of slavery. In the 1960s, African American writers and historians undertook the task of research-ing, understanding and dramatizing the legacy of U.S. slavery in the late-twentieth century. The great majority of these writers recognized that, a century after emancipation, the story of slavery was yet to be included, in detail, in the historical and literary imagination of the nation. In particu-

lar, writers from Margaret Walker to Ernest Gaines to Amiri Baraka to Alex
Haley recognized that general U.S. amnesia and amnesia even within the
black community about slavery was deeply implicated in the social in-
equities and ills of Civil Rights/Black Power era.

Johnson's *Oxherding Tale* not only argues against the racial particularism
and the formal, tragic realism of much of this work, it also diverges from
this tradition simply because it seems to take deep knowledge of the realities of slavery for granted. *Oxherding Tale*'s play with conventions presumes
a very knowledgeable, highly adept reader, one whose range of reference
would have to include the original slave narratives—both written and dic-
tated—the Black Codes, the one-drop rule, the prevalence of sexual abuse
of black women, the prohibitions against the education of slaves, and the
profound taboos against black male-white female sexual involvement. In
other words, *Oxherding Tale* is marked as a post-Civil Rights novel because
it depends upon the literature and historiography of the Civil Rights/
Black Power era. Without the work produced from the mid-'6os to the
early '7os, Johnson's playful, irreverent representation of slavery would be
virtually impossible.

Johnson's Andrew Hawkins/William Harris represents one extreme of
the spectrum of new black subjectivities postulated by the contemporary
narrative of slavery. The unease created in the reader by Andrew's con-
tented morphing into whiteness in the antebellum/Civil War-torn South
establishes an outer limit for the black subject. What George Lipsitz calls
"the possessive investment in whiteness," (Lipsitz vii) combined with phenotypical whiteness, finally and fully establish William as a white man. Intended as an argument for the fluidity of black identity, the protagonist
cannot fully function as such in a novel set in slavery. This is Johnson's most
resounding and disturbing anachronism: the representation of a "black"
slave transcending race in the U.S. South during slavery.

At the end of *Oxherding Tale,* Johnson leaves us with two models for
(black) subjectivity: Reb the Coffinmaker, who has passed into a state of ultimate Allmuseri/Buddhist enlightenment, and Andrew Hawkins/Wil-
liam Harris, bourgeois paterfamilias and householder passing for white. A
number of critics (myself included) have pointed out that Reb provides
the model for subjectivity consistently championed throughout the novel,
yet this model, like the model of Caliban, does not allow for reproduction.
Reb has no family. In fact, it is the loss of his family that teaches him the
first lessons of self-abnegation. As for Trishanku—Ezekiel Sykes-Withers's
teacher in Eastern philosophy—the loss of family and property is the
means by which Brahma shows the seeker the nature of Samsara, the world

of appearance. Reb's model is one only the few can follow, one void of sexual and material pleasures and satisfactions. In a certain sense, it is an intensification of the depredations of slavery, transformed because the emptiness and lack are chosen rather than merely inflicted by the master. Reb, to quote an old saying, makes a "Way" out of no way, but this way is an individual solution to a social problem.

Andrew's "Way" is also limited, based as it is upon passing, male identity, and the potential for social change embodied in the white American family in the Reconstruction South. Even if we think of Andrew's way as that of the householder irrespective of race, it still leaves something to be desired, since, like the Invisible Man's intention to come out of his hibernation and engage in social action, it is not (and perhaps cannot be) realized within the space of the novel. As noted above, this model is further limited by its dependence upon the subordination of women, both black and white.

The foregoing analyses have shown that adherence to Western philosophy, particularly Hegel's theories, provides a catalyst and a source of humor for much of Charles Johnson's work, yet also frustrates *Oxherding Tale*'s attempts to move beyond binary oppositions and the problems of individualism. It is not until the 1990 novel *Middle Passage* that Johnson begins to work his way out of the gender binary through his protagonist Rutherford Calhoun's adoption of Baleka, the only surviving Allmuseri from the journey of the slave ship *Republic*. Perhaps in a Johnson novel to come, an enslaved woman will transcend bondage and the narrow traps of individual and racial identity with the shape-shifting grace of Swamp Woman (from *Faith and the Good Thing*) and Reb's determination and craft.

I now turn from Morrison's and Johnson's historical novels of slavery to an Anglophone-Caribbean text that belongs to the second type of contemporary narratives of slavery: a work set in the present that examines the legacy of slavery in a small, neocolonial island nation.

The Chosen Place, The Timeless People

Late Capitalism in the Black Atlantic

Global structures of domination survive a differentiation that requires us to grasp the various, local postmodernities, as related, but not therefore homogeneous or identical. Our task as critics must be to retain a tension between what will remain an unsatisfactorily homogenizing term—postmodernism—and the heterogeneous local forms produced within and sometimes against its logic.

SANTIAGO COLÁS, "The Third World in Jameson's *Postmodernism, or The Cultural Logic of Late Capitalism*"

Herein lies the explanation of why the quest for identity becomes for certain peoples uncertain and ambiguous: there is a contradiction between a lived experience through which the community instinctively rejects the intrusive exclusiveness of a single History and an official way of thinking through which it passively consents in the ideology "represented" by its elite. Ambiguity is not always the sign of some shortcoming. . . .
    The struggle against a single History for the cross-fertilization of histories means repossessing both a true sense of one's time and identity: proposing in an unprecedented way a revaluation of power.

EDOUARD GLISSANT, *Caribbean Discourse*

Since the early 1960s, Paule Marshall's fiction has included a critique of capitalism in its imperialist and multinational phases, embedded in short stories and novels representing the lives of Caribbean and Caribbean American subjects. In *The Chosen Place, The Timeless People* (1969), Marshall explicitly addresses the economic system in which the characters find

themselves entangled and the ways in which their subjectivities are constructed through the system's differential effects. It is because of this overt
and oppositional engagement with capitalism in its various forms that I
have chosen to analyze Marshall's work in relation to what is arguably the
most influential Marxist account of contemporary culture, Fredric Jameson's *Postmodernism, or The Cultural Logic of Late Capitalism,* as well as his
contested essay "Third-World Literature in the Era of Multinational Capitalism." Though not writing theory-as-such, Marshall is indeed theorizing
late capitalism and the cultural forms and subjectivities to which it gives
rise. Marshall's novel represents a history of capitalism from its mercantile
phase (financed largely through the profits generated in the slave trade
and through plantation labor)[1] to its late phase. As Santiago Colás argues
in the passage that serves as an epigraph to this chapter, "Our task as critics must be to retain a tension between . . . postmodernism [as a general
term] . . . and the heterogeneous local forms produced within and sometimes against its logic" (267). This chapter maintains just such a tension
between Jameson's critical concept of postmodernism as "the cultural
logic of late capitalism" and Marshall's localized yet expansive vision of
one "Third World" cultural response to late capitalism. Without refuting
Jameson's analysis of late capitalism and postmodernism in the "First
World," this investigation expands the frame of his discussion of multinational capital and cultural resistance and analyzes the applicability of
the term "national allegory" to a novel like *The Chosen Place.*

Colás's insightful critique of Jameson's conceptualization and use of the
"Third World" in *Postmodernism* is critical to my analysis here. Colás argues
that the "'Third World' performs" a crucial but "paradoxical double function in . . . Jameson's theory of postmodernism."

> It is *both* the space whose final elimination by the inexorable logic of capi-
> talist development consolidates the social moment—late capitalism—whose
> cultural dominant is postmodernism, *and* the space that remains somehow
> untainted by and oppositional to those repressive social processes which have
> homogenized the real and imaginative terrain of the "First World" subject.
> The latter function then secretly makes possible that subject's attempts to
> gain a historical foothold through which to recall the past out of which the
> seemingly eternal, postmodern, present emerged; that is, to think the pre-
> sent historically and thus to think the possibility of transforming it. (258)

Colás demonstrates how Jameson's analysis of the "Third World" is in error, because in it, "'geographic differentiations then frequently appear to
be what they are not: mere historical residuals rather than *actively reconsti-*

tuted features within the capitalist mode of production'" (David Harvey, quoted in Colás 266). In other words, what looks like the past of the postmodernist "First World" is a new economic and social formation brought about by the action of late capitalism upon the "semi-colonial"[2] countries.

Central to Jameson's theory is the idea that postmodernism is the "cultural dominant" (*Postmodernism* 4) under late capitalism. He argues not that every cultural product is postmodernist, but that postmodernism is the field into which all cultural products—be they realist, modernist, or postmodernist—are introduced. After establishing the fact that late capitalism looks different in the Third World, we must ask whether it will produce the same "cultural dominant," that is, First World postmodernism. As Aijaz Ahmad has pointed out in "Jameson's Rhetoric of Otherness and the 'National Allegory,'" Jameson does not address the many contemporary First World literary works that still fall into the categories of realism and modernism, thus artificially highlighting the differences between First World and Third World fictional techniques. Furthermore, it is clear that late-capitalist conditions can produce a range of literary and cultural responses. As Colás argues in his critique of Jameson:

> One response to Jameson's work, then, is to confront his projected concept of global totality with the details of the various local forms of cultural politics, to which he may fail to attend, but whose existence and various specific characters he does not exclude. In this way, certain global categories operative within Jameson's model (or other global models of postmodernity) can be provisionally rewritten, with greater flexibility, to assist us in understanding and articulating the heterogeneous forms of resistance culture functioning around the world today. (268)

Colás then goes on to demonstrate how a particular Latin American literary form is indeed postmodernist, though it does not represent the "weakening of historicity" (*Postmodernism* 6) that is emblematic of historical fiction in Jameson's account.

Adapting Colás's critique, I contend not that *The Chosen Place* is a postmodernist novel, but that it articulates "a distinctly Afro-Caribbean notion of modernism" (Gikandi 168) that responds to the conditions of late capitalism. As such, it counters the violence of official history and the fragmentation wrought by the imperatives of multinational capital with a representation of countermemory and a desire for personal and cultural wholeness on the part of its fragmented subjects. Despite the fact that a unified, whole subjectivity is a fiction, for these characters (as for the characters in *Beloved*), it is a necessary fiction. Integrating the history of Bournehills' oppression and revolt with its present state of torpor (masking a will to revolt) is one of the Bournehills community's deepest needs, analogous to Merle's need to integrate her personal history of colonial and neo-colonial domination in the psychic realm. As Edouard Glissant maintains in the passage quoted as an epigraph to this chapter, identity becomes "uncertain and ambiguous" (93) for peoples trying to negotiate between their active rejection and passive acceptance of monolithic, official history. This is one of the primary struggles narrated in *The Chosen Place;* slavery and slave resistance are central to this struggle. To the rest of Bourne Island and the outside world, the villagers of Bournehills appear to be caught in a time warp, talking about Cuffee Ned's slave rebellion as if it happened yesterday and endlessly reliving it in their Carnival masquerade. Yet, as this chapter will show, the villagers are counterposing their sense of time and identity to an official narrative of history and progress—in which freedom and, later, political independence were granted to enslaved and colonized blacks in the Caribbean by benevolent English monarchs.

Through an analysis of Marshall's representation of late capitalism and Third World resistance to its economic and cultural hegemony in the Anglophone Caribbean, this chapter elaborates one way of addressing the most pressing of Jameson's questions, indeed the most pressing of questions for all who are trying to imagine and bring about social change in the present. Is it possible to "think the present historically and thus to think the possibility of transforming it" (Colás 258) under late capitalism? Once we recognize Third World economic and social formations, not as "the remains of older cultures in our general world capitalist system" ("Third-World Literature" 68) but as culturally distinct products of late capitalism brought into being coterminously with First World postmodernism, we can bring this question into clearer focus, no longer needing to maintain the idea of the Third World as a receptacle for the past of the West or as an imaginative staging ground for First World theories of liberation.

1. Late Capitalism in a Small Place

In *The Chosen Place, The Timeless People,* we find allusions not simply to capitalism but to late capitalism specifically. If we return to Ernest Mandel's elaboration of the concept in his book of the same title, it becomes clear that Marshall's novel accentuates a number of the signal features of late capitalism in the Third World. For example, the multinational character of capital is alluded to in a number of different ways throughout the novel. The car Vere acquires in order to restore his manhood is described thus:

It was a much used but fairly late model Opel Kapitän, the car made by the General Motors subsidiary in Germany, which combines features drawn from both countries: on one hand, a high-powered German motor, on the other, a long, sleek, low-slung American body that in motion, going very fast, looks like some powerful animal leaping forward to strike. (184)

Of course the car, a symbol of global corporate mergers, ultimately proves fatal to its owner. Furthermore, Unicor (United Corporation of America), the corporation in which Harriet Shippen's family holds a controlling interest, is a conglomerate composed of a number of formerly family-owned businesses that had their origin in the Atlantic slave trade. Unicor's holdings include "huge sugar refineries, a soft drink popular the world over, mammoth flour and paper mills, as well as major interests in other, more impressive, industries: iron, steel, oil, the large-scale manufacture of munitions, uranium mining, banking." Not only has this corporation vastly expanded its holdings, it has also "reached out to link up with other great trading and industrial empires abroad, including Kingsley and Sons, Ltd. [owners of the Bournehills plantation and sugar factory]" (37).

The massive unemployment and underemployment evident in Bournehills are also features of late capitalism in the Third World (Mandel 67–68). Many of the men in Bournehills work only half the year in the cultivation of cane (the "in crop" season, roughly from January/February to June); the other half of the year is the "out of crop" season (267), when the men have little to do besides drink in the rumshop and *lime* (or "idle"). Other men in Bournehills appear to be continuously unemployed, constituting the substantial reserve army of labor that, according to Mandel, has increased in size in the "underdeveloped" countries since the mid-nineteenth century. Mandel is eloquent on this point, arguing that Western European nations reduced their internal reserve army of labor (their continuously unemployed workers) by expanding their external markets.

As soon, however, as the accumulation of capital ceased to advance principally through the displacement of pre-capitalist classes on the internal market and turned instead to the expansion of the external market, it started to create more jobs than it destroyed in the metropolitan countries, *because the jobs it destroyed were henceforward located in the underdeveloped countries.* It is this that explains why the secular trend now came to be a gradual reduction of the industrial reserve army in the metropolitan countries and a gradual swelling of the reserve army in the underdeveloped lands, which in turn explains the increasing discrepancy of real wages in the two parts of the world. (363)

The "steelband boys" (288), who show the rigor and organization of which they are capable only during the Bournehills masque at Carnival (281), can thus be seen as part of the growing number of Third World men put out of work by the destruction of local craftsmanship and subsistence agriculture and the failure of significant local industry to take its place. The same forces drive some workers to travel to other islands, or to the metropoles, in search of employment opportunities and educational advancement. Later in this chapter, I will discuss how Merle and Vere are constructed as fragmented subjects by the imperatives of global capitalism. For the moment, it is important simply to note how alert Marshall is to the features of late capitalism in the post-independence Caribbean. As Hortense Spillers has argued, Marshall presents us with an incredibly detailed picture of this world as "a staged dialectics of human involvement" (*Conjuring* 152) operating at the economic, political, and interpersonal levels.

Finally, according to Mandel's definition, the development scheme that serves as the primary motor for the plot is yet another aspect of late capitalism. Mandel argues that

> [t]he growing export of elements of fixed capital . . . [machines, vehicles and equipment goods] leads to a growing interest by the largest monopoly groups in an incipient industrialization of the Third World. After all, it is not possible to sell machines to the semi-colonial countries, if they are not allowed to use them. In the final analysis it is this—and not any philanthropic or political consideration—which constitutes the main root of the whole "development ideology" which has been fostered in the Third World by the ruling classes of the metropolitan countries. (65)

While Saul Amron may be motivated to pursue development projects because of his political radicalism, Unicor funds the Philadelphia Research Institute and donates the lion's share of the budget of the Center for Applied Social Research (CASR), because it suits their economic interests to do so. The elites on Bourne Island feel as if the Bournehills people are simply ignorant and dedicated to their own backwardness, yet every scheme that has been imposed is an attempt to bring the Bournehills people into line with the interests of international capital. The most blatant of these were the attempts to make them grow bananas for export and the pottery factory, in which they would have made souvenirs for tourists, but the other plans also sought either to expropriate the villagers' land or to dictate how they would cultivate it and the kinds of housing they would inhabit. For the descendants of slaves who worked the land but couldn't lay claim to it, land ownership and the freedom to cultivate that land as they see fit is too precious to relinquish without the absolute certainty that what's being offered in exchange is as valuable as what's being surrendered. Trinidadians have a saying—"Land don't rot"—to express the value of real property and its capacity, when cultivated, to support a family and perhaps generate a bit of extra income.

Other gifts from the center of global capitalism that Bournehills refused include Rediffusion [radio reception] offered at low cost by the island government, a television set donated by a British firm for use in the "social center" (which "played one day and then mysteriously broke down"), and finally, a "jukebox from America" that "didn't last a week" (58). With a remarkable instinct for cultural self-preservation, the Bournehills people have refused the very instruments that would initiate them into the pleasures of underdevelopment and the desire for more of the dubious benefits of late capitalism. Lyle Hutson, the local barrister and senator who hosts Saul, Harriet, and Allen on their first night on Bourne Island, describes Bournehills thus:

> Bournehills, you see, is the thorn in our sides, the maverick in our midst, the black sheep of the family, if you will, which continues to disgrace us in spite of all our efforts to bring it into the fold. In other words, while we have been making quite considerable progress on this side of the island it has remained a backwater even with the large amounts of money that have been poured into it. The place is really quite unique in that respect. I don't believe you could find another like it in the whole of the West Indies or the world for that matter. . . . And it's not, you know, that it can't change, but rather, one almost begins to suspect, that it chooses not to, for some perverse reason. (62)

Clearly, it is necessary for Bourne Island's black elite to believe that increased tourism, more consumer goods, and an economy reliant on imported food products and monocrop agriculture constitute "progress."[3] If Merle serves as the moral center of the novel, Lyle Hutson fulfills the opposite role—he is the representative of the national bourgeoisie in deep complicity with the old British imperialist order and the new American one. Yet he betrays an acute understanding of the Bournehills people in this speech. They are held in place by allegiance to a history long past but still present in their deprivation. Marshall begins *The Chosen Place* with a proverb from the Tiv of West Africa: "Once a great wrong has been done, it never dies. People speak the words of peace but their hearts do not forgive. Generations perform ceremonies of reconciliation but there is no end" (n.p.). The great wrong in this case is, of course, New World slavery, and a number of critics, most notably Hortense Spillers and Barbara Christian, have articulated the ways in which the legacy of slavery persists in the daily lives of the Bournehills people and makes itself felt in their ritual observances. The problem of identity—its uncertainty and ambiguity—is directly linked to the process of diaspora, past and present.

2. The Process of Diaspora, The Problem of Identity

In *The Chosen Place,* Marshall represents diaspora as a continuing process, not as a fixed reality. The original African Diaspora, the scattering of Africans through the Atlantic slave trade, is repeated again and again through the operations of multinational capital and the still-powerful forces of the European imperialist powers. This continuation of diaspora, this repeated breaking and loss, is represented most clearly in the lives of Merle Kinbona and Vere Walkes. These two characters are the Bournehills people who are most beaten down and used up by the multinational military-industrial-agricultural-educational complex.[4]

Virtually every aspect of Vere's life represents the continuation of the diaspora and the consequent disruption of identity. He travels to the United States to cut cane in Florida and do farm work in New Jersey for agribusiness. Big agriculture's need for cheap labor—that motor of the Atlantic slave trade—is still operating here, driving Vere from home and his few remaining family members. "Success" in the United States would cement his natal alienation; it is only his failure to find a sympathetic friend or relative in the States that sends him back to Bournehills. The U.S. agricultural corporations have learned lessons from slavery, and the Farm Labor Scheme allows them to use black labor in its prime and then ensure that the laborers do not remain and become part of the permanent population.

Sexuality is another site of disturbance for Vere. Before he leaves Bournehills for the United States, he impregnates his girlfriend, a character identified only by her last name, MacFarland ("Black, White, and in Color" 285).[5] Both Merle and Vere's great-aunt contend that the infant boy died because of the mother's neglect or abuse (32, 85), though the woman herself declares that "from the day that child born you could tell it wasn't going to live any time. It was a sickly something!" (274). Determined to avenge the "wrongs" (275) done him by the Canterbury woman, Vere stalks her for several weeks upon his return to Bourne Island (apparently to increase her fear of him) and finally gives her a beating with a foreshortened cane that has been in his family for generations (in fact, his great-aunt Leesy beat him with it when he was a child). This is one of the novel's most disturbing scenes, largely because Vere's actions are represented as justifiable, and the Canterbury woman's defense of herself is not accorded any credibility by the text. As Spillers argues, "It seems that the narrator(s) chooses sides here and speaks *for* Bournehills society" ("Black, White. and in Color" 278–79) which is in full agreement with Vere. The young woman's dispassionate acceptance of the beating is presented as both a sign of her guilt and of her hardened nature. She responds with anguish only when Vere attacks her collection of white baby dolls, the surrogate children upon which she lavishes care and attention.

Vere's punishment of the Canterbury woman is the action that releases "all the bitterness and rage he had contained during his three years away"; he is deeply frustrated by the fact that "he would never be able to convey to her what it was he had been seeking in having her as his woman and giving her the child, and how deeply she had wronged him by denying him both" (275). As Spillers points out, the text here endorses "the hierarchical arrangements of father-law" ("Black, White, and in Color" 279). Having taken his revenge, Vere has more of the bearing of a mature man than the tentative, slightly boyish demeanor that was one of his characteristics before (303, 346). On Carnival night, he takes up with another woman (the dark-skinned Milly); very soon thereafter, he gets a job driving a tractor for the local soil-conservation program. The people of Bournehills attribute his newfound confidence and manhood to his car, his girlfriend, his job, or some combination of those factors, yet the decisive turn in his character can be traced directly back to the night of the beating. As disturbing as this aspect of the novel is, especially to a black feminist critic, it does reveal the extent to which "father-law" is and has been seen as a legitimate way of counteracting colonialism's denial of full manhood to Afro-Caribbean male subjects.[6] Vere's violence toward his ex-girlfriend is not his downfall; instead, his continued investment in Western technology brings about his death.

Though U.S. agribusiness ejects Vere once it has benefited from his labor, he retains an allegiance to the products of the fully industrialized West and decides to make himself a hero in his local community by rebuilding a car, that most American (in the narrow sense) symbol of independence, individuality, and manhood. It is Vere's great-aunt and caretaker from childhood who understands most clearly the nature of the threat posed by Western industrial machinery, especially the old, worn-out machinery available to the working class in the Third World.

It was as though she believed beyond question that all such things as cars, all machines, had human properties, minds and wills of their own, and that these

were constantly plotting against those whom they served. They were for her
the new gods who, in a far more tyrannical fashion than the old, demanded
their sacrifices. Something in her gaze as she stood there peering out, her face
as reamed and eaten away by time as the wood of the door, said she feared and
detested the Opel straddling Vere as much as she did the rollers at Cane Vale
which had crushed and killed her husband years ago. (185)

Of course, Leesy is prescient in her fear of the car, which finally kills Vere
in his moment of glory at the Whitmonday race. After repairing and con-
solidating his identity through a series of traditionally masculine behaviors,
he dies because of his belief in modern machinery and the ideal of technological mastery. But he has fathered an as-yet-unborn child, suggesting
that his interpersonal strategies for establishing manhood have been far
more successful than the ones involving First World technology. Milly will
certainly be a more conscientious mother than the Canterbury woman, as
symbolized by the way she stands at the site of the crash, "one hand . . .
clenched in a fist on her stomach as though to defend the child there from
the thing that had killed Vere" (368). Here again the novel reveals its investment in "father-law" for the colonized black man who has historically
been denied the full prerogatives of traditional masculinity.

Merle's life also represents the continuation of diaspora and psychic
fragmentation. Like so many West Indians in the mid-twentieth century,
she goes to Europe for higher education. Her travel to the metropole is
driven by forces virtually identical to those that drive Vere to the United
States. The deliberate underdevelopment of subsistence agriculture, local
industry, and local educational institutions before and (in many Caribbean
countries) after independence forces the Bournehills people and their
real-life counterparts to migrate in search of better opportunities.

While Vere is physically worn down and discouraged by his sojourn in
the First World, Merle undergoes a more profound psychological dissolu-
tion. Having returned to Bournehills after the tragic end of her marriage,
she holds herself together with a constant stream of talk and suffers break-
downs in which she becomes catatonic for days at a time. Clearly, she suffers from what Tsitsi Dangarembga, borrowing from Sartre, elaborates as
the "nervous condition" of the colonized. At several points within the
novel, we are reminded that Merle *is* Bournehills, despite her elite educational background and her years spent "Away."

Fanon's words about the psychic disorganization caused by metropolitan racism echo through Merle's description of her time in London. When
she narrates her tale to Saul, she makes it clear that uncertainty about her
sexual orientation was a part of that confusion. Sketching a portrait of her

English benefactress's character, she notes how much the woman wanted to be entertained and admits: "'yours truly did her share of the entertaining. In more ways'—the rushing voice slowed; she tried to shrug off the thought but her shoulders didn't quite lift—'than I care to say.'" That haunted pause in the middle of her sentence serves as one of the few acknowledgments of the sexual nature of her relationship with the Englishwoman. Merle also says of "the business between her and myself": "That had me so that I didn't know who or what I was." One of her reasons for finally leaving the Englishwoman (another nameless character) was "'to see if a man would maybe look at me twice. I wasn't any raving beauty but I had a way about me then'" (329). Merle's tragic personal history— as the daughter of a white planter who refuses to acknowledge her before she reaches high-school age and a black plantation worker who is shot to death in front of Merle by the planter's "Backra" wife when Merle is just two years old—clearly merged with the destabilizing power of white supremacy in England to make her deeply vulnerable to self-hatred, self-doubt, and exploitation. In the world of the novel, homosexual imperialist exploitation is clearly worse than its heterosexual counterpart, because, from a hetero-normative point of view, it disrupts the "natural" sexual order.

Ketu Kinbona, the African scientist and anti-colonial activist whom Merle marries in London, restores the "proper" racial and sexual order of things to her life. She deeply admires the purity of his revolutionary spirit and his ability to take from English culture the knowledge he needs, without feeling beholden to it or internalizing its messages about black inferiority. In relationship to Ketu, Merle is like the young George Lamming who, as he describes himself in *The Pleasures of Exile*, felt a deep envy of Africans because they had indigenous languages and cultures with which to combat the onslaught of colonial Othering (162). In terms of her sexuality, Merle credits Ketu with redeeming her from a confusion that was profoundly damaging to her self-esteem:

> "But most of all, he made me know I was a woman. Yes"—she nodded quietly—"that, above all else, is what that man did for me. After years of not being sure what I was, whether fish or fowl or what, I knew with him I was a woman and no one would ever again be able to make me believe otherwise. I still love him for that." (332)

In Merle's view, traditional sexual object choice is clearly a prerequisite for Caribbean true womanhood. While Marshall's critique of imperialist sexual exploitation is well-taken, this is the *only* way in which the novel repre-

sents gay/lesbian sexuality—as a decadent product of old and new metropolitan cultures. I will examine this issue again in the next section of this
essay, but drawing attention to it here allows me to highlight the extent to
which Marshall's novel is concerned with subjectivity and which subjectivities are appropriate for resistant Third World people. Ketu deems lesbian
relations with an Englishwoman to be both sexually perverse and counter-
revolutionary, and Merle accepts this judgment, wishing only that her husband had shown her more mercy and allowed her some contact with her
daughter.

We are meant to understand that Merle's natal alienation, her dis-ease
as a result of her encounter with metropolitan culture, her stasis, and her
seizures stand for analogous conditions in the Bournehills community as
a whole. Merle is, in a sense, a formal intellectual turned organic intellectual, yet it's clear that she doesn't have cures for what ails the community.
She must first find the courage to heal herself, to reconnect the sites of her
own diaspora, before she can effectively work toward social transformation
on Bourne Island. Her movement toward Africa at the novel's end—a journey that eschews the northern hemisphere in favor of the southern—is simultaneously a movement toward past *and* future, toward ancestors *and*
descendants. Speaking of the Bournehills community at large, Hortense
Spillers writes,

> Marshall does not mean that Bournehills is stuck, consequently, in its history
> of betrayal and oppression, but that the scene against which it enacts and
> reenacts its history has been decided by origins that must be appeased, at
> least recognized and named out loud. (*Conjuring* 158)

This is as true for the individuals within Bournehills as it is for the community as a whole. The need for each person to perform ceremonies of reconnection and reconciliation is further evidence of the extension of the
diaspora, the new ruptures that complicate the old.

In *The Chosen Place,* colonial and neo-colonial domination disrupts the
individual identities of the dominated by pushing them to move in search
of better educational and employment opportunities, by imposing white supremacy in the psychic realm, and by disturbing hetero-normative gender
roles. Vere and Merle are clearly subjects constructed under the aegis of international capital, and one is destroyed, the other nearly so, by this system
and its far-reaching physical and psychological effects. It is also important
to note that both Vere and Merle are motherless children, their personal
losses serving as a metaphor for their entire society's loss of connection to
"Mother" Africa. Thus, the novel can be read as an allegory, as Jameson uses

this term: the individual, psychological dramas are metaphors for the political dramas of the collective. Yet we must ask whether the group so allegorized is in fact the nation or some other collective entity.

Saul's final realization of the nature of the island's eastern side comes toward the end of the novel:

> Bournehills, its shabby woebegone hills and spent land, its odd people who at times seemed other than themselves, might have been selected as the repository of the history which reached beyond it to include the hemisphere north and south.
>
> And it would remain as such. . . . [D]eep down, at a depth to which only a few would be permitted to penetrate, it would remain fixed and rooted in that other time, serving in this way as a lasting testimony to all that had gone on then: those scenes hanging on the walls [Merle's collection of drawings of slavery and the Middle Passage], and as a reminder—painful but necessary—that it was not yet over, only the forms had changed, and the real work was still to be done; and finally as a memorial—crude in the extreme when you considered those ravaged hills and the blight visible everywhere, but no other existed, they had not been thought worthy of one—to the figures bound to the millwheel in the print and to each other in the packed airless hold of the ship in the drawing. (402)

This view of Bournehills—as testimony to and memorial of the Atlantic slave trade and plantation slave labor, as well as rebellions against slavery—is not merely Saul's partial view, it is the novel's perspective, the revelation to which the entire work directs its readers. What I want to emphasize is how thoroughly this perspective exceeds national consciousness or the idea of anti-colonial nation-building. Bournehills is the receptacle of these histories for the Americas as a whole, not simply for Bourne Island or the Caribbean. Though a number of critics have written persuasively about the concept of Caribbean nationalism in this novel, and despite Jameson's assertion that all Third World novels function as "national allegories," I contend that Marshall displays and advocates a post-national consciousness in *The Chosen Place*.

3. One, Two, Many Nationalisms

A variety of different discourses of Caribbean nationalism have proliferated since the period of decolonization, as evidenced by the title of Franklin Knight's book on the subject—*The Caribbean: The Genesis of a Frag-*

mented Nationalism. The European model of the nation-state held sway throughout the period of decolonization and is still influential today, despite the economic and political barriers to full sovereignty. Yet this European ideal of the nation-state has been haunted and disrupted by another concept of nation—the African ethnic groups from which the majority of Caribbean people descended. In another of her novels, *Praisesong for the Widow,* Marshall specifically invokes this other concept of the nation; Lebert Joseph, the Legba figure, asks the protagonist Avey Johnson, "And what you is? . . . What's your nation?" (166–7). In *Praisesong,* this African ethnic identity is intended to supersede Avey's identification as a part of the U.S. nation, calling her into an African-Diasporic imagined community. Though this concept is not as fully developed in *The Chosen Place,* Marshall is clearly moving toward this vision. One critic has designated *The Chosen Place* as "a Third World novel" (Ogundipe-Leslie 20); following Abena Busia, I would argue that it is a "diaspora novel" as well, one that requires "diaspora literacy" of its readers.[7] The novel is not centered upon the promise of Bourne Island becoming an independent nation-state—that promise has already been minimally fulfilled and quickly betrayed by neo-colonial power in league with the comprador bourgeoisie.

Numerous features of the novel lead me to argue that it is focused primarily on collectivities both smaller and larger than the nation-state. First, Bournehills, not Bourne Island, is the "chosen place"; the inhabitants of this small corner of the island are the "timeless people." The Bournehills people fall on the margins of the national imaginary of Bourne Island, as evidenced by the scorn directed toward their Carnival masque and by the elite's disgust at Bournehills' failure to transform itself by accepting development aid. Bournehills is, in short, the internal Other to the island's national consciousness.

Furthermore, Merle is portrayed as a citizen and representative of Bournehills, not Bourne Island. Her teaching of the local history of Bournehills—Cuffee Ned's revolt—is not acceptable to the powers that be in the national education system, since they are still clearly in the grip of its colonial past. While one can imagine Cuffee Ned serving as a revolutionary symbol for anti-colonial nationalists, that era has passed on Bourne Island. In an interview with 'Molara Ogundipe-Leslie, Marshall herself describes the character Lyle Hutson as "a devoted socialist" during his student days in London. She continues, "Yet when he returns home he fits into and conforms to the bourgeois mold and he abandons all his idealism, the radical position of his youth. I see that happening time and again, not only in West Indian societies, but in African societies and in black American society" (Ogundipe-Leslie 20). Clearly, Marshall is trying to address the failures of anti-colonial nationalism. By sketching one corner of a "semi-colonial," Third World nation-state, she gestures toward the particularity of a potentially revolutionary community denigrated by the nation as a whole *and* toward the transnational revolutionary potential in the African Diaspora and the Third World at large.

Further evidence for the expansion of the novel's vision beyond the national includes Merle's need to reconnect the sites of her own personal diaspora and the way in which the Cuban Revolution functions as a model for the kind of transformation that Bournehills' resistance might eventually bring about. At the end of *The Chosen Place*, Merle recognizes that, in order to heal, she must find her child in East Africa. She cannot fully recover from the psychological damage wrought by her colonized childhood and her sojourn in the metropole in the space of the nation-state. Kamau Brathwaite has praised Paule Marshall "as a novelist of the 'African Reconnection'" (quoted in Busia 197), and in *The Chosen Place*, Merle's literal African reconnection is a prerequisite for her effective political action in the future. Unlike Avey of *Praisesong for the Widow*, who is psychically healed by recognizing the traces of Africa in the New World, Merle must travel to the continent itself for a reconciliation with her personal and ethnic past.

The novel also imagines what a communal reconciliation with the past might make possible. During the Bourne Island Carnival, the image of the Cuban Revolution merges with the re-creation of Cuffee Ned's rebellion to prefigure a Bourne Island revolt in the future. The Bournehills band stirs the crowd, and marchers from other bands leave their groups to "jump behind" Bournehills, and in particular,

> [a] large contingent of the Twenty-sixth of July Guerrilla Band made up entirely of young people from the Heights. . . . Dressed in olive fatigues, heavy combat boots and helmets camouflaged with leaves, the young men sporting beards and puffing cigars and all of them, even the women, brandishing cardboard machetes and grenades, the members of the guerrilla band came charging toward Queen Street and the Bournehills troupe, singing the praises of Cuffee as they came and firing toy machine guns and pistols. (289)

Here the residents of the peri-urban shantytown called Harlem Heights, who have named their Carnival band after Fidel Castro's revolutionary movement, join forces with the disenfranchised peasantry of Bournehills. It is this purposeful tide of humanity that drags Harriet along with it; she believes they're marching toward their own doom and tries to prevent them from going into the sea. They, of course, know exactly where they're going and refuse to pay the slightest heed to her exhortations. The gen-

uine independence from colonial and neo-colonial domination that such
a revolt might bring is represented as a promise for which Bournehills will
"hold out . . . defying all efforts . . . to reclaim it; refusing to settle for anything less than what Cuffee had demanded in his time" (402). (Of course,
the weapons carried by the Carnival masqueraders are toys, an irony that
undercuts the revolutionary possibilities suggested by their performance.)
There is certainly a nationalist character to this representation of revolu-
tions past, present, and perhaps future, yet its pan-Caribbean aspect is
more pronounced. As the more recent history of Cuba and the crushing
of Maurice Bishop's New Jewel Movement in Grenada have made clear (if
this wasn't already clear from the aftermath of the Haitian Revolution), a
revolutionary movement against multinational capital in one of the Caribbean islands can just barely eke out an existence without the support of
other like-minded regimes in the region. Marshall is calling out for the creation of a new pan-Caribbean, Third World consciousness. In one interview, she says,

> I would like to see it [*The Chosen Place*] described as a Third World novel, be-
> cause it is set in a mythical island in the West Indies. Readers spend an awful
> lot of time trying to identify the place rather than seeing its larger meaning;
> the fact that it makes a statement about what is happening in the Third World
> in general [politically and psychologically]. (Ogundipe-Leslie 20–21)

In a variety of ways, then, *The Chosen Place* focuses upon communities
other than the nation-state; in fact, at some points the text is explicitly anti-
national. However, one aspect of the novel that links it to explicitly nationalist discourses is its curious subtext: its numerous, profoundly negative
representations of homosexuality.

Throughout the book, same-sex desire and sexuality are represented as
yet another plague visited upon Bourne Island and its people by decadent
metropolitan culture. From Mr. Hamilton, the American manager of the
Banyan Tree Hotel, who made sexual advances toward one of his "yard
boys" (76), to the gay white male tourists in Sugar's Nightclub, who prey
upon Bourne Island young men, to Allen Fuso, whose love and desire for
other men is the primary symptom of his deformation by U.S. culture, to
the Englishwoman who seduced Merle and subsequently destroyed her
marriage: same-sex desire is always located outside the Third World subject as a corrupting force to be reckoned with. Merle is particularly harsh
in her assessments of white gay men. She refers to Hamilton as "Miss
Hamilton" (78), and, despite her own sexual experience with another
woman, she fails to understand Allen's confession of a lack of desire for

women for what it really is and suggests to him that he should marry and have some children to cure his malaise. She simply refuses to countenance same-sex desire in a man she thinks of as a friend. This persistent stigmatization and externalization of homosexuality is what marks the text most clearly as a nationalist project; the gay or lesbian subject figured as alien to the national body dovetails with nationalist rhetoric rather than politically going beyond it. This contrasts with most of Marshall's representations. By failing to recognize the existence or even the possibility of gay and lesbian Caribbean subjects, Marshall writes them out of both the nation-state and the nation of African-descended ethnicity.

My primary interest here is not in simply labeling *The Chosen Place* homophobic. Marshall has written an important critique of sex tourism, both gay and straight, along with other interpersonal manifestations of colonial and neocolonial power. Yet it seems important to ascertain why the novel focuses so often upon same-sex sexual relations, none of which are even vaguely positive. I refer to the novel's homophobic subtext as a curious feature because many (if not most) Caribbean literary works from this period simply have nothing to say about homosexuality, which is one way of silencing it. In contrast, *The Chosen Place* seems mildly obsessed with same-sex desire. In "Not Just (Any) *Body* Can Be a Citizen: The Politics of Law, Sexuality and Postcoloniality in Trinidad and Tobago and the Bahamas," M. Jacqui Alexander notes that stringent legislation against same-sex sexual activity has been enacted in several Caribbean nation-states since independence (much like the laws in many U.S. states criminalizing same-sex sexual interaction). Alexander focuses on these laws to "argue that as the state moves to reconfigure the nation it simultaneously resuscitates the nation as hetero*sexual*" (6). Though she is addressing the Caribbean, post-independence nation-state at a later historical point than Marshall, her analysis illuminates this striking feature of *The Chosen Place*. According to Alexander, in Trinidad and Tobago and the Bahamas,

> The state's authority to rule is currently under siege; the ideological moorings of nationalism have been dislodged, partly because of major international political economic incursions that have in turn provoked an internal crisis of authority. I argue that in this context criminalization [of gay and lesbian sex, as well as prostitution] functions as a technology of control, and much like other technologies of control becomes an important site for the production and reproduction of state power. (6)

Linking the criminalization of gay and lesbian sex with the criminalization of prostitution is especially illuminating in relationship to *The Chosen Place*, because of the "Canterbury woman," Vere's one-time girlfriend and the mother of his child (who dies in infancy). Hortense Spillers's brilliant reading of this character identifies her as the one character in the text not granted an inner reality that would show why she behaves as she does. Spillers writes,

> Apparently a sign of Bournehills' Other, she [the Canterbury woman] marks, in effect, a tribal limit, and all her kin follows her status. Neither absorbed nor absolved by the structure of irony, this character without a *first* name, or a *last* one that would claim precise differentiation, enters the fiction and leaves it—is *abandoned* by it, more appropriately—as the single figure who is not exhausted by the work's rhetorical resources. . . .
>
> From the angle of stratagem and disguise, the Canterbury woman cannot turn round from the mirror to either the audience of the fiction, or the one outside it, since *to turn* would bring this figure into the one symbolic confrontation that all the parties have not engaged systematically, cannot engage at all, except in the most violent manner, as the scene depicts: *Who* is the "European" in me that the "African" in me need fear? (285)

As Spillers points out, the Canterbury woman is seen as the Other of Bournehills not merely because of her white skin but because of her psychic investment in whiteness. Leesy Walkes accuses her of killing Vere's child because it was "too black" (32). She is also stigmatized because she is a prostitute: we first encounter her in Sugar's Nightclub, flirting with a young officer (implied is that the officer is white and a foreigner) and later we are told that she occasionally brings officers and sailors home for the night. Prostitution (a virtually inevitable result of the island's economic situation) is here linked to the overvaluation of whiteness; thus there can be no sympathy for the woman who makes her living this way. Though resistant to the economic and cultural incursions of multinational capital, in this situation the collectivity of Bournehills functions like the Caribbean nation-states Alexander analyzes. She writes,

> Embedded here [in their legislation on sexuality] are powerful signifiers about appropriate sexuality, about the kind of sexuality that presumably imperils the nation and about the kind of sexuality that promotes citizenship. Not just (any) *body* can be a citizen any more, for *some* bodies have been marked by the state as non-procreative, in pursuit of sex only for pleasure, a sex that is non-productive of babies and of no economic gain. Having refused the heterosexual imperative of citizenship, *these* bodies, according to the state, pose a profound threat to the very survival of the nation. (6)

Thus, while generally moving away from a nationalist vision toward a vision of a resistant African-Diaspora community, *The Chosen Place* does in some ways participate in a discourse of nationalist exclusion, especially when it comes to non-heterosexual, non-procreative sexualities.

4. History, Memory, and Resistance

Throughout *The Chosen Place*, Marshall examines the problems—personal, interpersonal, social, economic and political—created by late capitalism, as well as the existing and potential resistance to this system. In so doing, she must address the vexed question of Caribbean histories, both hegemonic and insurgent. This chapter began with an epigraph from Edouard Glissant's *Caribbean Discourse*, in which he asserts that "[t]he struggle against a single History for the cross-fertilization of histories means repossessing both a true sense of one's time and identity: proposing in an unprecedented way a revaluation of power" (93). The story of Cuffee Ned—itself a contested history in its details—is counterposed to English and U.S. histories in which emancipation is a result of Queen Victoria's benevolence and U.S. military and economic interventions facilitate progress. Thus, the novel does "[propose] . . . a revaluation of power" but not in a simple fashion. Critic Simon Gikandi offers the most subtle and complex analysis of history in *The Chosen Place*. He very precisely identifies the Bournehills mas'—the reenactment of Cuffee Ned's rebellion—as "not simply the Freudian repressed that returns to haunt us, nor merely the unconscious of history; rather, it is also an attempt to capture and articulate the voice of the black subject in the categories of its own modernity" (190). As I noted in the introduction to this chapter, Jameson analyzes the Third World as the site of "the remains of older cultures in our general world capitalist system" ("Third-World Literature" 68). At first glance, Bournehills seems to embody this generalization; the residents could be interpreted as Lyle Hutson interprets them: as Luddites whose atavistic attachment to the wounds of slavery and the glory of slave resistance make them unfit for present-day life under neo-colonial late capitalism. Gikandi illuminates the nature of Cuffee Ned's story—it is not so much a remainder of an older culture as it is a modernist revision of that older culture necessary for survival and resistance under late capitalism.

> The African fragment has value precisely because it is the central focus of the rules—both conscious and unconscious—that govern black discourse. The limit of the Western version of history is shown to be its enslavement to lin-

ear development, the emphasis it places on the continuity of that history initiated by Columbus, a history of repression and pain, which always seems to
insist that the destiny of the Caribbean is to become European. And thus . . .
the primal scene of the West Indian object is marked by the paradoxes of a
society caught between colonial history and the longing for a national culture. (Gikandi 195–96)

Gikandi eloquently articulates the function of the "African fragment," not
as an atavism but as the node around which Afro-Caribbean modernist discourse and identity has developed and can grow. Yet, finally, I must part
company with Gikandi's analysis on account of its emphasis on the national.
The Chosen Place expresses the longing for a resistant, African-Diasporic culture not limited by the boundaries of the nation, a culture that can reach
across the sea and the colonial histories dividing the islands and recognize
other insurgent histories—Haiti's, Cuba's—as its own. Bournehills, the
chosen place with its timeless people, is the "African fragment" around
which such a diasporic community could imaginatively develop.

In "Third-World Literature," Jameson is imposing rather than recognizing the primacy of the national in his analysis of these literatures; that
is, he sees nationalism where other forms of social organization may be in-
cipient. In his chronology, nationalism, a concern supposedly "long since
liquidated here [in the United States] and rightly so," persists in the Third
World and determines the production of novels that "remind us of out-
moded stages of our own first-world cultural development" (65). Jameson
would have us believe that the national, in the European nation-state sense,
is the privileged, indeed, the only category of the collective that the Third
World novel discusses. In answer to his question, which might be posed as,
"Can the subaltern speak of anything but the nation?" Jameson has uttered
a resounding No! Yet this paraphrase of Spivak's question, like the original itself, raises the issue of hearing more than the issue of speech. The
subaltern can speak, but can the dominant culture hear what they are saying? In relation to novels like *The Chosen Place,* Jameson's chronology (in
which First World subjects might "urg[e] these nation states to outgrow it
[nationalism] as fast as possible," [65]) acts as yet another form of imperial history, silencing "the voice of the black subject in the categories of its
own modernity" (Gikandi 190). Looking at Gikandi's argument through
the lens of late capitalism, I want to suggest that, just as Paul Gilroy designates the "Black Atlantic" as a "counterculture of modernity" (*Black Atlantic* 1), Paule Marshall's diasporic vision of the Atlantic world, centered
in the Caribbean, is a counterculture of postmodernity. Marshall's post-na-
tionalist vision—in which mobile, fragmented black individuals attempt to

construct and maintain "migratory subjectivities" (Boyce Davies 1) while largely ignoring the vitiated rhetoric of nationalism issuing from the "semi-colonial" nation-state—is invisible to Jameson's First World gaze. Thus *The Chosen Place* is like the stone thrown in the eye of the Cyclops; though the novel does not provide a revolutionary solution for the people of Bourne-hills, it does suggest that Third World writers and critics, including those living in the First World, might function as the *griots* for the African-diasporic community the novel imagines, a community whose obsession with history and memory is not backward but visionary.

In an attempt to consider how to "think the present historically" under the pressures of late capitalism, this chapter has examined *The Chosen Place* and the cultural expressions represented within it as Caribbean modernist responses to multinational-capitalist exploitation in the Caribbean. The impasse that the novel reaches and represents—the fact that the spirit of resistance preserved in the Bournehills Carnival reenactment of Cuffee Ned's rebellion has not found an effective new form to inhabit—remains the Caribbean's critical dilemma. Toward the end of the novel, Saul finally realizes:

> Only an act on the scale of Cuffee's could redeem them. And only then would Bournehills itself, its mission fulfilled, perhaps forgo that wounding past and take on the present, the future. But it would hold out until then, re-sisting, defying all efforts, all the halfway measures, including his, to reclaim it; refusing to settle for anything less than what Cuffee had demanded in his time. (402)

The effectiveness of Cuffee Ned's mode of resistance has been outstripped by capitalism's ability to transform itself almost endlessly and adapt to vir-tually any attempt to thwart its growth and development. Thus we can see that in the later half of the 1960s, Marshall was presciently addressing the Caribbean's present-day predicament—over thirty years later, Caribbean people and communities continue to search for a form of resistance ade-quate to the racist, sexist, neo-colonialist, anti-human hydra that confronts them. At a historical moment when numerous other cultural figures were advocating resistance and revolution as pure solutions, Marshall was al-ready looking ahead to this "postcolonial," post–Civil Rights, postmodern moment, showing us the dark side of Louise Bennett's "Colonization in Re-verse," and even prefiguring the return of the emigrants to their Caribbean natal places. Finally though, the novel offers hope in the form of the Bournehills villagers' cooperative shipping of their sugarcane to another processing factory when the one they rely upon closes. This small act of community allows us to imagine the possibility of radical social transformation in "a small place."[8] Like the Ibo in her *Praisesong for the Widow*, Marshall, with her remarkable vision, encompasses the past, present, and future of the scatterlings of Africa now grounded—in both positive and negative ways—in the Caribbean.

The imbrication of the legacy of slavery with colonialism and neo-colonialism is a focus of virtually every Anglophone Caribbean contemporary narrative of slavery. The specifics of the relation between slavery and colonialism vary from text to text, but recognizing how these systems overlap and jointly influence the formation of black Caribbean or diasporic subjects is a critical task in these works. In *Dream on Monkey Mountain*, analyzed in the next chapter, Derek Walcott traces the lingering psychic wounds of slavery and imperialism through a surreal, dramatic allegory which follows the main character, Makak, in a journey from self-hatred to the recovery of his true name and human identity.

PERFORMANCE, IDENTITY, AND "MULATTO AESTHETICS" IN DEREK WALCOTT'S *DREAM ON MONKEY MOUNTAIN*

One day, one of the animals brought back a coconut, but Anansi came and stole it. While he was carrying it away, a tiger saw him and asked, "What are you eating?" Anansi said to Tiger he was eating a piece of his stones (testicles). Then Tiger said to him, "What, Anansi? How does it happen that your stones are so sweet?" He said, "Well, Daddy Tiger, how sweet yours must be that are so much bigger and fatter than mine." So Tiger asked him how he could break his stones off so that he could taste them. "Daddy, come to the corner, for a blacksmith is there and surely, with his hammer and anvil, he'll be able to break your stones." So they went there, and Anansi told Tiger to lay down. Just as he lay down, Anansi struck him with a hammer and broke his stones. Tiger died instantly. So he cut him to pieces, cooked him, and ate him up.

From a Surinamese folktale in Roger D. Abrahams, ed. and selec.,
Afro-American Folktales: Stories from Black Traditions in the New World

The children of slaves must sear their memory with a torch.

DEREK WALCOTT, "What the Twilight Says: An Overture"

Dream on Monkey Mountain's relation to slavery is more oblique than that of the other texts analyzed in this study. The play is primarily linked to the history of slavery through Derek Walcott's use of the animal characters of Afro-Caribbean trickster tales, tales with their origins in West Africa, profoundly transformed in the context of New World bondage. In Walcott's vision, the animal characters are fused with racist, imperialist images of blacks as less than human, specifically as apes. This fusion of animal allegory with imperialist stereotype enables an effective critique of both within this remarkable play. *Dream* also emphasizes the way in which the legacy of slavery is deepened and extended by the continuation of colonial rule.

The fierce, deadly ruse that Anancy[1] perpetrates on Tiger in the Surinamese folktale quoted above is a feature of trickster tales throughout the Caribbean. Often hailed as representations of slaves' resistance to the masters' authority and as examples of anti-hegemonic consciousness in Caribbean folk thought, these tales also have an anarchic quality. The weak but clever spider does not always defeat the stronger, larger beasts of prey, and sometimes, in his attempts to conquer the powerful, Anancy ruthlessly uses other animals as pawns or dupes. The ethic of cooperation among the weak animals against the strong is sometimes upheld and sometimes undermined by Anancy. From recent critiques of folk and literary trickster figures, it is clear that the ability of these figures to represent a mode of being beyond the binary oppositions of master-slave, colonizer-colonized is limited. Critic Patrick Taylor, author of *The Narrative of Liberation,* defines the Anancy stories as "mythical narrative." He argues that

> In situations of oppression, in the colonial situation, for example, these narrative forms are the vehicles through which the colonized lay out the terrain of social conflict, point to practices of resistance, call for rebellion, and provide hope for an alternative future. Mythical narrative reaches its limit, however, in the tragedy of endless repetition: everything is in flux, but nothing is very different; the weak defeat the strong, the strong defeat the weak; the weak become the strong. Lacking is the vision of a qualitatively new world free of human oppression. (xii)

What Taylor terms "liberating narrative" goes beyond the constraints of mythical narrative to envision the possibility of radical social transformation. He writes,

> From the slave period to the present, some forms of Caribbean narrative have shown how mythical patterns can be transformed with liberating significance. . . . The narrative of liberation reveals the limits of the struggle for a hallowed ancient past, the endurance of a wretched present, or the leap toward a utopian future; it engages the processes of historical transformation with a view to the possibility of creating a society based on human mutuality. (xii)

Walcott's *Dream on Monkey Mountain* clearly meets Taylor's criteria for liberating narrative, and Taylor analyzes the play as a literary text that goes beyond the politics of inversion. This reading is congruent with that of critic Tejumola Olaniyan, who, in an essay entitled "Corporeal/Discursive Bodies and the Subject: *Dream on Monkey Mountain* and the Poetics of Identity,"[2] analyzes *Dream* as a text that escapes from the Manichean logic of slavery and colonialism. Olaniyan analyzes Makak's transformation as a movement beyond binary oppositions.

> From being a slave to whiteness and then to an imaginary Africa, he is now his "real" West Indian self—a cultural mulatto—without any illusions. . . . Even the elements celebrate this rebirth: the sun appears in all its bright glory . . . as Makak is freed from prison, the symbolic prison of mental enslavement. This political gesture may be "small" but it is the pre-condition for any clear-sighted struggle in the social sphere. ("Corporeal" 164–65)

Walcott's play, first performed in 1967, was far ahead of its time in terms of its exploration of mixed racial and cultural identity in the West Indies, and I have chosen to discuss it, even in the company of much more contemporary works, because, like *The Chosen Place, The Timeless People,* it addresses so directly the issue of Afro-Caribbean subjectivity. *Dream* presents a model of dramatic representation in relation to identity that anticipates the theoretical work of a number of contemporary theorists of identity and performance.

The two critics cited above, Taylor and Olaniyan, have produced the most complex and compelling interpretations of Walcott's celebrated play, yet neither has addressed in detail the play's sexual and gender dynamics and its marginalized black female characters. (Olaniyan has critiqued the stereotyping of female characters—both the use of black women as mere background figures and the embodiment of all the evils of Eurocentrism in a white woman [*Scars* 109].) Other commentators on this play, and on Walcott's work in general, have either remained silent about his failure to represent black women characters and the concerns of black women, or they have criticized him (usually briefly) for this omission.[3] My purpose in discussing the masculinist aspect of Walcott's aesthetics in *Dream* is somewhat different. While I concur with those who label many of Walcott's works sexist at worst and inattentive to female characters at best, I want to move beyond that labeling to argue that his articulation of a specifically masculine sexuality imbricated with slavery and colonialism redefines a particular, black, New World masculine subjectivity, one which can be traced back to the trickster tales, and which Walcott's contemporaries represent in the Caribbean reconceptualizations of Caliban and in crucial texts of decolonization like Frantz Fanon's *Black Skin, White Masks,* to which

Dream often alludes. Delineating the features of this black, masculine, Caribbean subjectivity, this masculinized "mulatto aesthetics," will make clear the extent to which masculinism is not merely a default position or an atavistic response, but is, in part, created by slavery and colonialism's reconstructions of gender relations. My reading will also clarify the ways in which the omission of the enslaved or colonized woman is not accidental but necessary to the social schema of New World slavery and colonization that is represented and resisted in *Dream*. The play's failure to contest this absence is a measure of its inability to completely resist the terms established by the hegemonic culture. *Dream on Monkey Mountain* is able to break out of the Manichean world of slavery and of the Anancy stories to a certain extent, yet the play unfortunately preserves the masculinism of that world and its dramatic division between the roles assigned to white and black women. In this regard, it bears a striking resemblance to Charles Johnson's *Oxherding Tale* and my readings of both works address the consequences of these failures in the realm of the literary and cultural imaginary.

1. Performing Identities

In *Dream* and in numerous essays and interviews, Derek Walcott has articulated principles of performance that can be read as a theory of performance and identity in the Caribbean. In "What the Twilight Says," the introduction to Walcott's first published collection of dramatic works, he indicates the journey to reclaim their humanity that he believes each actor must make:

> If I see these [actors] as heroes it is because they have kept the sacred urge of actors everywhere: to record the anguish of the race. To do this, they must return through a darkness whose terminus is amnesia. The darkness which yawns before them is terrifying. It is the journey back from man to ape. Every actor should make this journey to articulate his origins, but for these who have been called not men but mimics, the darkness must be total, and the cave should not contain a single man-made, mnemonic object. Its noises should be elemental, the roar of rain, ocean, wind, and fire. Their first sound should be like the last, the cry. The voice must grovel in search of itself, until gesture and sound fuse and the blaze of their flesh astonishes them. The children of slaves must sear their memory with a torch. The actor must break up his body and feed it as ruminatively as ancestral story-tellers fed twigs to the fire. (5–6)

The Caribbean actor's journey represents that which the people must also undertake; it is the journey Makak, as Caribbean everyman, must complete in *Dream on Monkey Mountain*. Thus performance, in *Dream*, functions as "restored behavior," (3) as Joseph Roach, drawing from Richard Schechner's work, argues in *Cities of the Dead: Circum-Atlantic Performance*. "Performance, in other words, stands in for an elusive entity that it is not but that it must vainly aspire both to embody and to replace. Hence flourish the abiding yet vexed affinities between performance and memory, out of which blossom the most florid nostalgias for authenticity and origin" (3–4). In Walcott's play the "restored behaviors" are more negative than they are positive, however. The characters mostly perform identities from which they would like to escape rather than identities they want to maintain or bring into being. Here "origin" means the governing stereotypes that allowed people of African descent to be treated as subhuman. Makak must make the journey from ape to man and reclaim his human name.

In a 1971 interview with *The New Yorker* magazine, Walcott discusses the genesis of *Dream*, saying, "when I started to write this play, I remembered an almost inhuman man named Makak Rougier—I suppose his name meant 'Rougier's monkey,' because he worked for a man named Rougier—who used to come into town and get terrifyingly drunk. He'd roar up and down the main street, fling things around, and get arrested" (*New Yorker* 19). In a later interview, he says,

> The metaphor of *Dream* was, for me, an old man who looked like an ape, and above his shoulder, a round white full moon. And the journey of that moon which drew the man/ape through the cycle of one night multiplied (like all metaphors) into questions of human evolution, racial evolution, the search for self-respect and pride, and the reality which comes with the morning. (Ciccarelli 38)

Walcott's own account of the play's origins in his memory and imagination points to the society's denigration of those who are poor, dark-skinned, and possess facial features identified as African. It is not entirely clear from whom Makak Rougier acquired his nickname, but, more than likely, he was so named by other people of color in St. Lucia.[4] The problem of the enslaved and the colonized's internalization of white supremacy is inherent in this black man's designation as Makak Rougier, a sobriquet that erases his human name entirely. When coupled with the Anancy tale and its representation of human behavior through animal behavior, the folk practice through which Makak Rougier acquired his nickname forms the emotional basis for *Dream*.

Several contemporary theorists of performance and theater have articulated the ways in which physical movement, especially the highly stylized movement of drama or dance, can preserve and transmit gestures from the past. Roach uses the term "kinesthetic imagination" to refer to the faculty that performs this function. He writes, "This faculty, which flourishes in that mental space where imagination and memory converge, is a way of thinking through movements—at once remembered and reinvented—the otherwise unthinkable, just as dance is often said to be a way of expressing the unspeakable" (27). As Errol Hill has shown in his groundbreaking work *The Trinidad Carnival: Mandate for a National Theatre,* Carnival performance has been an exemplary vehicle for such transmission. Walcott borrowed heavily from Carnival, from storytelling, and from syncretic religious traditions (Vodun, Shango, Obeah) in the construction of *Dream,* and, based on accounts of the rehearsals for the play, he called upon the actors to access their own kinesthetic memory and imagination in developing their parts.[5] Because of its pervasive influence in the culture, Carnival performance would certainly have been a part of the performance lexicon of the original actors, whether they habitually "played mas'" or not. Thus it is clear that the play is a vehicle for memories accumulated in the bodies of its performers as well as a vehicle for Walcott's artistic appropriation and transformation of Caribbean traditions of vernacular performance.

At one level, Walcott's *Dream* is an attempt to create a subjectivity for Makak Rougier, the representative of the most "wretched of the earth." As such, the play engages in what Roach calls *"surrogation,"* the attempt to create substitutes for those who are no longer with us. Roach argues that, "[i]nto the cavities created by loss through death or other forms of departure . . . survivors attempt to fit satisfactory alternates" (2). While this may be an unconscious or unexamined process in organizations or communities, in Walcott's theatrical practice it is a conscious process that attempts to heal the colonized mind. I find it interesting in this context that Walcott's offhanded translation of Makak Rougier—"I suppose his name meant 'Rougier's monkey,' because he worked for a man named Rougier"—elides another possible meaning of the name. Rather than indicating the possessive, Makak Rougier may be meant to indicate that the black man is the false, degenerate version of the white man for whom he works: "makak" standing in for "mimic." Throughout the play, both potential meanings, the possessive which invokes the legacy of slavery and the imitative which invokes colonialism, come into play in dynamic ways. Walcott's conscious process of surrogation presents a possible internal life for a profoundly denigrated figure and demonstrates how such a figure might decolonize his own mind and the minds of his fellow men. Walcott's Makak "stands in for an elusive entity that it is not but that it must vainly aspire both to embody and to replace" (3). And, I would add, to explain.

Makak Rougier thus stands as an acknowledged absent presence in *Dream*. There are, however, a number of *un*acknowledged absent presences in the play—the black female characters fall into this category. They play a variety of supporting roles: "Sisters of the Revelation," "Market Women," "Wives of Makak" (209). They rarely speak and are not clearly differentiated from one another. The marginalization of the black female characters is particularly striking in a play that draws so heavily upon folk sources, since women play extremely important roles as storytellers of the Anancy tales and as practitioners of Obeah and Vodun. Walcott's play does not merely register the marginalization of black women in Caribbean society; it marginalizes these women, refusing to acknowledge the social power they actually possess. The playwright's biography supports this point. In discussions of his "folk" plays, Walcott has described another figure from his memory of childhood, his aunt Sidone, the teller of tales. He remembers her thus:

> When I was very young, I had an aunt whom we called Sidone who would tell us stories. She was an old woman—I can't remember her face too clearly, but she was a powerful woman and a terrific storyteller. . . . And two boys sitting there, not knowing that they wanted to write . . . or maybe beginning to be writers, listening to these amazing stories that were a combination of French and Creole, that obviously had African roots. And the role that she played was really a traditional tribal, sibylline role of the storyteller. And she was tremendous, because she could scare you. There were songs in the narration that she would sing, and they were very plaintive and very frightening, very beautiful songs. . . . Actually, it wasn't just storytelling; it was dramatization. She would change roles. So she became very frightening, but beautifully frightening. If ever there was a visible and audible Muse, then I think she must have been it, this woman, who probably could not write . . .
>
> So that's part of something, a memory that—I am sure, when I think of it—generated in the theater particularly, not necessarily in the poetry, but certainly in the theater, the impulse to tell stories based on the folk imagination and the folk memory, and in a setting that was turbulently beautiful in terms of what the landscape looked like, particularly at night in the moonlight. ("Animals" 269–70)

I quote from this lecture at length because, in it, Walcott clearly identifies his first encounter with theater and the way in which his aunt's dramatic talents led to his "impulse to tell stories based on the folk imagination and the folk memory." Yet Sidone, "this visible and audible Muse," has disappeared almost entirely from the work she helped to generate. Walcott has published a poem about her in *Midsummer*,[6] but in *Dream* she remains an unacknowledged, absent presence. From Walcott's description of Sidone, one can imagine her as the counterpart to Makak Rougier, the denigrated man *Dream* rehabilitates; she is also seen as powerful and frightening and connected to Africa. Behind the weak, interchangeable black women characters of *Dream*, I want to argue, stands this "powerful woman" and "terrific storyteller" who mesmerized the young Walcott and his twin brother. After analyzing what I've termed the Caribbean masculinist tradition in relation to *Dream*, I will return to this discussion of Sidone as an absence and potential presence in the play who might be brought into full being through performance.

2. Slavery, Colonialism, and Masculine Subjectivity in *Dream on Monkey Mountain*

Black male heterosexuality is a significant theme in *Dream*. Makak laments the ugliness which has brought him his nickname and driven women away. When he speaks of his vision of a white goddess who addresses him tenderly, he is viciously mocked by his fellow inmates Tigre (Tiger) and Souris (Mouse), and, later in the play, by his partner Moustique (Mosquito). Tigre says, "I can imagine your dreams. Masturbating in moonlight. Dreaming of women, cause you so damn ugly. You should walk on all fours" (225). "Which woman ever look at you, once, much less a white one?" Moustique asks (241). Makak has completely internalized these assessments of his physical appearance. He himself says, "I have live all my life/Like a wild beast in hiding. Without child, without wife./ . . . Is thirty years now I have look in no mirror,/Not a pool of cold water, when I must drink,/I stir my hands first, to break up my image" (226). Makak's goddess/vision exercises great power over him, both because she represents a white beauty ideal and because she contradicts everything he has been told about his appearance. She also calls him by his real name, not the derogatory nickname by which he is generally known. Makak, revealing his vision to Moustique, recalls, "[S]he say something I will never forget. She say I should not live so any more, here in the forest, frighten of people because I think I ugly. She say that I come from the family of lions and kings" (236). While *Dream*, in the end, critiques both Eurocentricity and Afrocentricity, in this passage we can see the importance of the Afrocentric impulse to decolonizing not only the mind but also the body. It is only through reference to a beauty standard other than that of Europe that Makak is able to transform his self-image, to think of himself as something other than an ugly monkey. Yet, of course, it is European hegemony that has led to the need for an Afrocentric response. As Tejumola Olaniyan so eloquently argues,

> Makak's suspicion of his vision . . . is an implicit critique of reverse discourse as a method of resistance. It dawns on him that his dream of a pristine, glorious Africa is ironically an acceptance still of whiteness as a measure of value (i.e., to *exhibit* his black heritage, to counterpose it to whiteness in the fashion of a binary opposition, not necessarily because he believes in it). And remember it is a *white* woman that set him on the wild utopian chase. In other words, Makak's reverse discourse is operating within, and therefore already circumscribed by, the Manichean terrains of the dominant discourse. ("Corporeal" 163)

When he beheads the white goddess near the end of the play, and refuses the white mask that is a physical remnant of her, Makak retains his true identity, as "a cultural mulatto" ("Corporeal" 165) named Felix Hobain. This ending resolves most, but not all, of the play's tensions; it provides dramatic, but not narrative, closure. Still unsettled is the question of a mate for Makak. At several crucial points within the play, Makak laments his wifeless, childless state: first in the previously quoted passage from the Prologue, then in part 1, scene 1 (236), and finally in part 2, scene 3, shortly before he beheads the white goddess. Recounting one of his lonely reveries, Makak says,

> I ask myself, in a voice I do not know: Who you are, *negre?* I say to the voice and to my hands, with the black coal in the cuts, I say, your name is what—an old man without a mirror. And I went in the little rain barrel behind my hut and look down in the quiet, quiet water at my face, an old, cracked, burn-up face, with the hair turning white. And it was Makak. So I say, if you dead now, if you dead now. Well what? No woman will cry for you, no child will look at your face in death, as if it was the first time. The water in the rain barrel will show the cloud changing, and, as it have no memory, will forget your face. (318)

Though killing the white "mother of civilization" and "confounder of blackness" (319) may offset Makak's "big, big loneliness" (318) to some degree, this action cannot supply the other things Makak longs for: female companionship and a child to provide a sense of his life continuing beyond his inevitable death.

One can look at the major relationships in the play as a series of dyads: between black man and black man (e.g., Makak and Moustique, Tigre and Souris), between black man and white man (with Corporal Lestrade representing white patriarchal rule), and between black man and white woman (Makak and his white goddess). If we accept the black man as the center of the drama, the missing dyad, of course, is between the black man and the black woman. This dyad is also missing from Fanon's *Black Skin, White Masks,* from most Caribbean revisions of Caliban, and from the trickster tales, which rarely address sexual relations among the enslaved/colonized. These omissions indicate the extent to which sexual relations among the colonized, both real and psychological, have been disrupted by imperialist notions of beauty, sexual attractiveness, and proper mating, and the extent to which resistance has been imagined and represented in masculine terms. The black woman's absence from *Dream* is akin to her absence from Shakespeare's *The Tempest,* the play that functioned as an important site of resistance for black Caribbean (primarily male) intellectuals in the struggle for decolonization.[7] In her essay "Beyond Miranda's Meanings: Un/silencing the 'Demonic Ground' of Caliban's 'Woman,'" critic Sylvia Wynter addresses the absence of representations of the black woman and shows how New World slavery and colonialism transformed gender relations: for the first time in Western history, women (that is, white women) were consistently in a relationship of power over men (that is, black men). Wynter argues,

> [W]ith the shift to the secular, the primary code of difference now became that between "men" and "natives," with the traditional "male" and "female" distinctions now coming to play a secondary—if none the less powerful—reinforcing role within the system of symbolic representations. . . . (358)

Wynter reads this transformation through *The Tempest;* her contention is that the play enacts "this mutational shift from the primacy of the *anatomical* model of sexual difference as the referential model of mimetic ordering, to that of the *physiognomic* model of racial/*cultural* difference (Wynter 358). Furthermore, the play enacts the contemporaneous

> mutation from primarily religiously defined modes of human being to the first, partly secularizing ones. . . . [B]oth mutations, each as the condition of the other, are nowhere more clearly put into play than in the relations between Miranda the daughter of Prospero, and Caliban, the once original owner of the island now enslaved by Prospero as a function of the latter's expropriation of the island. That is, in the relations of enforced dominance and subordination between Miranda, though "female," and Caliban, though

"male"; relations in which *sex-gender attributes* are no longer the primary index of "deferent" difference. (Wynter 358)

The white woman's dominance over the black man, initiated by New World
slavery and colonialism, is one of the primary themes of *Dream on Monkey
Mountain*. The white goddess is responsible both for Makak's self-loathing
and for his reflexive self-aggrandizement. Until he beheads her, she directs
his actions, even his apparent rebellion against Eurocentrism. Before colonialism and the rise of the secular, what defined a man was, at least in part,
dominance over women. The addition of modern racial classification to
this system of "sexual-anatomical" ordering (Wynter 358) produced the
denigration of the man of color; he became the "native," and as such do-
minion over a particular group of women was denied him, therefore trun-
cating his masculinity as defined in a traditional sense. At the same time,
white women gained limited access to the "rational nature" (Wynter 362)
accorded white men while Caliban was barred in perpetuity from this status. This is the wound that *Dream* primarily seeks to display and to heal. Exclusion or marginalization of the black woman within this work is not an
accident; it is a necessary condition of the play's internal logic. Wynter, in
her discussion of *The Tempest*, calls this "the most significant absence of all,
that of Caliban's Woman, of Caliban's physiognomically complementary
mate" (360). She continues,

> For nowhere in Shakespeare's play, and in its system of image-making, one
> which would be foundational to the emergence of the first form of a secular
> world system, our present Western world system, does Caliban's mate appear
> as an alternative sexual-erotic model of desire; as an alternative source of an
> alternative system of meanings. (Wynter 360)

Despite the decolonizing impulse of Walcott's play, it still falls short of representing this "alternative sexual-erotic model of desire . . . an alternative
source of an alternative system of meanings." The play rejects the Eurocentric "sexual-erotic model of desire" in which the white woman is the
only appropriate focus of masculine sexual longing, but no other model is
created to fill its place. In fact, fraternal bonding between black men takes
the place of relations between black men and black women that might indicate that Eurocentric ideals of beauty had been not only expunged but
replaced by a mulatto aesthetics of physical attractiveness. By utilizing the
term "mulatto aesthetics" (a phrase Olaniyan uses in passing), I mean to
indicate standards of beauty in cultural production and physical appearance that value creolization and hybridization rather than purity (especially

because, in the colonial and postcolonial context, purity has for the most part meant whiteness). As he comes to a recognition of himself as a "cultural mulatto" (*Scars* 109), one might expect that his own physical self-image and his notions of beauty more generally might have shifted.

But despite the transformation of his consciousness in *Dream,* Makak seems to return to his acceptance of the village's assessment of his looks; in the end, as in the beginning, he says, "And they calling me Makak, for my face, you see? Is as I so ugly" (322). However, at the play's end, Lestrade casually dismisses Makak's self-denigrating explanation with the comment, "I see uglier than that already, friend" (323). The reunited friends, Makak and Moustique, walk off toward Monkey Mountain together. Lestrade's brief assurance to Makak that he is not as ugly as he thinks he is, and the brotherly love of his friend Moustique, replace the extravagant, phantasmatic protestations of the white goddess/vision, while one might have expected that this space would be filled by an image of the black Caribbean woman. Since the play seems to be operating within a hetero-normative model of sexual desire and mating, Makak's grief and longing for a sexual partner are never resolved. Throughout the play, the caretaking relationship between these two men has served as a surrogate for the norm of heterosexual marriage. In scene 1, as he makes coffee for the two of them, Moustique reminisces about how Makak saved him from his previous life.

MOUSTIQUE: . . . And I remember how you find me.

MAKAK: True?

MOUSTIQUE : True. Drunk. Soaking drunk, with this twist foot God give me. Sleeping anywhere, and one morning when you come to market, you find me in the gutter, and you pick me up like a wet fly in the dust, and we establish in this charcoal business. You cut, burn and so on, and I sell, until we make enough to buy the donkey. . . . You was the only one to make me believe a breakfoot nigger could go somewhere in this life. (233–34)

Later, after Makak has related his dream of the white woman, Moustique tries to talk some sense into him.

MOUSTIQUE: You remember one morning I come up and from the time I break the bush, I see you by the side of the hut trembling and talking, your eyes like you crazy, and was I had to gather bush, light a fire and make you sweat out that madness? Which white lady? You is nothing. You black, ugly, poor, so you worse than nothing. You like me. Small, ugly, with a foot like a "S." Man together two of us is minus one. (237)

These two passages establish the love that Makak and Moustique have for one another; they also show that these men take care of each other because none of the women in their social sphere will have them. These actual, potentially available women, Makak and Moustique's female counterparts, are never represented; their lack of desire for these two social outcasts is a given. They are present neither as objects of desire nor as desiring subjects. As Wynter writes of *The Tempest*, "there, on the New World island, as the only woman, Miranda and her mode of physiognomic being, defined by the philogenically 'idealized' features of straight hair and thin lips is canonized as the 'rational' object of desire" (360). The white female apparition in *Dream* is a version of Miranda, and when she is beheaded, a gap is created that the play never fills. The black women in the play, though at one point called upon to represent "Wives of Makak" (209), do not carry symbolic weight sufficient to counterbalance that of "Venus, the Virgin, the Sleeping Beauty" (*Dream* 319). In the heterosexual world of the play, Makak remains celibate rather than finding his "physiognomically complementary" mate. In Wynter's analysis of *The Tempest*,

> the absence of Caliban's woman as Caliban's sexual reproductive mate functions to ontologically negate their progeny/population group, forcing this group to serve as the allegorical incarnation of "pure" sensory nature. (362)

In *Dream*, Walcott seeks to transform Makak's stigmatization and self-perception as a representative of "'pure' sensory nature," or, in Lestrade's terms, a member of the "one tribe . . . that lingered behind [the rest of mankind], . . . the nigger" (*Dream* 217). Yet the absence of Makak's "woman" "ontologically negate[s]" the progeny of this black Caribbean everyman and limits the possible effects of his transformed consciousness. While, in Patrick Taylor's words, "Makak is the Caribbean peasant or working-class person who has completed the liberating journey of self-recovery" (Taylor 223), in truth Makak is the Caribbean *man* who has completed this journey. (As the previous chapter on *The Chosen Place* makes clear, the Caribbean woman's journey to self-recovery looks different in several respects.) While Makak's achievement is a significant one, he cannot take further steps on one road toward liberation without his "physiognomically complementary mate" and their "*potential* progeny" (Wynter 360–61).

Traditionally in Western culture, women have been seen as the property of men—either fathers, husbands, brothers, or other male relatives. Unlike white men, whose claims upon women (both white women and women of color) are limited only by the claims of other individual white men, black men's claims to white women are continually foreclosed by white patriarchy. Furthermore, the black mán's claims to "his own" women may also be limited by the claims of white men, "masters" in the factual or the metaphorical sense.[8] When we understand the elevation of white women that took place in the context of slavery and colonialism, it becomes clear why a white woman is chosen to embody the evils of European hegemony in Walcott's play. Mainstream feminism may interpret this use of the female body as merely another way in which women are made to signify concepts. However, mainstream European and American feminism fails to recognize that, with the inception of New World slavery and colonialism, white women gained power, both material and symbolic, over black men and black women. The fact that the conquest of the Americas and plantation slavery provided white women with previously unattainable power and privilege cannot be separated from the fact that men of color became "natives" at this point and the fact that women of color were located even further down on the scale of human rationality. While in some cases white women have been forced to function as "pawns" through whom white men subjugate black men (as in lynching in the U.S.), in other ways, white women have gained unprecedented authority over men and women of color through the racial arrangements of slavery and imperialism. This power is not merely phantasmatic, like the white apparition's power over Makak's self-image. The slave narratives, primarily from the U.S. but also from the Anglophone Caribbean via England, register white women's everyday exercise of power over the enslaved, both male and female.[9] Wynter's critical reworking of *The Tempest* highlights these new, New World configurations of race and gender: she has moved beyond the other Caribbean writers who drew upon and drastically revised the play in an earlier moment in the process of decolonization. Walcott's Caribbean male contemporaries "seized upon *The Tempest* as a way of amplifying their calls for decolonization within the bounds of the dominant cultures" (Nixon 558). It is instructive to look at these West Indian revisions of Caliban in relationship to Walcott's articulation, in *Dream,* of a "real West Indian self . . . without any illusions" (Olaniyan, *Scars* 109).

The Rehabilitation of Caliban and *Black Skin, White Masks*

Caliban was particularly appropriate as a potential hero for the Caribbean anti-colonial movement, because he provided a way to speak about slavery and colonization simultaneously, and because he demonstrated how profoundly Anglophone Caribbean writers in the 1950s and '60s felt the lack of an established, indigenous literary tradition.[10] As critic Rob Nixon argues in an article entitled "Caribbean and African Appropriations of *The Tempest*," from the 1950s through the 1970s, a number of Caribbean writers,

> adopted the play as a founding text in an oppositional lineage which issued from a geopolitically and historically specific set of cultural ambitions. They perceived that the play could contribute to their self-definition during a period of great flux. (558)

The figure of Caliban represented the slave who had learned his master's language but still resisted his master's domination. One can easily see how such a figure, re-incarnated in a revolutionary moment, could serve the same function as the slave narrators in the United States—Caliban helped to create a history of resistance. The colonized, Caribbean writer had much to gain from using Caliban as his model and metaphor for resistance. First, he (and I use the pronoun advisedly) achieved recognition in the metropole, merely by his choice of subject. He also gained a lever with which to overthrow the discourse of colonialism: we can see Caliban as the deconstructive figure in Shakespeare's text, the element that reveals the play's subtext, which is about labor and who is designed to perform it. The third advantage the colonial writer gained was shock value, for refusing to accept the supposed inviolateness and transcendent literary value of Shakespeare and his work. Finally, Caliban is, in a peculiar sense, a literary ancestor, a written record of resistance. Therefore, one can see why using a figure like this would be particularly attractive to a writer. Having the will and the ability to manipulate this character is evidence of mastery of the dominant tradition, and, in the words of Errol Miller, "mastery of the Anglo-culture, particularly mastery of the English language, became the most important criterion of upward social mobility through education" in the British Caribbean colonies (Miller 207–8). Though using Caliban to state their unequivocal desire for independence, colonial intellectuals at the same time revealed their need to be accepted as masters of language by English standards. Caliban's "literariness" was both an advantage and a cage.

There were other significant problems involved in using Caliban. Nixon notes that "the plot ran out" (576); that is to say, after the initial moment of decolonization, the play had little to say about the relations between the former colonizer, the formerly colonized masses, and the colonial intellectual. He also briefly mentions the fact that the play included no model of colonized women's resistance, the issue that drives Wynter's analysis of

The Tempest. There is an other problem with Caliban that is ontological or perhaps genealogical: he is a fictional character, not an actual revolutionary. This means that there was only a limited extent to which one could reflect upon his construction as a revolutionary subject. Caliban's curses and his mimicry reveal, in Homi Bhabha's terms,

> a discursive process by which the excess or slippage produced by the *ambivalence* of mimicry (almost the same, *but not quite*) does not merely "rupture" the discourse, but becomes transformed into an uncertainty which fixes the colonial subject as a "partial" presence. By "partial" I mean both "incomplete" and "virtual." It is as if the very emergence of the "colonial" is dependent for its representation upon some strategic limitation or prohibition *within* the authoritative discourse itself. The success of colonial appropriation depends on a proliferation of inappropriate objects that ensure its strategic failure, so that mimicry is at once resemblance and menace. (Bhabha 127)

Thus the Caliban of Shakespeare's play embodies this "resemblance and menace" yet has no independent being; he is an effect of the splitting of colonial discourse. He is as much a product of imperialism as the colonies themselves—an impossible symbol around which to build an indigenous Caribbean tradition of revolt.

For Caribbean intellectuals during decolonization, there were (and continue to be) two primary tasks: first, overthrowing the discourse and the social and economic arrangements of colonialism, and second, recognizing and extending (in some cases creating) indigenous, creolized cultural forms.[11] Caliban could address the first task but not the second; he was appropriate for dramatizing the relationship to the colonizer but not for dramatizing the relationship of the descendant of Africa to his/her past and present reality in the Caribbean. Caliban looks outward rather than inward; hence other models are necessary for the creation of an indigenous tradition. This is of course why George Lamming, in *The Pleasures of Exile,* brings Toussaint L'Ouverture (via C. L. R. James) into his discussion of Caliban; however, his placement of L'Ouverture within the framework of Shakespeare's play works against his ultimate objective, in large part because he glorifies the individual and slights the collective nature of the Haitian Revolution. Overall, the use of Caliban as a revolutionary symbol privileges written sources over oral sources, European models over Caribbean/creolized models, individual achievement over collective achievement, and men's over women's revolts in the representation of slavery and colonization.[12]

In Caribbean literature's revisions of *The Tempest,* the black woman's absence mirrors her absence in the original play. Though these "repeated, reinforcing, transgressive appropriations" (Nixon 558) clearly sought to overturn the logic and the power relations of slavery and imperialism, they, like *Dream,* were unable to fully escape from the "new behaviour-regulatory narrative schema" in which the absence of the black woman is "an onto- logical absence, . . . central" to the operation of this new schema (Wynter 363). Rejected by Miranda, Caliban never imagines a mate similar to him- self with whom he might people "[t]his isle with Calibans" (*The Tempest* 1.2.350); without the creation of such a community of resistance, as op- posed to a single resistant subjectivity, his rebellion cannot progress. (I am not arguing that sexual reproduction is the only way to generate a com- munity of resistance, but it is one potent way of imagining and represent- ing the creation of such a community.)

Walcott, though creating *Dream* during this historical period, already perceived the problems of Afrocentricity as a corrective to Eurocentricity. *Dream* moves beyond Lamming's despair and complicates the resistance of Césaire's Caliban. Early in his career, Walcott chose a model for a Carib- bean creative subjectivity significantly different from Caliban—the figure of Robinson Crusoe. In a lecture from 1965, "The Figure of Crusoe," pub- lished only recently, Walcott articulates his appropriation of Defoe's cast- away.

My Crusoe, then, is Adam. . . .

I have tried to say this. That given a virgin world, a paradise, any sound, any act of naming something, like Adam baptizing the creatures, because that action is anthropomorphic, that is, like the pathetic fallacy, it projects it- self by a sound onto something else, such a sound is not really prose, but po- etry, is not simile, but metaphor. . . .

I am claiming, then, that poets and prose writers who are West Indians, despite the contaminations around us, are in the position of Crusoe, the namer. Like him, they have behind them, borne from England, from India, or from Africa, that dead bush, that morphology I mentioned earlier, but what is more important is that these utterances, these words, when written, are as fresh, as truly textured, as when Crusoe sets them down in the first West Indian novel. . . . Besides, it is the figure of Crusoe, as certain critics have found in the figure of Prospero, that supplies the anguish of authority, of the conscience of empire, rule, benign power. The metaphor can be stretched too far. There is now a fashionable, Marxist-evolved method of analysing figures from literature as if they were guilty. These analyses, we have seen them happen in brilliant re-creations, to Prospero as the white imperi- alist, and to Caliban as the ugly savage. If, as I shall, I draw a similar parallel to Crusoe and Friday, it is because all such dialectic is there in the text. It exists in Defoe the pamphleteer as it does in Defoe as a novelist, not a poet, and a novelist deals with the human condition under pressure. In *Robinson Crusoe* the pressure is that of isolation and survival. . . .

 I am claiming nothing exaggerated when I state that Crusoe, through Defoe's multiple combination of adventure story, religious Protestant tract of trust and self-reliance, and Christian zeal for converting brutish tribes, not with the belligerence of Kipling, but with honest, tender belief in the superiority of his kind, has given us a more real symbol than critics claim for Prospero and Caliban. Crusoe is no lord of magic, duke, prince. He does not possess the island he inhabits. He is alone, he is a craftsman, his beginnings are humble. He acts, not by authority, but by conscience. ("Crusoe" 35–37)

Walcott goes on to analyze Crusoe's salvation through writing and to describe Crusoe's loss of his new, New World self in the process of converting Friday. This critical reading and transformation of Defoe's Crusoe is, as Walcott suggests above, a move similar to the Caribbean reconstructions of *The Tempest,* yet its valence is profoundly different. Walcott chooses to inhabit the position of greatest power, while at the same time being aware of and critiquing the ways in which that power can be misused. I have quoted this passage at length to demonstrate that Walcott had in fact considered the viability of Caliban as a model for an emergent Caribbean subjectivity and then had rejected that possibility before (or during the time) he wrote *Dream on Monkey Mountain.* He explored the idea of Crusoe in a book of poems entitled *The Castaway,* published in 1965. It is clear that Makak's ability to move beyond a reflexive Afrocentrism (embodied, for example, in Césaire's Caliban) is the result of the development of Walcott's very different strand of thought about the legacy of Europe and Africa in the Caribbean. Yet like those writers who celebrated Caliban, Walcott perpetuates the representational dynamics of European colonialism in his omission of significant representations of black women. As we turn to yet another text of decolonization, we can examine the ways in which one of the most influential anti-colonial theorists and activists, Frantz Fanon, articulates the problems of men and women of color under colonial domination.

 In many ways, Walcott's *Dream on Monkey Mountain* can be seen as a dramatic analogue to *Black Skin, White Masks.* Both are fundamentally concerned with the loss of identity, power, and honor for black men under slavery and colonialism. Though fifteen years separate the dates of publication for the two books,[13] they register roughly the same moment in the psychic processes of decolonization. Furthermore, Walcott directly alludes to Fanon's book by employing a white mask as a signifier of Makak's dreams of whiteness and of a glorious heritage from a fictive Africa. The white apparition/goddess in *Dream* and Makak's response to her reflect the attitudes of the black men whom Fanon analyzes in chapter 3 of *Black Skin, White Masks,* "The Man of Color and the White Woman."

Unlike Walcott and the Caribbean champions of Caliban, Fanon appears to take into account the wounds and complexes of women of color under colonial circumstances. In fact, the controversial second chapter of Fanon's book, "The Woman of Color and the White Man," examines the preference for white men among French Caribbean women of color through an analysis of Mayotte Capécia's *Je suis Martiniquaise,* through anecdotes about such women in France, and through a piece of fiction by Abdoulaye Sadji, entitled *Nini* (published in *Présence Africaine*). Although Fanon recognizes that "[i]t is because the Negress feels inferior that she aspires to win admittance into the white world" (60), this chapter of the book is, nevertheless, primarily a complaint against black women's rejection of men of color. In discussing the man of color and the white woman, Fanon recognizes the loss of manhood that drives black men from the colonies to seek out white women. He writes,

> Out of the blackest part of my soul, across the zebra striping of my mind, surges this desire to be suddenly *white.*
>
> I wish to be acknowledged not as *black* but as *white.*
>
> Now—and this is a form of recognition that Hegel had not envisaged—who but a white woman can do this for me? By loving me she proves that I am worthy of white love. I am loved like a white man.
>
> I am a white man.
>
> Her love takes me onto the noble road that leads to total realization. . . .
>
> I marry white culture, white beauty, white whiteness.
>
> When my restless hands caress those white breasts, they grasp white civilization and dignity and make them mine. (63)

Fanon clearly understands the inferiority complex vis-à-vis white men that compels the colonized man of color to pursue idealized white female beauty. Yet he does not perceive the plight of the woman of color in the same terms; he refuses to recognize that women of color have been cut off from the general category of "woman" in the same way that men of color have been cut off from the general category of "man." As Sylvia Wynter states,

> [I]f, before the sixteenth century, what Irigaray terms as *"patriarchal discourse"* had erected itself on the "silenced ground" of women, from then on, the new

primarily silenced ground (which at the same time now enables the partial
liberation of Miranda's hitherto stifled speech), would be that of the majority
population-groups of the globe—all signified now as the "natives" (Caliban's) [*sic*] to the "men" of Prospero and Fernando, with Miranda becoming both a co-participant, if to a lesser . . . extent, in the power and privileges
generated by the empirical supremacy of her own population; and as well,
the beneficiary of a mode of privilege unique to her, that of being the meta-
physically invested and "idealized" object of desire for all classes . . . and all
population-groups. (363)

In other words, the black man is sundered from manhood, as embodied by
Prospero and Fernando, and the black woman is sundered from womanhood, as embodied by Miranda; furthermore, the white woman becomes the
object of desire for all men, regardless of race or class. The colonized women
of color whom Fanon so harshly critiques are clearly seeking to share the
"mode of privilege unique to" the white woman, in the same way that colonized men of color seek to experience the manhood that has been denied
them. While Fanon chastises these women for rejecting black men, he does
not make a similar case against black men whose sexual desire settles primarily upon white women; that is, their primary crime is not against the
black women whom they implicitly or explicitly reject as being incapable of
fully confirming their manhood. Fanon's basic complaint against women of
color—that in their longing to be white they reject men of color in favor
of white men—is partly a complaint against these women's agency as desiring subjects; they are critiqued not only because they choose white men, but
because they *choose*. Their place, as women, is to be selected.[14]

Like Walcott in *Dream*, Fanon in *Black Skin, White Masks* inadvertently
weakens the revolutionary character of his message and participates in the
dismissal of the black woman initiated by the Western, secular "behaviour-
regulatory schema" (Wynter 363). In *Dream on Monkey Mountain*, in the
Caribbean appropriations of *The Tempest*, and in *Black Skin, White Masks*,
the black man is revivified "as an alternative source of an alternative system of meanings" (Wynter 360), while the black woman remains in her
place in the hegemonic hierarchy, the native's native.

The Death of Anancy

I include the Caribbean trickster tales within the black Caribbean masculinist tradition for two reasons: first, because the animal characters of
the Anancy stories are almost exclusively male, and second, because the
tales address the power dynamics of slavery and colonialism, which have

traditionally been cast as problems of freedom and self-determination for the black man. Walcott's *Dream* borrows not only the animal characters of these African-based trickster tales, it also borrows from the tales a vision of slavery and colonialism as struggles of wit and strength between men, in which women play primarily symbolic roles. Though in one way Walcott's play works against the "mythical narrative" of Anancy, in another way it buys into the masculinism of the spider-trickster's *modus operandi*. Patrick Taylor argues that, "Though Moustique is associated with a spider in Makak's dream, there is no indication that this spider is Anancy the trickster" (217). My contention is that the white spider *is* Anancy and that the spider's death, while seen at first as a sign of impending tragedy, is actually a symbol that the trickster is dead, that his particular mode of Caribbean masculinity has little to offer in the future and must be superseded.

The spider suggests Anancy for several reasons. First, as noted above, the characters in *Dream* call to mind the characters of the Anancy stories, for many of them are called by animal names. Within this context, the appearance of a spider, not once but at two significant points in the play, points toward the well-known spider-trickster. Moustique first touches the spider when he reaches underneath a bench in Makak's hut for a crocus bag of coals. The stage directions read, "[*He puts his hand under the bench, then withdraws it slowly in horror*]" (238). He screams, kills the spider, and then asks Makak, "Well. What you looking at? [*Pause*] Is a bad sign?" (238) Makak replies in the affirmative, and then Moustique says,

Yes. [*Holds out his hand, which is trembling*] To hell with that! I don't believe that. I not no savage. Every man have to die. It have a million ways to die. But no spider with white eggs will bring it. [*Silence*] You believe that, of course. You . . . you . . . you living like a beast, and you believe everything! [*Points at the spider*]. (239)

It is not merely superstition that causes Makak to read impending death in the appearance of the white spider with eggs; the white goddess/apparition has told him that he "will see signs" (239) and he takes this to be one of them. Thus the white spider is associated with the white goddess. This connection is emphasized by the fact that when next Moustique reaches under the bench for the coal sack, he finds "*a white mask with long coarse hair*" (239), a mask that represents the white goddess throughout the play. The death of the spider foreshadows Moustique's dream-death in the play, as well as the final beheading of the goddess and the discarding of the white mask.

This association of the spider-trickster with the representative of idealized whiteness in the play may appear counterintuitive at first, since Anancy is an African-derived, creole folk character. However, when we look at the consequences of the spider's appearance and at recent analyses of the trickster tales in the Francophone Caribbean, their connection begins to make sense. The "sign" of the spider's appearance and death reinforces the goddess's advice and precipitates Makak's deluded journey to an "Africa of the mind" (*Scars* 104). The next time the spider appears is in part 1, scene 3, when Moustique impersonates Makak in Quatre Chemin (Four Roads/Crossroads) Market. He has just convinced the villagers to give him food and drink in exchange for his blessing when a spider runs over his hand. He drops the bowl that he has just raised to his lips, but then tries to pretend that the spider simply startled him, rather than revealing his mortal dread. Corporal Lestrade and Basil the carpenter call his bluff; when they put the spider on Moustique/Makak's body, he winces visibly. Basil then recognizes him as Moustique and reveals his ruse to the villagers. Moustique shouts,

> What you want me to say? "I am the resurrection, I am the life"? . . . or you all want me, as if this hand hold magic, to stretch it and like a flash of lightning to make you all white? God after god you change, promise after promise you believe, and you still covered with dirt; so why not believe me. All I have is this [*Shows the white mask*], black faces, white masks! I tried like you. Moustique then! Moustique! [*Spits at them*] That is my name! Do what you want! (271)

With cries of "Kill him! Break his legs! Beat him! Kill him!" (271), the crowd attacks Moustique, inflicting deadly wounds. He later dies in Makak's arms. In this scene, Moustique has been playing Anancy, deceiving his fellow "creatures" in the way that Anancy often does, and he is caught and punished with a ferocity characteristic of the trickster tales.[15] Here, the play registers the harm that the trickster ethos inflicts upon the community. Tricksterism, continued beyond the abolition of the slave system, works mostly at the expense of the other members of the colonized community. The fact that Moustique castigates the villagers for their stupidity in believing the stories about Makak, while holding up the white mask, further cements the connection between *Dream*'s spiders, Anancy, and the ideal of whiteness embodied by the goddess.

It is largely because of tricksterism's connection to plantation slavery and its negative consequences in the post-slavery era that contemporary commentators on Caribbean folklore question the continuing relevance of trickster characters. A. James Arnold, in an article entitled "Animal Tales, Historic Dispossession, and Creole Identity in the French West Indies," summarizes and analyzes a number of readings of creole animal tales. Highlighting her critical writing, Arnold contends that, for Guadeloupean novelist Maryse Condé,

> the characteristics of Rabbit [the French West Indian folktale hero/anti-hero who resembles Anancy] are those the slaveholding class attributed to the slaves. In other words, conceived in the slaves' interiorization of the image their masters had of them, the animal characters of the traditional tales constituted the very face and expression of the culture of slavery. Through their own folktales, the slaves had incorporated and expressed others' stereotypes of them. In Condé's analysis, that which seems to be indisputably the slaves' own popular cultural production—the traditional folktale—has its origin in someone else's vision. (259)

Though both Condé and Arnold are commenting on the folktale in the Caribbean islands now designated as overseas departments of France, their critiques are relevant to the Anglophone Caribbean folktale as well.[16] As noted in the introduction to this chapter, one of Walcott's most brilliant strokes in *Dream on Monkey Mountain,* a strategy that foregrounds the problematic genealogy of the creole folktales, is the connection between the negative history of black men/people being associated with apes and the legacy of the animal tales, which, like folktales in many other cultures, continue "the tradition of exploring animal creation as the source of metaphorical analogies for aspects of human experience" (Poynting 212). These two traditions—the Western tradition of dehumanizing blacks by associating them with "dumb" animals, and the tradition of metaphorically discussing and analyzing human behavior through reference to animal behavior—are brought into an edgy, fruitful interaction in Walcott's play. The latter, virtually universal tradition is degraded through its connection to the former, which justified chattel slavery by linking Africans with non-human primates and beasts of burden. The creole folktale is inextricably tied to the system of labor which brought it into being, not only through the identity of its original tellers but through the plantation system's valuation of these enslaved storytellers as so much livestock. This ambivalent legacy of the creole animal tale and other cultural, economic, and social legacies of slavery persist into the post-slavery era represented in *Dream.* Makak's escape from "the symbolic prison of mental enslavement" (*Scars* 109) is effected through his assertion of his human, not animal, name, Felix Hobain. "Felix," of course, means fortunate; Makak's fall into the dream turns out to be a *felix culpa* or happy fall that leads to a positive redefinition of self.

3. "Writing the Absent Potential"

While *Dream* does not question the masculinism of the trickster tales, it is possible to use the play's rejection of the Anancy ethos to critique the masculine bias inherent in that ethos. In recognizing how beholden the trickster is to the racial arrangements of slavery and colonialism, and in rejecting Eurocentrism and reflexive Afrocentrism, Walcott's *Dream on Monkey Mountain* has taken a crucial first step toward "the possibility of creating a society based on human mutuality" (Taylor xii). This society must feature mutual recognition and respect, not only between races, but between genders as well. Perhaps if we look behind the creole folktales at those who are often the tellers—black women like Walcott's aunt Sidone, whom he credits with his understanding of the dramatic significance of the traditional stories[17]—we can uncover the continuing significance of the tales, which lies more in their function than in their content. Behind the trickster tale, the black female teller is revealed as a powerful "source of an alternative system of meanings" (Wynter 360), keeping alive the idea of story and passing it on to a new generation, shifting shapes and embodying other realities, "very frightening, but beautifully frightening" (Walcott, "Animals" 270).[18]

In an illuminating critical essay on African American drama, Sandra Richards writes about the "absent potential" that exists in the written text of a play. She uses this concept to discuss how she would circumvent the masculine bias in August Wilson's "Ma Rainey's Black Bottom," if she were to direct the play. While the stories of the male band members are told in the written text of the play, Ma Rainey is given "no comparable narrative" (Richards 81). Citing the transformative potential of performance, Richards finds a space within Wilson's play where she would add Rainey performing one of her songs.

> Having just finished jockeying for respect with her white producers, and left in the company of her two most trusted band members, Ma might indulge the luxury of laying aside her aggressive defensiveness, she might begin to sing, thereby displaying some of the vulnerability and self-reflexivity that fuel the blues singer's stance. Dependent upon the carriage of the body, the quality of the actress's unadorned voice, and spectators' own sense of the terrors life poses, a moment of transcendence might occur when those assembled

experience why "[T]his be an empty world without the blues." In this moment, absent from the printed page but wonderfully charged in performance, Ma's particular blues performance can be constructed. (83)

Applying Richards's principle to *Dream on Monkey Mountain,* one can imagine at least one space where the black female teller of tales might be brought into view. The "Conteur," whose singing voice opens the drama, could be played by a woman and appear onstage (rather than singing offstage with the chorus as the stage directions now indicate). This would suggest the importance of female agency in the transmission and transformation of folk culture, an agency Walcott acknowledges not only in his comments on Sidone but in the notes on the first production of *Dream,* which appear at the beginning of the published text of the play. Walcott writes "Scene 11, the healing scene, owes an obvious debt to 'Spirit,' choreographed for the Little Carib Company by Beryl MacBurnie" [*sic*] (208). Walcott biographer Bruce King argues that "[a]s a result of seeing McBurnie's company, Derek Walcott would want to create an acting style which was West Indian in body movement and gestures, a style of acting close to dance" (*Caribbean Life* 124). Beryl McBurnie was a Trinidadian dancer and choreographer who had studied modern dance in the United States and returned to Trinidad to form her own company. McBurnie's genius as a choreographer using folk forms is a partially acknowledged presence standing behind some aspects of *Dream;* this fact provides yet another incentive for "writing the absent potential" of female agency in Caribbean art and culture. Perhaps by acknowledging and incorporating a wide range of modes of Caribbean womanhood—the black woman as lover, poet, mother, choreographer, narrator, healer, dramatist—as well as a wide range of modes of Caribbean manhood, we can actually move beyond the "narrative schema, powerfully re-enacted in the plot line of *The Tempest*" (Wynter 362), which Walcott and the Caribbean revisers of Shakespeare sought to destabilize. Perhaps we can then move closer to the "terrain . . . of a new science of human discourse, of human 'life' beyond the 'master discourse' of our governing 'privileged text,' and its sub/versions. Beyond Miranda's meanings" (Wynter 366).

Though Walcott, writing in the late 1960s, was not able to envision the extent to which New World cultural representations and societies would have to be transformed in order to deconstruct the "master discourse," he paved the way for later writers to explore the complex relationships between men and women, blacks and whites, myth and history, and storytellers and their tales in the Caribbean and in the United States.

The foregoing chapters have explored the black subjects created by

African American and Afro-Caribbean writers in works written in the wake of the Civil Rights Movement and West Indian anti-colonial struggles. In choosing these works, I have tried to represent the range and variety of the contemporary narrative of slavery. One of these works, *Beloved,* is a historical novel of slavery; indeed, it has become the classic of the genre. Another, *Oxherding Tale,* is a postmodernist historical novel of slavery in which the image of the past is continually disrupted by the idiom of the present. In the novel *The Chosen Place, The Timeless People,* and the play *Dream on Monkey Mountain,* the present is haunted by lingering memories of the past, sustained by a social structure still profoundly linked to slavery and colonialism. The final work I analyze in this study, Carolivia Herron's *Thereafter Johnnie,* enacts the past, present, and future of U.S. slave society. Its temporal range and epic scope distinguish it from every other contemporary narrative of slavery, and its apocalyptic vision makes the chapter devoted to it a fitting end to this book.

THE GEOGRAPHY OF THE APOCALYPSE

Incest, Mythology, and the Fall of Washington City in Carolivia Herron's *Thereafter Johnnie*

The childhood experience that determines spatial practices later develops its effects, proliferates, floods private and public spaces, undoes their readable surfaces, and creates within the planned city a "metaphorical" or mobile city, like the one Kandinsky dreamed of: "a great city built according to all the rules of architecture and then suddenly shaken by a force that defies all calculation."

MICHEL DE CERTEAU, *The Practice of Everyday Life*

There are, in the district of Columbia, several slave prisons, or "Negro pens," as they are termed. . . . By order of her master, Clotel was removed from Richmond and placed in one of these prisons, to await the sailing of a vessel for New Orleans. The prison in which she was put stands midway between the capitol at Washington and the President's house.

WILLIAM WELLS BROWN, *Clotel, or The President's Daughter*

Perhaps the most disturbing aspects of Carolivia Herron's 1991 novel *Thereafter Johnnie* are the eroticized incestuous relationships between a middle-class black father and daughter in the present and a white slavemaster, his son, and their black daughter/sister in the past. John Christopher Snowdon, a black surgeon in present-day Washington, D.C., sexually molests one of his three daughters, Patricia, when she is about two years old. The novel connects this molestation to Patricia's adult sexual obsession with her father; the two have seemingly consensual sex when Patricia is seventeen, and Patricia gives birth to a daughter, whom she names Johnnie. John

Christopher's sexual abuse of his daughter is linked to a history of incestuous sexual abuse in slavery. One of the primary questions that *Thereafter Johnnie* poses is: What is the connection between the incestuous sexual abuse of black girls/women by their black fathers and the incestuous sexual abuse of enslaved black girls/women by their white father-masters? The novel itself posits answers to this question in a number of different ways, and this chapter will elucidate the intimate associations between geography, gender, mythology, race, power, and sexuality in Herron's representation of this problem of historical influence and continuity.

Through realist narration, myth, fairy tale, prophecy, classical and biblical allusions, and allusions to African American literature and culture, *Thereafter Johnnie* tells the tale of the Snowdon family's development, crisis, and disintegration in a dizzying, layered, epic structure of 24 books (like the *Iliad,* the *Odyssey,* and the Hebrew Bible).[1] The novel employs virtually all of its characters as narrators: John Christopher Snowdon, the family patriarch; Camille, John Christopher's wife and the mother of their three daughters; Cynthia Jane, the oldest daughter, who leaves home to become a nun as the family is being destroyed by incest; Patricia, the daughter whose name indicates her special attachment to the father; Eva, the woman-identified sister who is raped on the same night John Christopher and Patricia consummate their incestuous passion; Diotima, the Afro-Mexican woman who becomes Patricia's companion and Johnnie's caretaker; and Johnnie herself, a messianic figure who is simultaneously John Christopher's daughter and granddaughter, Patricia's daughter and half-sister. Most of the novel takes place over the course of about thirty-five years, from the time of Camille and John Christopher's courtship and marriage to the family's demise at the end of the twentieth century. The final chapter flashes back to the slave past, introducing Laetitia and Rowena, an enslaved mother and daughter who are ancestors of the twentieth-century Snowdon women and whose story is a modern, near-pornographic re-telling of scenes from *Incidents in the Life of a Slave Girl, Iola Leroy,* and *Clotel, or The President's Daughter.* The last few pages of the novel flash forward to the new millennium, in which Washington, D.C., and the United States have been destroyed. The reader finally learns that the narrator whose voice frames the novel is a descendant of Diotima, an epic storyteller who calls down Johnnie as her muse and relates the final tragedy of Johnnie's destiny.

"Kill the boys and rape the girls" (Herron 242). This stark injunction, attributed to European slavers and slaveholders in *Thereafter Johnnie,* encapsulates the curse on what I call the House of Africa, the descendants of African slaves whose history is represented, in the novel, by the Snowdon family. The full curse reads thus:

"The females shall be raped and the males shall be murdered." And the males that are not murdered shall be sold, and to certain ones of the males that are neither murdered nor sold, to certain of those few males come late into the house marrying, and to certain of the males born to the house but who nevertheless survive murder and slavery—to these shall be given the power of revenge upon the females of their own house who consented with the white males for their destruction, these males shall be given the female children of their own house, and these shall be raped. And raped again. (Herron 239–40)

The novel presents this curse as the primary link between white slavemasters' sexual abuse of black women in the past and black men's sexual abuse of black women in the present. As a device within the text, the curse connects classical Western myth and biblical imagery, the history of American slavery, and the psychology and economics of domination. Yet, as an explanation of historical phenomena, the curse is a deliberate provocation, begging the questions that it appears to answer. For the modern/postmodern writer and reader, the curse is first and foremost a literary device, a complex allusion to Greco-Roman mythology in general and to the curse of the House of Atreus in particular.[2] Though gods both ancient and modern are invoked in the novel, their presence or absence is not responsible for the motion of history, except in the sense that patriarchal religious beliefs structure social behavior. The question thus becomes, through what mechanisms *does* this curse operate?

The ideological and material means through which the curse operates across American history fall into three broad and overlapping categories: the continuities of racial oppression, the continuities of patriarchal oppression, and the continuities in victims' responses to sexual abuse and domination. In the novel, these categories are linked by being embedded in a capitalist framework. Herron foregrounds the concept of ownership in all three, building a subtle connection between the moral and economic values of patriarchal slaveholders and middle-class property owners. The nation's inability to turn away from these values brings about the apocalyptic end of the society as we know it.

In order to illuminate these historical continuities, Herron uses two distinct but converging strategies: she employs geography as a major metaphor and structural principle, and she examines psychoanalytic and psychotherapeutic analyses of incest, invoking and critiquing the Freudian view of incest as phantasmatic and representative of the daughter's desire. The formation of the main characters as female subjects of patriarchy is inscribed in and through geography and incestuous sexual abuse. To put it another way, the psychodynamics of incest—as both familial and cultural pathology—are spatialized in the novel.

Thereafter Johnnie takes full advantage of the ability of geography to render the relations of power, an ability explicated by Michel Foucault in the interview "Questions on Geography,"

> I think through them [spatial obsessions] I did come to what I had basically been looking for: the relations that are possible between power and knowledge. Once knowledge can be analysed in terms of region, domain, implantation, displacement, transposition, one is able to capture the process by which knowledge functions as a form of power and disseminates the effects of power. There is an administration of knowledge, a politics of knowledge, relations of power which pass via knowledge and which, if one tries to transcribe them, lead one to consider forms of domination designated by such notions as field, region and territory. (69)

If we understand knowledge, and in particular scholarly learning, to be a major concern of the novel—the book does begin and end, after all, in a library—and if we recognize that the novel seeks to problematize power and resistance, then we can see how important it is to analyze the novel's modes of representing the relationships between knowledge and power. Herron's allusions to Greco-Roman mythology, the Old and New Testaments, and the founding texts of African American literary history (slave narratives and anti-slavery novels) combine to critique Western culture as a culture of incest. In her review of *Thereafter Johnnie*, Barbara Christian identifies this critique as one of the major reasons for the novel's constant references to the classical and biblical traditions: "Herron's unrelenting vision illuminates our Western origins, the incestuous nature of the Gods our civilization has created and the consequences of that creation" (7). Herron's novel chronicles and mythologizes the creation of middle-class, black female identities (and enslaved female identities) through incestuous sexual molestation, "seduction" by the father, and rape, as well as through education in classical Western myth and Christian tradition, especially the many tales of Zeus's seduction of his earthly daughters (Europa and Leda, for example) and the story of Lot and his daughters. When in "Matin," the final chapter, the white slaveholding master and son decide to establish their enslaved mistress Laetitia in a home of her own, they educate her so she can pass as a white widow, "teaching her all proper language, diction, speech, and the long tale of the wandering God who begot Jesus Christ upon Mary his daughter" (Herron 237). The slave's education in Christianity is an initiation that justifies her father's and brother's incestuous abuse of her. Likewise, Patricia's intense study of classical languages and cultures predisposes her toward domination by the father, both psychological and sexual. The relations of coercion, complicity, and resistance—between masters and slaves, fathers and daughters, and patriarchal culture and its female subjects—are represented spatially throughout the novel.

Thereafter Johnnie is obsessed with location in general and with the geography of Washington, D.C., in particular. Herron uses the geography of the capital city metaphorically to make concrete and visible the "relations of power which pass via knowledge." Virtually every chapter contains detailed references to places in the city; characters view and imagine the city from various vantage points. Upon examination, it becomes clear that monumental, patriarchal architecture and masculinist views of landscape are contrasted with daughters' geographies of the ocean, rivers, gardens, and islands. Monumental architecture and masculinist perspectives of space establish continuities of patriarchal domination and female submission and resistance across historical periods and racial boundaries. These same racial boundaries are also spatially represented; the complexion, both literal and figurative, of various neighborhoods is outlined as the female characters discuss or traverse these locations. The daughters' construction as female subjects of patriarchy is inscribed in and through geography, specifically the geography of the nation's capital. The knowledges that shape the sisters' identities are also represented spatially: Patricia's obsession with classical languages and the Greco-Roman world in general, Cynthia Jane's Christian orientation toward the father, both divine and human, and Eva's intimate acquaintance with the black community are all plotted onto specific coordinates within the city. Johnnie, the product of John Christopher Snowdon's incestuous relationship with his daughter Patricia, is able, for a time, to negotiate a more egalitarian relation to the patriarchal architecture of the city, but she ends her life as a disembodied light floating through the Old Carnegie Library.

The choice of Washington, D.C., as the site of the novel's action is a critical one. Washington is commonly thought of as the political capital of the West, in addition to being the governmental and symbolic center of the United States. Throughout U.S. history, the city has often served as a stage for the national drama of race; in the passage from *Clotel* quoted at the beginning of this chapter one can see clearly how William Wells Brown employs the monuments and their symbolic meaning to enhance his anti-slavery argument. However, in *Thereafter Johnnie*, Washington does not serve as merely a backdrop; the city itself is an actor in the tragedy of race and gender that Herron mounts—its stones speak and its monuments carry the grandeur and the contradictions of Greco-Roman and Christian mythologies. The major monuments in Washington were designed to connect American democracy with its glorious precursors, the city-states of Greece and the Roman Empire. Herron's use of the architecture of the city constantly reminds the reader that these republics, both ancient and modern, were profoundly male-dominated and depended upon slave labor. Throughout *Thereafter Johnnie*, the ideas of the past haunt the present through location. To quote feminist geographer Doreen Massey, "[S]ince social relations are bearers of power what is at issue is a geography of power relations in which spatial form is an important element in the constitution of power itself" (22).

Constructing a literal and figurative map of *Thereafter Johnnie*'s Washington is a complex undertaking, because of the sheer number of geographical references in the novel and the way in which many chapters focus upon a variety of sites rather than one or two. The book has several main characters, and while one can plot the movements of a number of these, no clear pattern arises from an attempt to plot the work as a whole onto a map of the city.[3] Instead the movements of each of the characters—both physical and psychological—describe personal, partial geographies of Washington that reflect and are constitutive of their subjectivities.

Though *Thereafter Johnnie* is one of a number of African American novels by women that deal with incestuous sexual abuse, Herron's novel is set apart from the others in this tradition by several factors. Critic Hortense Spillers has asserted that "incest fiction, even written by women, never, as far as I know, establishes the agency of the incestuous act inside the female character" ("The Permanent Obliquity" 132). *Thereafter Johnnie* appears to break with this convention by presenting a daughter who pursues her father. It also presents an extremely articulate, learned incest survivor, in contrast to the many black female incest victims in literature who are mute or who become articulate only with great difficulty.[4] Because of the disturbing ways in which the novel evokes Electra and the daughters of Lot, and refigures African American women writers' traditional representations of incestuous sexual abuse, it is necessary to examine its depiction of father-daughter incest in detail.

Herron both invokes and critiques mythological, biblical, pornographic, and psychoanalytic accounts of incest, arriving at an evocation of this type of abuse which registers its destructive and perversely generative power, its ambivalent legacy. In addition to being concerned with the relationship between past and present sexual abuse of black women, the novel is also obsessed with the relationship between sexual coercion and complicity.

Thus, in the second section of the chapter, I focus on psychoanalytic and psychotherapeutic analyses of incest in relationship to the parallel incest plots in *Thereafter Johnnie,* and the ways in which these analyses are brought together. While the novel's depictions of incest represent the excesses endemic to slaveholding and bourgeois families, the geographical, architectural, and gestural spatial representations provide a means of insisting upon the material reality of the body in space, the material reality of the sexually abused, powerful, frightened, desired and desiring black woman's body.

1. The Father's Geography, The Daughters' Geographies

Thereafter Johnnie creates a system of spatial representations that dramatizes the struggle between masculine and feminine power in the novel. Herron uses individual characters' spatial practices to indicate the extent of their complicity with or resistance to hegemonic power. As John Christopher, Cynthia Jane, Patricia, Eva, Camille, and Johnnie move around the city, they create what Michel de Certeau calls a "*migrational,* or metaphorical, city" which "slips into the clear text of the planned and readable city" (93). Racial and gender dynamics are played out through the use of space, especially through place names and the accumulated history of city landmarks. Through these representations, Herron creates a new city, a Washington in whose stones are embedded the histories of patriarchal domination, white supremacy, and black women's complicity with and resistance to both.

A Solar Eye, Looking Down Like a God[5]

The centrality of the father is established through three major spatial constructs: John Christopher's relationship to the city landscape, the places that are associated with him by name, and the monumental architecture of Washington. When John Christopher stands on Howard Hill on the night he finds his daughters playing in the snow, he commands a view of the city that feminist cultural geographers would define as masculinist. Geographer Gillian Rose, in *Feminism and Geography,* summarizes cultural geographers' recent writings about landscape, in which they argue that "landscape is a form of representation and not an empirical object" (89). Employing feminist film theory and art criticism, Rose expands upon these primarily class-oriented critiques of landscape-as-ideology with a reading of landscape as phallocentric. She argues that "[t]he particular dominant gaze constructs access to knowledge of geography as a white bourgeois heterosexual masculine privilege. And this gaze is not only the gaze at the land, although its dynamics are most clearly revealed there: it is also a gaze at what are constituted as objects of knowledge, whether environmental, social, political or cultural" (109).

John Christopher, the black father, is both included in and excluded from this analysis of the masculine gaze, and Herron's placement of him atop Howard Hill perfectly reflects the ambivalence of his social position. He stands on the Howard University campus at Founder's Library, an architectural landmark with connections to the Greco-Roman past and the origins of the United States. It was modeled on Independence Hall in Philadelphia, and it incorporates Doric, Ionic, and Corinthian columns.[6] Yet Founder's Library and the entire institution of Howard University are also integral parts of African American academic and social history; as such, they are profoundly important from one perspective and profoundly marginalized from another. Howard is, of course, one of the oldest black universities in the country and perhaps the most prestigious. Within this world, John Christopher Snowdon is almost certainly a "black first," a star surgeon, a master of medical technology, a kind of god. Yet his blackness marks him as marginalized and, in the terms of the novel's curse, as a target for murder. The passage detailing John Christopher's view of the city incorporates both his elevated status as male viewer and his position as denigrated Other.

From this Howard Hill location, laden with historical significance, John Christopher surveys the entire city. His panoramic gaze begins at Kennedy Stadium and pans "[f]rom the southeast to the southwest [in] a clear line," taking in "the Capitol dome" and "the spire of the Washington Monument" (Herron 47). He sees the Jefferson Memorial, the Lincoln Memorial, and other august structures; he also sees "Georgia Avenue, little Africa" and "Clifton Terrace . . . where the black children and their jump ropes and balls and jacks and bicycles are one day to be the last and only protection left to the great city" (Herron 48). Finally, though, the view changes significantly: "[T]he hill curves down toward Georgetown, stopping for a moment at Dumbarton Oaks, shuddering before descending to the Potomac and the Tidal Basin and southward toward that sea where so many of our ancestors lie fathoms deep. So many. Fifteen million black Africans undone by death" (Herron 48). John Christopher's panoramic view of the city is narrated as a single sentence whose period marks the encounter between his gaze and an object it cannot penetrate—"that sea where so many of our ancestors lie fathoms deep." John Christopher's access to the patriarchal power of the gaze is delimited symbolically by the

Atlantic Ocean's evidence of Euro-American whites' crimes against Africans during the slave trade.

It is instructive to compare John Christopher's view of Washington with an excerpt from de Certeau's *The Practice of Everyday Life*. Chapter 7, "Walking in the City," begins with a panoramic view of Manhattan from the 110th floor of the World Trade Center.

> Beneath the haze stirred up by the winds, the urban island, a sea in the middle of the sea, lifts up the skyscrapers over Wall Street, sinks down at Greenwich, then rises again to the crests of Midtown, quietly passes over Central Park and finally undulates off into the distance beyond Harlem. A wave of verticals. Its agitation is momentarily arrested by vision. The gigantic mass is immobilized before the eyes. It is transformed into a texturology in which extremes coincide—*extremes of ambition and degradation, brutal oppositions of races and styles* . . .
>
> To what erotics of knowledge does the ecstasy of reading such a cosmos belong? Having taken a voluptuous pleasure in it, I wonder what is the source of this pleasure of "seeing the whole," of looking down on, totalizing the most immoderate of human texts.
>
> To be lifted to the summit of the World Trade Center is to be lifted out of the city's grasp. . . . When one goes up there, he leaves behind the mass that carries off and mixes up in itself any identity of authors or spectators. An Icarus flying above these waters, he can ignore the devices of Daedalus in mobile and endless labyrinths far below. His elevation transfigures him into a voyeur. It puts him at a distance. It transforms the bewitching world by which one was "possessed" into a text that lies before one's eyes. It allows one to read it, to be a solar Eye, looking down like a god. The exaltation of a scopic and gnostic drive: the fiction of knowledge is related to this lust to be a viewpoint and nothing more. (91–92, my emphasis)

In this passage, de Certeau has identified the voyeuristic pleasure of viewing a complex, multifaceted city from on high. (Nothing in de Certeau's description contradicts Gillian Rose's contention that this pleasure is primarily a masculine one.) John Christopher views Washington from a position akin to that of de Certeau's voyeur. He also seems to experience "[t]he exaltation of a scopic and gnostic drive," and his claims to god-like knowledge and power in the next chapter, "The King of Hearts," can be seen as another manifestation of this drive. In response to de Certeau's question, "To what erotics of knowledge does the ecstasy of reading such a cosmos belong?" one might answer, the same "erotics of knowledge" governing John Christopher's decision to use his surgical mastery "to break the affection among [his] daughters and pull all that affection toward [him]self" (Herron 54); the same "erotics of knowledge" that his skilled hands exercise over the bodies of his wife and daughter. He turns his "totalizing" gaze from the city to the powerful circle of his daughters' lyric play, and his threatened, sexualized response is an urge to convert his mastery of the landscape into mastery of his daughters' deepest attachments.

Yet the racial subjugation of black men complicates the description of the geography of the black father. John Christopher is a patriarchal figure, but he and the other black men whom he represents are also victims of white patriarchy ("kill the boys"). Thus, it is necessary to contextualize John Christopher's relationship to space and domination of the women within his domestic sphere. His sexual molestation and rape/seduction of his daughter Patricia are explained by the curse as a form of revenge for black women's supposed collusion with white men in black men's oppression. Yet despite the remarkable power and brilliance of her evocation of the curse dooming black boys to death and black girls to rape and incest, Herron does not flesh out the curse's material effects on black boys and men. John Christopher, the black father, appears almost as powerful as the novel's white, slaveholding father. The victimization of black men is alluded to but not enacted, except in John Christopher's placement on Howard Hill, and in two other subtle ways, discussed below.

St. John

A number of spaces in *Thereafter Johnnie* are connected to John Christopher by name and/or by his dominance within them. These connections are made through a series of allusions to St. John, Christ's "beloved disciple" and John Christopher's namesake.[7] The most striking of these allusions is to San Juan, Puerto Rico, where John Christopher and Patricia have sex for the first time. By specifying the city, whose name is the Spanish equivalent of St. John, in which their incestuous relationship is consummated, Herron emphasizes the fact that, although Patricia pursues her father, the balance of power is on John Christopher's side. Their "adult" incestuous relationship comes into being in a space that is marked as his.

Another significant space associated with John Christopher is Atlanta, Georgia, which is in turn associated with the lost city of Atlantis. The chapter "Atlantis" recounts an episode from his Atlanta boyhood, concatenating several disparate elements: the young boy's journey out of the house alone and his encounter with the chicken-pox vagabond, a sermon on the three Greek words for love in the original text of the New Testament, a sermon on Lot and his daughters, the manifestation of the curse in John Christopher's life, and the cities of Atlanta and Atlantis. The young John Christopher, wearing red, white, and blue, makes a pact for his own salvation with a poor, ragged black man, at once a real character and a devil figure. Later in life, after seeing his daughters play in the snow, John Christopher is indeed saved from the threat of their power "like Lot was saved" (Herron 82); but his seed, which engenders Johnnie, does not save his civilization from ruin. Instead, his incest with Patricia perpetuates the curse which will bring down the entire society. Though this chapter is meant to provide a sense of John Christopher as a young, vulnerable black boy, potentially a victim of the curse, it does not fully satisfy this purpose. The vagabond's teasing threat that he will "take a stone and tie it around [his] neck and throw [him] in the ocean" (Herron 82) does not seem grave enough to warrant the symbolic weight it is given.[8] In addition, John Christopher's biblical musings as he is lost in the woods are strained so that they can connect this incident to his later molestation of Patricia. He murmurs to himself, "I have to find an island of Pat but I'm afraid of the island I'm afraid" (Herron 82). The link between Patricia and Patmos here is a less than resonant one.

The references to San Juan, Puerto Rico, and Plato's Atlantis foreground the concept of imperialism. In the *Timaeus*, Plato makes it clear that Atlantis was an imperialist power threatening Athens, and that the Athenians were able to defeat it, despite its technological sophistication. Traditionally, the United States has seen itself as the New World Athens; in the world of *Thereafter Johnnie*, the United States is Atlantis, the North American technological behemoth over which the Third World nations will triumph. John Christopher is a figure with a foot in both worlds. While his identification by name with San Juan suggests his masculine dominance over Patricia, through its colonial connotations it also indicates his racial subordination within the United States.

The Lesson of Rome

Reviews of *Thereafter Johnnie* have noted the importance of Greco-Roman mythology in the novel. What has not been elaborated is the way in which Herron represents the influence of ancient myth on life in the present through the neoclassical architecture of Washington. Five buildings in particular are highlighted throughout *Thereafter Johnnie*: the Washington Monument, the Jefferson Memorial, the Lincoln Memorial, the amphitheater at Dumbarton Oaks, and the Capitol Building, especially its dome. All five

directly invoke the architecture of classical Greece and Rome. The first
three, the monuments to the presidents, are referred to many times in the
novel, and the numerous mentions of them constitute double allusions—
references to the founding models of Western culture and to the Founding Fathers of the United States. When these buildings were erected, they
were intended to invoke the glories of Greco-Roman civilization and to
connect American democracy to its classical forerunners. Of course,
Greco-Roman civilization and American democracy are also connected
through their shared practice of slavery, and Herron is able to allude to
this as well. Within the context of African American literature and history,
Washington and Jefferson, the Founding Fathers, are recognized as slaveholders who somehow found it possible to reconcile their belief in human
freedom with the practice of human bondage. In *Thereafter Johnnie*, their
monuments become bearers of this ambivalent legacy.

De Certeau notes that "[o]bjects and words . . . have hollow places in
which a past sleeps" (108), and Herron pushes the reader to recognize
these hollow places and the pasts held within them. In *Fathering the Nation*,
Russ Castronovo quotes Daniel Webster's comments on the Washington
Monument to demonstrate the way in which architectural form was understood in relation to that which it memorialized: "Washington! . . . The
structure now standing before us, by its uprightness, its solidity, its dura-
bility, is no unfit emblem of his [George Washington's] character. His public virtues and public principles were as firm as the earth on which it stands;
his personal motives as pure as the serene heaven in which its summit is
lost" (138).[9] Webster's view is clearly the response that architects of the
monument and nationalism more generally were attempting to elicit; however, when Herron refers to the Washington Monument repeatedly in a
text foregrounding the legacies of slavery, readers are encouraged to re-
member that Washington accumulated wealth through the use of unfree
labor. In view of the indictment of slaveholders and their sexual relations
with female slaves contained in the *Thereafter Johnnie*'s final chapter, references to Jefferson inexorably bring to mind his relationship with Sally
Hemings, his slave "mistress." His monument memorializes not only the
heights of his career as a philosopher of democracy but also the contradictions and hypocrisies contained in his democratic philosophy and practice. The novel invites us to examine Lincoln in a similar fashion. Again,
in view of the novel's content, references to the Lincoln Memorial bring
to mind both the positive aspects and the limitations of the Great Emancipator's deeds. While it is not possible in the context of this chapter to
give a detailed explication of *Thereafter Johnnie*'s meditation on the concept
of freedom, suffice it to say that the idea of freedom as merely the absence

of chattel slavery (the idea invoked by Lincoln's designation as 'the Great Emancipator') is consistently challenged.[10]

The constant clustering of three monuments of presidents within the novel deserves attention as well. These buildings are usually referred to as a group, and references to them usually allude to their tops—for example, "Washington has a pointed top, Jefferson has a round top, Lincoln has a flat top" (Herron 179). As a group, these buildings invoke the ideals of pure form upon which classical architecture and neoclassical revivals are based. The Swiss-French architect Le Corbusier, in his arguments for allegiance to purity of form, drafted a sketch entitled "The Lesson of Rome" to demonstrate how basic geometrical forms were combined harmoniously to produce the glories of Roman architecture (see figure 1).

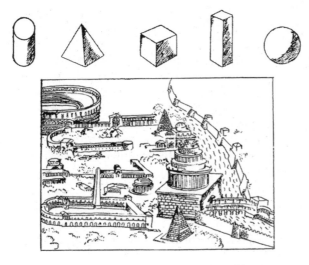

FIG. 1. Le Corbusier, *The Lesson of Rome* (illustration from *L'esprit nouveau*, no. 14, n.d. [1922–23]). © 2004 Artists Rights Society (ARS), New York/ADAGP, Paris/FLC.

Le Corbusier's drawing represents the standard forms of classical architecture, including the form of each of the buildings obsessively referred to in *Thereafter Johnnie*. Such buildings, both in ancient Rome and in Washington, D.C., pay homage to the Platonic ideal of pure form. However, the ideal of pure form cannot be entirely separated from other cultural values, like the imperialism Plato himself warned against in his accounts of the city of Atlantis. These exemplars of neoclassical architecture are, at the end of the novel, buried under sand, as drowned as the ruins of Atlantis. Only the pure pyramid—the pointed top of the Washington Monument—marks the space where the city once stood.

John Christopher, the father in the novel, is connected to these Founding Fathers through his gender and his domination of the women in his domestic sphere. (He is separated from them by his racial subjugation.) Yet he is also connected to them by his and Patricia's bizarre interaction in the space that the monuments delineate. Johnnie's "auntsister" (Herron 88) Cynthia Jane relates the story of how Patricia pleaded for John Christopher to make love to her on the Mall, between the Washington Monument and the Reflecting Pool. The setting of Patricia's attempted seduction of her father is striking in its peculiarity. It is January when this occurs, and, in Cynthia Jane's words, "she [Patricia] lay on the cold ground and begged him to make love to her" (Herron 191). The Mall is bounded on one end by the Washington Monument, phallic symbol *par excellence,* and, on the other end, by the Lincoln Memorial, another building commemorating a historical father. The space in which Patricia attempts to seduce her father lies between the Monument and the Reflecting Pool, between patriarchal architecture and that which confirms it. Though the Reflecting Pool is a body of water, it is not associated with the female, as are other bodies of water in the novel. It is a "man-made" body of water, and its purpose architecturally, as its name indicates, is to reflect the soaring obelisk that is the Monument. The spatial relationship between the phallic Washington Monument and the pool that gives back its image are an analogue for John Christopher and Patricia's relationship. Patricia's sexuality has become a mirror of her father's; her desire for him reflects the perverse desire that led him to molest her when she was two. One can read this tableau as an example of what Doreen Massey means by "a geography of power relations in which spatial form is an important element in the constitution of power itself" (22).

In one sense, *Thereafter Johnnie* reinforces the traditional dichotomy between masculine Culture and feminine Nature. The father is associated with monumental architecture and an all-encompassing view of landscape. The feminine—in the persons of Camille the mother, the three daughters, and Diotima the storyteller—is associated with gardening, with the Potomac River and the Atlantic Ocean, and with islands—in short, with the natural world. Yet this dichotomy is not as simple as it at first appears. The daughters' connection to patriarchal culture, and to John Christopher in particular, is often indicated by their proximity to the geography and architecture associated with the father.

Voyeurs or Walkers

Cynthia Jane's perspective on Washington is almost identical to her father's, signaling the fact that she is, in Barbara Christian's words, "infected by father-myths" (7). While trying to write a poem, she remembers being inspired by a panoramic view of Washington from Howard Hill: "She stood at the top of the hill that cuts through the city, the hill with Howard University on one end and Georgetown University on the other. . . . She saw how it [the city] lay before her from Kennedy Stadium westward toward the blue of the White House to the fog that rose out of the Potomac as it passed Georgetown" (Herron 91). Not only does her viewpoint almost exactly mimic her father's, both in its epic sweep and in the objects it touches, Cynthia Jane focuses on the most phallic object in this landscape, the Washington Monument. She thinks: "O lord what a beautiful city. And its Monument. . . . A shaft of blue-tinted marble from earth to heaven. No genial presidential face grinning cheery comfort across the city; no romantic portraits; no round or wispy additions muddling its corners—the obelisk is hard" (Herron 92). Cynthia Jane's appreciation of the phallic shape and erect position of this landmark needs no elucidation. Viewing the city and its Monument in these terms does not facilitate her writing: "The poem is not ready yet, it still won't come" (Herron 92).

The fact that Cynthia Jane is utterly in thrall to the father's geography is congruent with her placing on Patricia all blame for her incestuous relationship with John Christopher. Though Cynthia Jane is aware of the ways in which their father preferred Patricia to her and of the fact that his jealous fear of the daughters' circle drove him to destroy it in order to redirect their affection to himself, she still believes that the "awful trinity" of the sisters, especially Patricia, "destroyed [their] father" (Herron 213). Despite the evidence before her, she refuses to see the father's desire and guilt, assenting to the myth of the "Seductive Daughter" which Western culture uses to disguise incestuous sexual abuse.[11]

Patricia is the daughter most susceptible to the seduction of the father and of patriarchal culture in general. In the book's second chapter, "The Last Time," Patricia takes the baby Johnnie to Dumbarton Oaks to while away the day, because John Christopher has told her he cannot visit until the following day. The first site she visits with Johnnie is the amphitheater. As Patricia looks at the amphitheater, she remembers having being taken there as a child, and being told that "once there had been concerts in the amphitheater of Dumbarton Oaks that was so eaten away now with grass and ice and ancient mud washed up beneath leaves cracking the bricks with gray water" (Herron 10). Her reverie continues,

> Even when Patricia was a little girl it was a long time ago when there had been concerts. That was almost before everything. That was almost the beginning. The amphitheater is not like the surrounding gardens but is unkempt, complicated. There are entwined bamboo and evergreen and autumn winter trees so that at all times the leaves are thick the steps crumbling the smell aboriginal mold for Patricia, a holy place secluded a place final as a sea with raw chill and blank decomposition to damp mulch. (10)

Patricia, the scholar of classical languages and mythologies, stands before the ruins of the amphitheater, and, symbolically, the ruins of the classical tradition. Her meditation upon the amphitheater follows a dense series of classical allusions in the first chapter and makes clear the pressure this tradition brings to bear upon the present and the pressure the novel brings to bear upon this tradition. The decaying amphitheater at Dumbarton Oaks is a spatial referent establishing both the influence and obsolescence of classical mythology, literature, and philosophy. The persistence of classical tradition is not merely abstract; it is made material through this location and others. One can trace not only Patricia's movements through "real" space but also her mind's movements through the layers of history stratifying the very air of historical sites in Washington. Her spatial practices both support and help to create her mythic vision of herself. Her movement from the Dumbarton Oaks amphitheater into the museum takes us from classical to biblical allusions.

Patricia surveys the items on display until her gaze settles upon "a porphyry rattlesnake St. John of Patmos cup, vial, chalice, grail. All by himself. Alone. Holy Cup Vial Chalice Grail Urn Skull Cup. Alone" (Herron 11). The reference to this object reveals two of the levels at which classical and biblical allusions operate in the novel: the structure of the entire book is inflected by them, and individual characters use them to organize and articulate their personal mythologies and viewpoints. As noted above, John Christopher is associated throughout the book with St. John of Patmos; Johnnie is connected to the Apostle John as well, by name and because "the child is the second coming prophesied in Revelation" (Daly 472), which John received on the island of Patmos. Of course, Johnnie's association with St. John is part of Patricia's obsession with her father. Thus, the chalice fits perfectly into Patricia's personal and familial mythology; it is connected to her father and her child, and, in the description of the artifact before her, she inserts the image she has of herself, that of an empty skull. The classical and biblical allusions serve as a system directing the reader to important concepts in the novel, as most allusions do, but they function at another level as well. The novel's characters are aware of the symbolic meaning and function of these references within their individual stories. Patricia imagines herself as a martyred Virgin Mary, whose sacrifice of her life to her father and to a patriarchal culture in decline will bring about the salvation of the city and the nation through the new messiah, Johnnie. Not only does she project the image of herself as an empty skull onto the objects in the Dumbarton Oaks Museum, she also projects this vision onto the Capitol dome. In a sexist, racist, imperialist nation, the spirit of the law has left the Capitol Building; Patricia imagines that Johnnie will restore it. Eva tells Johnnie, "in her pregnancy [Patricia] believed that you embodied the city's lost soul. Washington had lost its soul according to her and she would restore it through you, through her child" (Herron 105).

Patricia's suicide at Three Sisters Island is an event that spatially dramatizes the conflict between the geography of the father and that of the daughters. Though Patricia is captivated by the mythology and geography of the father, her favorite place in the city is near Three Sisters Island, an actual place that Herron uses as she uses Washington's neoclassical monuments—to deepen and extend her literary, mythological, and biblical allusions. The novel is laden with references to *Macbeth,* beginning with a dedication that reads, "When Shall We Three Meet Again?" These words are repeated at other points in the text: Cynthia Jane quotes them to Johnnie when she is discussing the power of the sisters' circle, and John Christopher alludes to his daughters as "three witches, three weird sisters" (Herron 46) by whom it is his fate to be destroyed. Yet beneath these references to the witches in *Macbeth* who lure the knight/king to his downfall are references to *King Lear,* in which a foolish king extracts professions of love from his daughters and thereby brings about the downfall of his kingdom. In the chapter "Three Witches," in which John Christopher finds his daughters playing in the snow, he thinks, "[A]lways there are stories of three witches and the fourth is always a king who is betrayed to his death. You were the king. They were the witches, girls, daughters, your daughters. The king must be killed through the power of the witches but if the king could overcome the witches he could save himself" (Herron 50). John Christopher's "uncanny fear" of his daughters is also mixed with sexual arousal; Johnnie narrates his thoughts thus:

> You discovered that you feared something about them and you wanted power over them, you felt the terrifying warning of that power in the fire that stirred upon your thigh. You were in hell, it was hell, this stirring of the fire upon your thigh at the vision of your daughters dancing, you could not escape. (50–51)

The threat of his daughters' power mixes Western mythology and literature with sexual desire to create a motive for John Christopher's decision to destroy the sisters' bond and redirect their love toward himself. The circle of the girls' love for one another and the power of their inspired, hybrid, literary-spiritual singing is broken forever. Its only recurrence is in Johnnie's stream-of-consciousness meditation at the scene of her mother's suicide:[12]

> [A]nd my mother Patricia raised her arms toward her sisters and her sisters
> came to her from out of the City of Washington those three met again above
> Three Sisters Island above the Potomac with my mother who raised her arms
> above her face her hair her embrace held the city her invocation of Wash-
> ington in her happiness [. . .]it flushed her cold body threw back her head
> loved her in the sparkling rain she tried to think of a name she wanted a
> name for it prayed for a name she would stand there until she found a name
> and that name was joy [. . .] and the three sisters moved in a circle singing.
> (Herron 158–59)

One can imagine a feminist revision of *King Lear* in which the destruction of the sisters by the patriarch's demand for love and power is the center of the story, the primary loss mourned by the narrative. In one sense, *Thereafter Johnnie* is just such a revision. The emphasis on the three sisters, reinforced through the geographical reference to Three Sisters Island and through Johnnie's mythic vision of the sisters' reunion above the Island and the river, revises a traditional plot and re-focuses it upon the female characters.

Eva, the youngest of John Christopher and Camille's daughters, is the one least affected by father-myths and most connected both to feminine geography and the geography of the black community. Christian notes that "[w]oman-bonding is primarily associated with Eva" (7), and when Eva tells Johnnie her story, she also provides a partial map of Washington's black community: "Fourteenth and U streets Northwest is the crossroad intersection of the black community. . . . The Northeast center is Eighth and H streets" (Herron 98–9). Not only does Eva, the prophet, foretell the fall of Washington and Johnnie's incarnation as the second coming; in her spatial practices she foretells Johnnie's (analyzed below). Eva experiences the city at ground level; she is a walker, not a voyeur. Cynthia Jane describes her passage through the city thus: "She walks the streets like riotfire, she arouses them and keeps walking, keeps returning as if each return were pure and she a virgin, in the parks, in the slums, from Connecticut Avenue to Deanwood, she lies down in apartments, up against alley fences, or getting high in lesbian bars" (Herron 93).

Despite the sisters' mythology of Eva as an eternal virgin, her geography is centered around racial-sexual subjugation; her mental plan of the city radiates out from the stone next to the Old Carnegie Library, the spot where she was raped. Eva obsessively repeats the word *stone* throughout her story, which is told in the chapter "The Story of the Stone." In Eva's story, the tension between coercion and complicity comes together with geography. Eva's sexual promiscuity and her peculiar assent to an act she consistently refers to as rape are plotted onto specific coordinates within the city. The rape is certainly a trauma, but her assent to the rape reveals that her inner turmoil precedes that event. In her account of the story, she tells Johnnie,

> I lay silently on the stone, Johnnie, naked, and so silently. He talked to me at first and I answered but then he was quiet and I was as silent as if I were his bride, I loved the silence, Johnnie, no one can believe this but I love the silence in which violence has no voice because the pain of that silence is stronger than the pain in my mind, the violence comes from outside of me and pierces me and hurts me so that for one moment I don't have to think my own thoughts. *I imagined chains within the silence, to bind my wrists, to spread my ankles,* I wanted to forget what I was thinking, desperately, passionately, I wanted to forget. (Herron 102; my emphasis)

Though Eva is not "held in the air in the shape of an X in order to be fornicated" (Herron 238), as Laetitia, the enslaved ancestor in "Matin," is, she imagines her body in the shape of an X as she is raped. This spatial figure, explicitly connected to slavery by the word "chains," links Eva to both Patricia and Laetitia. Her meditation on the usefulness of violence in easing the mind is very close, in tone and content, to Patricia's meditation on love and slavery, in which Patricia asserts,

> The beauty of torture, the delight of slavery, the joy of being tied up bound down whipped beaten drawn quartered stretched broken into the ground is this—the mind is free. . . . Free at last. Released from complications of survival, from the necessity to devise its own release, caught then forever, in flame, tarred and feathered, castrated, raped the mind discovers infinite stillness—there are no decisions to make. It's just like love. (Herron 21–22)[13]

Patricia's conflation of love and slavery is a result of her father's incestuous sexual abuse, and there is at least one hint in the text that Eva may have been fondled by John Christopher as well.[14] Thus Eva, though somewhat removed from the profound influence of the father's geography and mythology upon Cynthia Jane and Patricia, still has not escaped or surmounted her formation through patriarchal dominance. Both her body and her geography of the city are marked by the patriarchal geographical imaginary.

On Ground Level, with Footsteps

Johnnie is the character who delineates a profoundly different view of the city. As Christian has observed, "Johnnie is a fruit of incest nurtured in isolation, . . . completely in the company of women" (7). Perhaps this is why her geography of the city is so different from that of the father; it takes shape at street level and acknowledges regular human speech, action, and graffiti—in short, the muddle of human life in an urban setting. Two chapters highlight Johnnie's relationship to space in Washington, D.C.: "Dilation and Cutterage" [*sic*] and "My Grandparents' Door." In these chapters, Johnnie travels across the city on foot, minutely observing the details of city life that she passes. She sees the city as a walker rather than as a voyeur. In "Dilation and Cutterage," she leaves Georgetown for the first time in panic after her mother's suicide. Diotima has told her that if anything ever happens, she must go to Eva's, and she has shown her the way. As a seventeen-year-old girl who has never left home alone before, Johnnie experiences every step of her journey intensely:

> Run. P Street. I made it to P Street. This is P Street. I can read it, P Street. I found it. I found it. Wisconsin Avenue. P Street. Neams Market. Chocolate Shoppe. This is the way Diotima showed me. . . . This way is Washington City. . . . Washington. Presbyterian Congregational Church. . . . Rock Creek and Potomac Parkway. Strange buildings. Diotima brought me here. She brought me this far. Right here. Here. Where the brick sidewalk stops. Step over. I can't. I don't know how. Step over. I never stepped over before. Mommy and Diotima told me, Johnnie, don't ever step over. Don't step off the brick sidewalk. Run down P Street. I can't. The sidewalk changes. Step. (Herron 162–63)

Johnnie's view of the geography of Washington is the complete opposite of John Christopher's and Cynthia Jane's panoptic views. The contrast between these ways of viewing the city is made clear and reinforced by Johnnie's encounters with masculinist architecture and black men hanging out on the street. As Johnnie reaches Fifteenth Street, she sees the Washington Monument for the first time. Her concentration on the monument is broken by a comment from a black man on the street.

Look down there. It's the Washington Monument way down there. Look at
it. A smooth white column with a point on top.
   "Hey sugaaaah!"
   The Washington Monument.
   "Hey sugaaaah baby doll sweetheart dahlin'—I like yo' style but yuh gots
tuh git outa thuh street honey chile." (Herron 164)

Johnnie's first encounter with the phallic architecture of the Monument
is punctuated and reinforced by her interpellation as a "baby doll sweetheart dahlin'." A symbol of white male power dominates the skyline, while
black men's style of occupying public space in Washington dominates the
streets. This passage illustrates "the intricacy and profundity of the connection of space and place with gender and the construction of gender relations" (Massey 2). Johnnie, heretofore virtually invisible, is constructed
as an attractive sexual object by the gaze and the speech of the men she
encounters. They continue, "Sweet thang! . . . you talk about a black stack
. . . you somethin' else honey chile . . . when the berry's that black an'
round you know the juice be done gots tuh be sweeeeet" (Herron 164).
However, Johnnie partially escapes this interpellation because of the isolation of her upbringing. She has absolutely no idea what the men are talking about until another man intervenes in standard English. At the end of
the chapter, just before entering Eva's house, Johnnie sees the tower of
Founder's Library at Howard University, another phallic structure, this
one explicitly connected to John Christopher. Her first solo trip into Washington City has been, at least in part, an education in the patriarchal domination of public space. Yet her view of the city, from street level, remains
democratic; she takes in every element without arranging the elements in
hierarchical order.
   One can see Johnnie's non-hierarchizing tendency again in the chapter
in which she travels to her grandparents' house. In the course of this chapter, she walks about five blocks, from Sixteenth Street and Colorado Avenue, where she gets off the bus, to Sixteenth and Kennedy Street, where
the older Snowdons live. As she walks, she describes minutely the diverse
people and sights she sees; the result is an international and multiethnic
chronicle of this small section of the city. "[A] lively brown wife talking and
gesturing," "an orange husband who was laughing and trying to find a
break to answer back" (Herron 216), two white students, a black student,
a little boy, a teenager in a plaid skirt, a Mexican man, a "Krishna worship-
per" (219): these are the people she passes and makes note of in her journey. The buildings are equally heterogeneous, both in their architecture
and in what they house: "Carter Barron Amphitheater" (217), "Iglesia

Evangelica Menonita Hispanica" (217–18), "[a] house of red brick and wood, more modern than the others with a sign, AFRICAN SISTER, in red and black and green. Gigantic block letters were stretched across the next house, Chù Chiàc Hoàng, with a hundred tall flags waving in a row behind the windows BUDDHIST CONGREGATIONAL CHURCH OF AMERICA and a smaller note on the door, 'Indra's Bow'" (219).

Johnnie does not make metaphors from the things she sees; she simply records them and her reactions to them directly and vividly. From the point of view of de Certeau's voyeur, she has suffered "[a]n Icarian fall" "into the dark space where crowds move back and forth" (92). Yet she is also performing "the process of *appropriation* of the topographical system on the part of the pedestrian (just as the speaker appropriates and takes on the language)" (de Certeau 97–98). That is to say, Johnnie creates her own geography of Washington as she walks. As de Certeau argues,

> The long poem of walking manipulates spatial organizations, no matter how panoptic they may be: it is neither foreign to them (it can take place only within them) nor in conformity with them (it does not receive its identity from them). It creates shadows and ambiguities within them. It inserts its multitudinous references and citations into them (social models, cultural mores, personal factors). (101)

This is how Johnnie's spatial practices revise the official, panoptic view of the city embraced by John Christopher, Cynthia Jane, and, to some extent, Camille.[15] Johnnie's passage through the city undoes the official valuation of its constitutive elements and emphasizes an equal juxtaposition of "high" and "low," sacred and secular, black and white. Her geography approximates the "paradoxical geography" of "the subject of feminism" articulated by Gillian Rose in *Feminism and Geography*:

> The subject of feminism, then, depends on a paradoxical geography in order to acknowledge both the power of hegemonic discourses and to insist on the possibility of resistance. This geography describes that subjectivity as that of both prisoner and exile; it allows the subject of feminism to occupy both the centre and the margin, the inside and the outside. . . . It is a geography which is as multiple and contradictory and different as the subjectivity imagining it. I have already suggested how some of the founding antinomies of Western geographical thought are negated by this feminist subjectivity: its embodiment which overcomes the distinction between mind and body; its refusal to distinguish between real and metaphorical space; its refusal to separate experience and emotion from the interpretation of

places. All these threaten the polarities which structure the dominant geographical imagination. They fragment the dead weight of masculinist space and rupture its exclusions. Above all, they allow for the possibility of a different kind of space through which difference is tolerated rather than erased. (155)

Though Johnnie's "long poem of walking" does indeed "allow for the possibility of a different kind of space through which difference is tolerated rather than erased," her resistant practices of space do not prevail. In the apocalyptic conclusion to the novel, both hegemonic and resistant spatial practices are rendered immaterial.

In the Shape of an X

A final spatial element in *Thereafter Johnnie* functions somewhat differently from the geography and architecture of Washington, D.C.; it connects all of the sexually violent acts perpetrated on female characters. As noted above, Eva, Patricia and Laetitia, the three women characters in the novel who are victims of rape or incestuous sexual abuse, are associated through kinship, through references to slavery, and through the shape of the X. Patricia's body goes "into an X shape and [won't] come out of it" (Herron 180) on the night she is first molested by her father. Later, she dances in an X shape; this dance marks the point at which her father begins to give in to the second wave of his sexual desire for her (Herron 203–4). After she first has intercourse with her father, "her body stiffens into a catatonic X of horror, violation violently enforced pleasure and pain" (Herron 121) as she remembers his molestation of her. Laetitia, the enslaved ancestor of Patricia and Eva, is held in the shape of an X by her father and half-brother as they have sex with her simultaneously (Herron 238). Though not a victim of rape, Camille, the mother, is linked to her abused kinswomen by the X shape made by the roach she kills as she elopes with John Christopher (Herron 230), and she is certainly sexually dominated by her husband, as demonstrated in the chapter "Monopoly." Even the female dog upon whom John Christopher operates is described in a spread-eagled position (Herron 59), and it is his operation on the "bitch" that decisively turns the adolescent Patricia toward her father. Though several critics have noted the recurrence of the X shape to mark significant points in the novel, no extended analysis of this element has been undertaken.[16] When one examines *Thereafter Johnnie* in terms of geography, architecture, and spatial practices and symbols, the X can be interpreted as a spatial signifier employed to illuminate the sexually charged intersections of coercion and complicity. The X marks the female body, in particular the black female body, for sexual exploitation by both white and black men. It serves as a representation of the woman's body, spread-eagled, and it also designates the female chromosome.[17] The X shape obviously alludes to crucifixion as well: the sacrifice of these women's bodies fulfills the curse upon the Snowdon family and the nation as a whole. Yet these crucifixions do not lead to salvation. Instead, the light of the second coming (that is, Johnnie) is buried under sand for eternity. All of the women in *Thereafter Johnnie* (with the possible exceptions of woman-identified Diotima and Johnnie herself) are caught up in obedience to authority, enforced pleasures, and resistance. The destiny of black women in this novel, as women and as blacks, is encoded in their genes and represented spatially and transhistorically by the sign of the X. From this analysis of the shape assigned to the abused female body in the novel, let us now turn to an analysis of the shape of desire created in the psyche of the childhood victim of sexual molestation.

2. "In the Time of the Daughters and the Fathers"

[T]he most insidious part of sexual abuse is in the creation of desire in the molested child, the way it forms a shape for desire that can never again be fulfilled, only compulsively substituted for and repeated . . .

MICHAEL RYAN, *Secret Life: An Autobiography*

Consent and choice are concepts that apply to the relationships of peers. They have no meaning in the relations of adults and children, any more than in the relations of freemen and slaves. Instances in which an unusually assertive child was able to discourage an adult's sexual advances do exist. Similarly, in the days of slavery, some exceptional slaves were doubtless able to talk their masters out of beating them, or selling their children, or copulating with their wives, or doing whatever it was that they intended. But just as, in those cases, the final decision rested with the master, the final choice in the matter of sexual relations between adults and children rests with the adult.

JUDITH HERMAN WITH LISA HIRSCHMAN, *Father-Daughter Incest*

I know of no slaveholding society in which a master, when so inclined, could not exact sexual services from his female slaves.

ORLANDO PATTERSON, *Slavery and Social Death: A Comparative Study*

The title of this section refers to Hortense Spillers's landmark article "The Permanent Obliquity of an In(pha)llibly Straight: In the Time of the Daughters and the Fathers," which examines the applicability of Freudian psychoanalysis to representations of father-daughter incest in African American literature. Spillers concludes that, because of the ways in which black families were disrupted by slavery, the Freudian model applies "only by accident" (148) to father-daughter incest in African American contexts. "The Permanent Obliquity" was published before Carolivia Herron and her novel *Thereafter Johnnie* "swe[pt] into our literary tradition like a fourth Fury and [left] very few things untouched" (Herron n.p.), in the words of critic Henry Louis Gates, Jr., Herron's novel, with its vision of father-daughter incest in a black middle-class family, challenges Spillers's conclusions and forces us to look again at this issue in the African American literary tradition and in the African American family.

Spillers's analysis divides black and white paternity, and for very good reasons. On the one hand, under slavery,

> [T]he African father is figuratively banished; fatherhood, at best a cultural courtesy, since only mother knows for sure, is not a social fiction into which he enters. Participation in the life of his children, indeed the rights of patriarchal privilege, is extended to him at someone else's behest. (130)

The black father cannot function as a father in any real sense under the conditions of "the peculiar institution." What, then, of white men who fathered children with enslaved black women? Spillers continues,

> [T]he "master" and his class—those subjects of an alternative fatherhood— cannot be said to be "fathers" of African-American children at all (without the benefit of quotation marks) since, by their own law, the newborn follows the "condition" of the mother. But in those instances where they were begetters of children, the puzzle of the father is fully elaborated. As "owners" of human "property," they offer impediment to the operations of kinship; by denial of kinship, they act out symbolically the ambiguous character of fatherhood itself, perpetuating it in this case as blank parody. (130)

Thus, for Spillers, the white father's denial of kinship in favor of ownership puts him outside of the black family, such as it is, altogether.

Herron's novel both acts out and revises Spillers's argument. In the final chapter of *Thereafter Johnnie*, "Matin," Herron reinserts the white father into the story of the African American family. Johnnie's story in this chapter traces her family line (through the mother, necessarily) back to her "mother's mother's mother's mother's mother's mother," "the nameless one" (235) who was brought from Africa to the United States, raped first by the captain of the slave ship and then by her owner (a lawyer) in Virginia. This is the root of the story that grows into an incestuous family tree.

> Not for long did she tend the small family garden before the young lawyer availing himself of his property rights tendered her with himself, she thence conceiving and bringing forth a female child, Laetitia, brown-eyed Laetitia of alabaster skin. Also at that time had the young master taken unto himself a wife, . . . white blue-eyed blond, and yea also, she thus conceiving, and she did bring forth a male child. Time passed and husband and wife and slave concubine and female slave child and male child grew older and the fate of the black one, the nameless one, is hidden from us. But the child Laetitia grew in beauty and tenderness and desire and before her twentieth year had she received within herself the sperm of both her white father and of the white male child, her father's son, her half-brother. The child life of both had she held within herself. (Herron 235–36)

The slave-owning father in this literary representation goes far beyond "perpetuating" "the ambiguous character of fatherhood" "as blank parody." The white slaveholding lawyer commits incest, not because the roles of father and daughter are not differentiated enough, but because his legal ownership of Laetitia amplifies the power relationship between them. The Law of the Father is not erased, as in Spillers's account of the black father-daughter relationship. Here, the Law of the Father exceeds itself and will not be contained—it has provided itself a legal means to facilitate its movement outside of its proper boundaries. *Thereafter Johnnie* proposes that virtually the same thing happens in "single-race" families in which father-daughter incest occurs: the Law of the Father exceeds itself and will not be contained by conventional morality.

But what of the daughter and her response to the father's illicit desire? Readers of *Thereafter Johnnie* have been profoundly disturbed and, I believe, repelled from analyzing the novel because of Patricia's apparent aggression in her "adult" incestuous relationship with her father. Re-analyzing Patricia's pursuit of her father in the light of his sexual molestation of her is the first step toward re-interpreting her behavior. In the novel's third chapter, "Faerie Tale," Johnnie describes her mother Patricia's obsession with their father, John Christopher. This representation of Patricia's mental disturbance (quoted briefly in an earlier section of this chapter) identifies "[t]he beauty of torture, the delight of slavery." It continues thus:

[T]he joy of being tied up bound down whipped beaten drawn quartered stretched broken into the ground is this—the mind is free. Is this, this, there is no way out, giving up is simplified. With warm flesh in shreds, limbs broken torn, guts lashed slashed hung hooked, body held down trussed up bent over, skin fingernails toenails stripped off, breasts cheeks ears eyes stuck stung pierced, . . . limbs pinned open spread askew separated detached, genitals mauled, split, sliced, eliminated it's easy, so easy, so finally and absolutely easy. It must be endured. In such extremity the impulse toward life, living, is uncomplicated, smooth with minimal variation. . . . There is nothing that can be done. The mind can rest. After so much perturbation, so much weighing of possibility, so much consideration of choice, opportunity, alteration, adjustment, coercion, influence, reversal, reconsideration—nothing. Nothing can be done. The mind is free, free, free indeed. Free at last. . . . caught then forever, in flame, tarred and feathered, castrated, raped the mind discovers infinite stillness—there are no decisions to make. It's just like love. (21–22)

This meditation on slavery and love is one of the most important passages in the novel.[18] Looking at love through the lens of torture, Patricia arrives at a twisted view, but this twisted view must be seen in the context of her molestation, and in the context of her ancestor Laetitia's forced sexual relations with her father and half-brother. While the Western religious and literary tradition maintains an ideal of love that comes down to us (like Diotima's name and the story of Atlantis) from Plato, Herron's novel traces the warping of love through ideologies of ownership and control of other human beings, a practice as old as Plato's ideal. In addition, the romantic idea of being incapacitated by love, of falling in love and being unable to extricate oneself, even if one so desires—this concept of love is linked here to the inescapability of the torture imposed by the master upon the slave, which is in turn linked to the inescapability of the molestation visited by the father upon the daughter.

Critic Brenda Daly interprets Patricia's analogy between slavery and love as mere confusion: "Confusing slavery with love . . . Patricia re-enacts the history of her race's enslavement" (481).[19] But it is not Patricia who "re-enacts" the story of "her race's enslavement"; the history of the race's enslavement *has been re-enacted upon her body*. The curse on Patricia's family, what I call the House of Africa, should be remembered here:

[T]o certain of the males born to the house but who nevertheless survive murder and slavery—to these shall be given the power of revenge upon the females of their own house who consented with the white males for their destruction, these males shall be given the female children of their own house, and these shall be raped. And raped again. (Herron 239–40)

It should not be surprising that the adult Patricia equates physical coercion, and even torture, with love. Patricia has been sexually molested by her father as an infant—this is confirmed through three different characters' viewpoints[20]—and she remembers this first sexual abuse when she and her father have sex. She is not yet eighteen at the time of this first intercourse.

Patricia seduces John Christopher by joining him in the bath, but at the last moment, when they are about to have intercourse, she pulls away and then turns back to him.

> Then he plays her body, all of her, her legs and her stomach and her arms, he feels for the warm places, her ears, knees and suddenly the first kiss full in her mouth, their damp bodies close upon each other, *and she has never expected this. She has not imagined that something could happen.* She struggles to push him away, kicks and twists from under him wrestling his arms from around her body, she turns him away from her and she means it. He knows that she intends truly to push him away and he doesn't fight for her but lies surprised on his back with her holding his shoulders away from her. And she almost rejects him entirely right then except she oddly changes her mind as a strangeness begins its slow circles within her. (118–19, my emphasis)

This passage represents the ambivalence and naiveté of Patricia's seduction of John Christopher. The italicized phrases make it clear that she is not capable of fully understanding her pursuit of her father, nor is she fully in control of it. In the section that follows, the reader finds out why. After they both climax, Patricia remembers the first time her father ever touched her clitoris, when she was two years old, and whispers her ambivalent feelings about him "in her forgotten baby voice" (120):

> "[W]hat are you doing to me Daddy, that hurts me, is it a fire Daddy? it hurts me, did your finger put a fire on me Daddy?" . . . Whispering the words she had no words for in the beginning, during the first time, as he sleeps *fifteen years later* her body stiffens into a catatonic X of horror, violation violently enforced pleasure and pain, she whispers possessed by the words she did not have at the beginning, "Daddy, Daddy, Daddy. I hate you, I love you, I hate you, I love you, I hate you, I love you, I love you, I love you, Daddy, Daddy, Daddy." (121, my emphasis)

As an infant, she experiences John Christopher's sexual touch as primarily painful, but it still produces her later, ambivalent desire for sex with him. Patricia's violation as an infant and her status as his seventeen-year-old daughter at the time of their first "adult" sexual episode put John Christopher's actions clearly in the realm of coercion.

As noted in the epigraph from Judith Herman's *Father-Daughter Incest,* "just as, . . . [in slavery], the final decision rested with the master, the final choice in the matter of sexual relations between adults and children rests with the adult" (27). In fact, John Christopher himself tells his wife Camille that he raped Patricia (181), though his account does not tally entirely with the one told in "The First Time." Perhaps in telling Camille that he raped their daughter, John Christopher is acknowledging his early molestation of Patricia and his responsibility for Patricia's incestuous sexual obsession. This is not to say that Patricia, at seventeen, is entirely free of responsibility for her sexual relationship with her father. However, her agency has been severely compromised by her molestation and by the patriarchal myths to which she is attached. While I agree with Daly's contention that "Patricia does not value the love of Diotima, her sisters, or her mother . . . she chooses her father and death" (481), I would argue that Patricia makes this choice under coercive conditions and that molestation by her father has compromised her ability to value the love of women. If one examines the character of Patricia in light of contemporary, feminist, psychotherapeutic literature on incest, it becomes clear that she has been psychologically damaged by incestuous sexual abuse and that Herron is subtly critiquing the Freudian view of incest as phantasmatic and representative of the daughter's desire. Here, I am not attempting to psychoanalyze the female characters in *Thereafter Johnnie;* instead, I am arguing that these characters have been constructed with the contemporary psychoanalytic and psychotherapeutic literature in mind. By so creating her characters, Herron is able to make a critical intervention into the discourse on father-daughter incest, incorporating into it the hidden history of incest in slavery.

In a remarkable article entitled "Soul Murder and Slavery: Toward a Fully Loaded Cost Accounting," historian Nell Irvin Painter argues that not enough effort has been made to analyze the sexual abuse, incest, child abuse, and malign and benign neglect prevalent in slavery using the psychoanalytic and psychotherapeutic tools now available to us. Contemporary African American and Caribbean novels focused on New World slavery provide an especially appropriate occasion for such an analysis. In this section of the chapter, I read Freud's work and contemporary feminist, psychotherapeutic analyses of father-daughter incest as intertexts for *Thereafter Johnnie.*

In order to use Freudian psychoanalysis to analyze the place of incest in both master-slave families and in bourgeois, "single-race" families, it is necessary to decide which Freud one wishes to deploy. If one accepts the official Freud, one will locate desire in female children, black and white, and treat the acts of incest as fantasy. Or, if one accepts the acts of incest as real, one will identify the daughter as the seducer. Herman argues that this is in fact what has happened throughout most of the century since Freud uncovered incest in the modern bourgeois family (7–21). If, however, one accepts Freud's early belief that "seduction" by the father or another adult relative was the cause of hysteria, and, further, if one accepts that Freud reversed this position because he could not bring himself to attest publicly to the fact that so many seemingly respectable men were capable of child molestation, then one will have a very different picture of the family tableau.[21] My contention is that Herron is able to link the father/master-daughter/slave relationship and father-daughter incest in the bourgeois family because she accepts the latter view, that father-daughter incest is desired and initiated by fathers and produces psychological trauma in its young victims. *Thereafter Johnnie* represents the sexual abuse of female children as a problem endemic to the master-slave and bourgeois families, because of the way the concept of the father's ownership of his family members structures these families. Herron is both invoking and critiquing psychoanalytic interpretations of incest by creating a character who appears to fit the Electra role and then revealing what has been masked by the Electra myth: the daughter whose molestation by the father has produced the desire for him by which she is defined.

Herron takes the concept of ownership, obvious in the context of slavery, and foregrounds it in the black bourgeois family. In the sexual encounter between Camille and John Christopher in the chapter aptly titled "Monopoly," there is the appearance of mutual claiming between the lovers, but finally, John Christopher's dominance becomes clear. By arousing his sexually inexperienced fiancée and by withholding the contact that she desires almost painfully, John Christopher gets Camille to claim his body. But he has made up the game and she can only play by his rules. He has initiated their love play by almost bankrupting Camille in a game of Monopoly. As Daly argues, "Camille's desire is contained by John Christopher's claim to possess her. Camille's temporary possession of her future husband's penis dispossesses her, for in marriage he legally owns his wife as well as their children" (476). John Christopher's position vis-à-vis Patricia is even clearer. The last time they make love he says, "I own you my dear, I own you. I can do what I want with you now. Come here now and do what I tell you to do" (Herron 14). These statements echo those of the slaveholding father and son portrayed in the final chapter, "Matin"; they tell their enslaved granddaughter/daughter: "[Y]ou and your Ma both are niggers, we can fuck her like this 'cause she's our nigger, and you're our nigger too, you're a nigger slave, . . . we got papers to show that you and your Ma are niggers. . . . We can sell you or rape you any day of the week" (238). The bourgeois father's ownership of his wife and children and the slavemaster's ownership of black women and the children he fathered with them are here closely equated with one another. This equation is elaborated in other ways throughout the novel. Incest is not incidental to these family configurations; it is a pathology manifested throughout Johnnie's family line and, by implication, throughout U.S. society.[22]

Judith Herman's *Father-Daughter Incest* is one of the major contemporary psychotherapeutic works on incest, and perhaps the only such work that analyzes incest consistently in feminist terms. According to Herman, "[T]he victims of incest [grew] up to become archetypally feminine women . . . In their own flesh, they bore repeated punishment for the crimes committed against them in childhood" (108). Like many of the incest survivors interviewed by Herman and Lisa Hirschman, Patricia finds it impossible to separate pleasure and pain, hatred and love, either in the past or in her current sexual encounter with her father. What distinguishes Patricia from other survivors of incestuous childhood sexual abuse is that she does not find a substitute sexual partner; her compulsive desire will accept only the father as a love object.

One of the most important connections between Herman's *Father-Daughter Incest* and Herron's *Thereafter Johnnie* lies in their analyses of the incestuous nature of certain cultural stories or myths. In a chapter entitled "The Question of Blame," Herman introduces us to "the two major culprits in the incest romance, the Seductive Daughter and the Collusive Mother" (36). She argues that historically, these two figures have been made to bear the responsibility for the actions of incestuous fathers: "Ensnared by the charms of a small temptress, or driven to her arms by a frigid, unloving wife, Poor Father can hardly help himself, or so his defenders would have us believe. Often he believes it himself" (36). Herman maintains that "[t]he image of the Seductive Daughter is part of the literary and religious tradition" (36), and she analyzes the biblical story of Lot and his daughters and the literary tale of Lolita and Humbert Humbert in this context. In her reading, Lot

managed to impregnate both his daughters while apparently maintaining complete innocence of the matter. Initiative for the sexual encounters is ascribed entirely to the daughters, and Lot is spared even the responsibility of conscious memory through the merciful effects of alcohol. (36)

The author goes on to quote a longer section of the same biblical passage that Herron has Patricia quote to her sister Cynthia Jane: "Come, let us make our father drink wine, and we will lie with him, that we may preserve the seed of our father" (Herman 37; Herron 207). Herman notes that in the biblical tale of the Seductive Daughter, the actions of the daughters "at least have the dignity of a serious motive. . . . Thus, even though the daughters are portrayed as entirely responsible for the incest, their actions are to some extent excused" (37). In contrast, secular representations of the Seductive Daughter declare her motives to be "entirely perverse," and Nabokov's *Lolita* is the prototype for this "perverse" character. Herman discusses *Lolita* as, at least on one level of analysis, "a brilliant apologia for an incestuous father" (37). Nabokov's novel has spawned numerous pornographic offspring:

> Lolita has become the model for countless nymphets who appear, unredeemed by Nabokov's elegant prose, in the literature of male sexual fantasy. . . . Thus the Seductive Daughter lives on, an active inhabitant of the fantasy life of the millions of ordinary citizens who constitute the readership of *Chic, Hustler, Playboy, Penthouse,* and the like. (38–39)

Finally, Herman shows how prevalent the idea of the Seductive Daughter has been in psychoanalytic and psychotherapeutic literature. Even in cases where adult male relatives have used force in molesting female children, the psychotherapeutic literature has "tended to focus on qualities in the child victims which might have fostered the development of an incestuous relationship" (39). The cultural influence of the myth of the Seductive Daughter, from the biblical to the literary to the pornographic to the psychoanalytic, is of great importance in interpreting Herron's novel. In *Thereafter Johnnie,* Herron brings together these four forms of representing the supposedly Seductive Daughter, and complicates them with representations of father-daughter incest from the point of view of the child-victim and the teenage-victim/participant. While Patricia appears to be the Seductive Daughter incarnate, using the biblical story of Lot and his daughters to confirm her desire for her father, her pursuit of John Christopher is not only, as Daly argues, "obsessive and unmistakable"; it is also fraught with resistance, bravado, desperation, and grief. These aspects of her apparent pursuit of her father are also present in the clinical testimony of incest survivors quoted in Herman and Hirschman's study.

In *Father-Daughter Incest,* the authors have recorded the words of many survivors of the experience, both clients in therapy and women who have written and published books about their trauma. One unexpected aspect of some clients' responses to their molestation was their acceptance and dramatization of the wickedness socially ascribed to them.

> Many women felt that what set them apart from others was their own evilness. With depressing regularity, these women referred to themselves as bitches, witches, and whores. . . . Some women even embraced their identity as sinners with a kind of defiance and pride. As initiates into forbidden sexual knowledge, they felt themselves to possess almost magical powers, particularly the power to attract men. They seemed to believe that they had seduced their fathers and could therefore seduce any man. (97)

This tendency on the part of incest victims to assent to and act out their own "evilness" is represented in Patricia's behavior. In conversations with her sister Cynthia Jane, Patricia positively revels in the wickedness of her actions. When Cynthia Jane protests Patricia's description of love-making with their father, saying "Oh, Patricia, I wish you wouldn't talk about it like that! It's awful. I don't like to hear about it," Patricia replies, "Ha-ha, it's not awful, Janie. It's warm and brown like pumpernickel you know, ha-ha, the bread that can feed the five thousand and then some, the bread that can be broken and still rise to feed again, and let it rise, Janie, let it rise again and again . . ." (207). This attitude of bravado and pride in her ability to seduce her father is a magnification of the attitudes expressed by actual survivors of incest and it should be understood in this context. Without this context, Patricia is Electra gone round the bend, a crazed, sexually obsessed woman seeking the most desirable and most inappropriate object. Herman, however, presents another way of seeing this behavior and the contradictory attitudes and behaviors that surround it. She analyzes abused daughters' fantasies of power in this way:

> Several . . . women . . . spoke of feeling that they had extraordinary powers over others, especially sexual powers over men, and destructive powers over both men and women. One woman described herself as a "bad witch" and expressed the fear that she could cause other people to sicken with her thoughts. These fantasies uniformly dated back to the incestuous situation in childhood. In part they represented a defense against the feeling, which these women had so often experienced, of being dominated and overwhelmed by their fathers. In part they were expressions of the sense of specialness and privilege which they had derived from being their fathers' favorites. Finally, these fantasies represented the reality that for many years these women had had the potential power to destroy their families. . . . All children, no doubt, have fantasies of secret powers that could be used to de-

stroy their parents. Few children, however, are in possession of knowledge
that could make this fantasy come true. (98)

Patricia, the magnified, mythologized, mythologizing incest victim, realizes, like the actual women to whom Herman refers, that her carnal knowledge of her father has the power to destroy her family. Unlike the incest
victims interviewed by Herman and Hirschman, she takes on the power
given to her by her father's molestation, and actually proceeds to destroy
her family. When Eva asks her what she will do with John Christopher when
he falls in love with her, she says, "'I don't care what happens then, I want
everything to fall down'" (196).

   It is important to recognize that Patricia's pursuit of her father is partly
driven by a desire for revenge against him for his molestation of her. This
is indicated in at least two passages in the novel. As noted above, after the
first time John Christopher and Patricia have sex, she remembers his molestation of her and speaks from the perspective of her two-year-old self.
She says, among other things, "I don't like you, stop hurting me, don't you
hurt me any more, you're mean to me, if you hurt me any more I'm going to kill you when I grow up . . ." (120). In an argument with Cynthia
Jane over her seduction of their father, Patricia says, "I like him angry. I
enjoy the heat that leaps from him when he yells at me, when he breaks
against me, screaming and pleading for his life. He has my life too. He has
had my life. And I'll have him" (207). This expression of power, like those
of the incest victims quoted in Herman's study, is ultimately disempower-
ing. That is, Patricia's perception of her power over her father is only
partly accurate. In a peculiar way, Patricia does kill her father, using
Johnnie as her instrument, because it is in the presence of his seventeen-
year-old daughter that John Christopher dies. Johnnie is the child that
John Christopher wanted to abort. Her entry into his life and her words
("You never should have touched my mother" [83]) seem to bring about
his death.[23] Yet, as noted above, John Christopher has wielded enormous
power over Patricia throughout her lifetime, and she chooses his birthday
as the day on which to commit suicide. In the end, the two of them destroy each other. Since in real situations of incest, the daughter's mental
and emotional health is always damaged, while the father appears to suf-
fer few, if any consequences (unless criminally prosecuted), perhaps this
fictional daughter's infliction of psychic pain upon her father does constitute a significant dilution of his power, a revenge of a sort. It is, at best,
a Pyrrhic victory.

   While one might wish, in feminist terms, to see Patricia turn her back
on her father and patriarchal myths, the fact that she overvalues her father

and patriarchal culture is quite in keeping with her incest history. As Judith Herman writes,

> The majority of the incest victims, in fact, tended to overvalue and idealize men. In their pursuit of sexual intimacy, they sought to recapture the specialness that they had felt in the relationship with their fathers. Many had affairs with much older or married men, in which they relived the secrecy and excitement of the incestuous relationship. As the "other woman," however, they had little power to define the terms of the relationship, and they had to content themselves with lovers who were capricious and often unavailable. . . . With the exception of those who had become conscious feminists, most of the incest victims seemed to regard all women, including themselves, with contempt. At times, remembering their privileged position as their fathers' favorites, they exempted themselves from their general condemnation of women. In adult life, their only possible source of self-esteem was to maintain an identification with their powerful fathers. But more often, on a deeper level, they identified with the mothers they despised, and included themselves among the ranks of fallen and worthless women. (103)

This feminist analysis of the patriarchal leanings of incest victims describes Patricia so well that one might think it was written with her in mind. In Herron's critique, this Electra, and, by implication, the Electra figure in general, stands revealed as the daughter whose desire for her father and hatred of her mother are both coerced by her molestation. She is the product, not the initiator, of father-daughter incest.[24] Patricia achieves a certain sense of power by inhabiting and mythologizing the role she has been assigned, but, finally, her incestuous relationship with John Christopher leads to her madness and death.

Patricia's ancestor Laetitia, an enslaved woman who is the sexual servant of both her father and her half-brother, also has an identity constructed through incestuous sexual abuse. Herron represents Laetitia assenting to her sexual violation and even stating that she takes some pleasure from it. However, her acceptance of her own abuse is partial payment for a guarantee from her masters that they will not abuse her daughter in a similar fashion.

> [W]hen the hand of the young master would have lifted to touch the young Rowena, the innocent child, then did Laetitia cry nay, never. And because of their jealousies [the father and son's] having money and power of her own, having status and capital, did she say "Forever will I receive upon my body the father and the son my masters nor will I say I have no pleasure in them

for I have pleasure to give myself to father and brother, infolding the life of the one with the other until I know well how deeply we have sinned, but not shall you lift your hand to touch my child, which is the child of US." (237)

Laetitia, like Patricia, has some measure of power within the sexually coercive master-slave/father-daughter relationship. While she cannot extricate herself from the relationship, she can insist that the masters refrain from extending their incestuous attentions to their granddaughter-daughter. Again, like Patricia and other incest victims, Laetitia has absorbed the value system of her molesters. Before she dies, she writes to her daughter Rowena and asks her to visit. However, Rowena has married an Indian man and her child is visibly black; if she brings the baby with her on her visit, Laetitia's blackness will be revealed to the neighbors. The ideology of white supremacy is so powerful within Laetitia that she cannot allow this to happen. Despite the fact that she has resisted the power of her masters by protecting Rowena and sending her away, she has absorbed and assented to the ideology of her masters in other ways. Patricia stands in a similar position vis-à-vis patriarchy.

In summary, Herron takes the tangle of emotions identified in victims of father-daughter incest and amplifies them through the addition of a mythic dimension, a critique of "the incestuous nature of the Gods our civilization has created and the consequences of that creation" (Christian 7). She also takes that tangle of emotions and reads it back into the slave past, imagining Laetitia as an incest victim like Patricia. Neither Patricia nor Laetitia can be seen as sexually autonomous women giving consent or making choices; they are involved in coercive sexual relations whose nature is thinly disguised by the victims' accommodation to situations they cannot fundamentally alter. However, their victimization cannot be oversimplified either. The perverse desire produced by childhood sexual abuse, so elegantly summarized by Michael Ryan in one of the epigraphs to this chapter, and the other emotions created by the betrayal of trust inherent in father-daughter incest are complex and contradictory and must be represented as such. Thus, neither Patricia's pursuit of John Christopher nor Laetitia's statement that she takes pleasure in her sexual relations with her father and brother can be taken at face value or fully dismissed. In the context of incest survivors' testimony, the complex, indeed, deeply paradoxical nature of Patricia and Laetitia's actions and statements becomes intelligible.

Herron is signifying both on the myth/stereotype of the Seductive Daughter/Electra figure and the ways it is and has been used to disguise fathers' sexual desires and abuses, and on the myth/stereotype of the promiscuous black woman and the ways it is and has been used to disguise white men's sexual desires for and abuses of enslaved or free black women. What also becomes clear in the historical linkage between these two incidents of father-daughter incest is Herron's vision of incest as a national, cultural pathology. As Christian writes, "*Thereafter Johnnie*... demonstrates that *sex* is *religion* is *nation*, that, to use a Freudian term, 'family romance' is a nation's soul. In the United States that soul originated in bloody sexual violence" (6). The rape of "the nameless one," the African maternal ancestor, by her owner, a European-American lawyer, engenders a history of genocidal violence. In Laetitia's reference to Rowena as "the child of US," the final word must be read both as "us" and as "U. S." Here, Herron is signaling that Rowena, the issue of incest between master and slave, is a "pure product of America," to borrow William Carlos Williams's phrase. Of course, Johnnie is as well. Patricia's mythology about Johnnie, that she will "restore the soul of the city, . . . be the light in the skull" (Herron 214), is Patricia's hope for the salvation of a city and country destroying themselves through racist and sexist determinism.

Johnnie, the last woman in the family line and the nation's potential savior—"god's holy black virgin" (169)—cannot reverse the tragedy brought about by the racial and gender determinism of the city's "byword": "Kill the boys and rape the girls" (242). The tragic ending of the novel reveals that Washington was not able to give up this motto and Johnnie's beautiful dream for the new millennium was destroyed by fire. Like Plato's lost city of Atlantis, to which Herron is clearly alluding, U.S. civilization, though formed by democratic ideals and technologically advanced, is destroyed by excessive greed and imperialism; American racism and racist sexism are shown, in *Thereafter Johnnie*, to be an inextricable part of the negative tendencies of U.S. capitalist society.

3. The Geography of the Apocalypse

Johnnie's physical state and her location are the focus of both the beginning and the end of the novel. At the end of the first chapter, "Vesperus," the epic storyteller, whom we later find out is a Diotima, says of Johnnie, "She knows she is a small dark space in a small dark box in an empty city at the bottom of the sea in drought. She does not know that she has become a light" (Herron 7). The small dark box is the Old Carnegie Library, where Johnnie is condemned to roam the halls for eternity; like the heroes in many Greek myths, she has been transformed into a non-human, literally "a light." Her special knowledge and messianic power are trapped in this abandoned building, endowed by and named for a wealthy industrial capitalist, symbolic of the greed and imperialism destroying the nation. In the final chapter, "Matin," we learn that "the sea in drought" is the sand covering the city of Washington and the surrounding area. We have been prepared for this ending from the very beginning of the novel; Herron's epigraph is a quotation from the Old Testament Book of Lamentations:

> How doth the city sit solitary,
> that was full of people! how is
> she become as a widow! she that was
> great among the nations, and
> princess among the provinces, how
> is she become tributary!
> —Lamentations I:1 [25]

Eva has had a vision of the fate of the city in the aftermath of her rape, a vision in which a group of teenagers playing in a field come across a pointed stone that they cannot move. In her vision, the gods are asking her to identify the stone. She says, "'It is a stone, the stumbling block, the beautiful smooth white piercing stone upon which my city has fallen, it is the Washington Monument that, in fulfillment of the dreams of the people, shall stand forever, covered under a field of sand'" (Herron 130). Herron's representations have moved from the geography of the library's interior and the city streets to the geography of epic, myth, or fairy tale, all forms that the novel invokes and critiques. Both of these geographies, the quotidian and the epic, are buried under sand at the novel's end, "shaken by a force that defies all calculation."[26]

The Diotimas (members of a Mexican storytelling tribe established by Johnnie's caretaker) have become the New World *omeros*, the blind poet-historians generally called Homer. Unlike the original Diotima, the Diotima of the third millennium does not speak through the voice of a patriarch of Western culture (that is, Plato). She and her descendants call down Johnnie as the immortal goddess who will authorize their speech, and they tell the story of "what has passed in the north and why there is such great silence there" (Herron 241) polyphonically, in a framework that radically revises the *Odyssey*. One critic reads this conclusion in a positive way, as the creation of a "new mother-land" (Daly 474). I read Herron's tale as a tragedy, an apocalyptic, cautionary tale for the end of the twentieth century. Adherence to patriarchal mythology, religion, and philosophy, combined with racist ideology and uncontrolled imperialistic drives, has overcome the possibilities presented by the circle of the singing, prophesying, poetic sisters and by Johnnie's dream for the new millennium. It is our own society that has been so destroyed, and to look upon this destruction benignly, because it brings about a seemingly more woman-centered society, is to avoid what the novel is trying to tell us about the fate of subjects constructed in a society abandoned by its own gods for its inability to turn from its "byword forever for its grand family of Northern Europe and Africa, forever, 'Kill the boys and rape the girls'" (Herron 242). *Thereafter Johnnie* proposes that the Law of the Father, the patriarchal "rules of architecture" and geography, and the feminist transformations of these rules may finally be overwhelmed by an even greater force and become in the end merely a cautionary epic for another emerging civilization.

Conclusion

"One Lives by Memory, Not by Truth"

Identities are the names we give to the different ways we are positioned by, and position ourselves within, the narratives of the past.

STUART HALL, "Cultural Identity and Diaspora"

As postmemorial writers, Morrison, Johnson, Marshall, Walcott, and Herron demonstrate the myriad ways in which narratives of the past structure identity. They show how one can "change the joke and slip the yoke" (*Shadow and Act* 45) of identity by changing one's relationship to these narratives, and, conversely, how certain aspects of narratives of slavery can prove inescapable and profoundly determinative of subjectivity. Walter Benjamin, discussing the importance of resistant historiographical practices, writes,

> To articulate the past historically does not mean to recognize it "the way it really was." . . . It means to seize hold of a memory as it flashes up at a moment of danger. Historical materialism wishes to retain that image of the past which unexpectedly appears to man singled out by history at a moment of danger. The danger affects both the content of the tradition and its receivers. The same threat hangs over both: that of becoming a tool of the ruling classes. In every era the attempt must be made anew to wrest tradition away from a conformism that is about to overpower it. . . . Only that historian will have the gift of fanning the spark of hope in the past who is firmly convinced that *even the dead* will not be safe from the enemy if he wins. (Benjamin 255)

Throughout this book, I have argued that contemporary African American and Caribbean writers have taken up the task Benjamin outlines for the historian in this passage. In the "moment of danger" in which we live, these writers have seized hold of slavery as an existential condition through which to articulate the difficult coming-into-being of the black subject in the New World.

This conclusion's title—one lives by memory, not by truth—is a provocative declaration Rita Dove has used as a spur to her writing.[1] When I began this book in 1995, as a dissertation, I hung these words above my desk because they emphatically, yet mysteriously, articulate a central theme of this project. Cultural memory is of critical importance in the process of self-creation, but its function is complicated by the forms that accompany and succeed it, namely, postmemory and history. I undertook *Black Subjects* because, like the writers whose work is examined here, I felt haunted by the history of slavery and its legacies to the present. The differing truth claims made by each of these major means of calling up the past—memory, postmemory, and history—are elaborately intertwined with one another in the contemporary narrative of slavery.

In my research, I came across the story of the journey the Surinamese Bush Negro chiefs made to Ghana in 1970 in order to reconnect with their ancestral culture. The ancestors of the present-day Bush Negroes were enslaved West Africans who escaped from their captors almost immediately upon their arrival in Surinam. They thus retained a remarkable number of their original customs and were so successful as a Maroon society that they eventually signed a treaty with the Dutch that allowed them to remain free. During the course of their trip, the chiefs met with Ghanaian and Nigerian dignitaries. After one lavish meal, one of the Bush Negro chiefs said, "It is a fine meal, . . . probably paid for with the money that was earned by selling us as slaves" (De Groot 396). This astonishing statement, which shrinks time so profoundly that a fine meal in 1970 might have been paid for with money from a transaction made 200 years before, is one end of a spectrum of thought about the beginning of the African Diaspora. At the other end of that spectrum stands the ludic, postmodern fiction of Charles Johnson and Ishmael Reed. As she defines postmemory and analyzes postmemorial art, Marianne Hirsch explicitly addresses the difficulties that arise when succeeding generations too readily appropriate the experiences of their ancestors. She writes, "The challenge for the postmemorial artist is precisely to find the balance that allows the spectator to enter the image, to imagine the disaster, but that disallows an overappropriative identification that makes the distances disappear, creating too available, too easy an access to this particular past" ("Projected Memory" 10). Most African American and Afro-Caribbean postmemorial writers and artists have achieved this balance admirably, using a wide range of strategies.

In an illuminating essay on *Beloved,* Valerie Smith argues that Morrison powerfully evokes yet also holds at one remove the pain of slavery:

> My sense is that by representing the inaccessibility of the suffering of former slaves, Morrison reveals the limits of hegemonic, authoritarian systems of knowledge. The novel challenges us to use our interpretive skills, but finally turns them back upon themselves. By representing the inexpressibility of its subject, the novel asserts and reasserts the subjectivity of the former slaves and the depth of their suffering. The novel reminds us that our critical acumen and narrative capacities notwithstanding, we can never know what they endured. We can never enjoy a complacent understanding of lives lived under slavery. To the extent that *Beloved* returns the slaves to themselves, the novel humbles contemporary readers before the unknown and finally unknowable horrors the slaves endured. ("Circling the Subject" 354)

Morrison encourages readers to undertake the task of "attempt[ing] to put oneself in the other's position without taking the other's place," a task that Dominick LaCapra deems necessary for non-survivors as they approach representations of the Holocaust (quoted in "Projected Memory" 16). Johnson uses anachronism and humor as distancing mechanisms in his works on slavery; as I argue in chapter 2, his work sometimes seems too parodic, floating free of the gravity of real bodies in pain. Marshall leans in the other direction, identifying the present-day inhabitants of Bournehills with their enslaved ancestors. Yet in representing their static, albeit powerful, annual re-enactment of Cuffee Ned's rebellion and their inability to find an effective form in the present for their revolutionary spirit, *The Chosen Place* acknowledges the differences between slavery and oppression in late-capitalist society. Walcott stages Makak's spiritual journey as a dream, using theatrical techniques (Brechtian techniques among others) designed to maintain the audience's distance from the play. Herron almost completely conflates the enslaved victim of incestuous abuse with the contemporary incest victim; in *Thereafter Johnnie,* American history is a tragedy of endless repetition leading to a final apocalypse. The epic structure of the novel—as a tale told by a member of a storytelling clan who calls on Johnnie as the muse/goddess who will authorize her speech—is its primary strategy for keeping readers from identifying too readily with the enslaved. Yet this alienating mechanism is undercut by erotic representations of incestuous sex that implicate the reader in illicit desire, making us aware of the prurience of our engagement with the text. All of these writers, and the other contemporary narrators of slavery whose works are not examined here, strive to bring the slave past into a coherent relationship with the present, without collapsing the two.

The range of contemporary narratives of slavery reaches far beyond the boundaries of this study. In addition to numerous other works of fiction and drama, collections of poetry like Kamau Brathwaite's *The Arrivants* trilogy and the mixed-media art objects of Glenn Ligon and Marianetta Porter, including this book's cover, also contribute to this vibrant new movement in Afro-Caribbean and African American literary and visual arts. If I had world enough and time, this book would have included analyses of Black British contributions to the contemporary narrative of slavery such as Caryl Phillips's *Cambridge* and Fred D'Aguiar's *The Longest Memory*. A significant number of white fiction writers have taken up the theme of slavery since William Styron's foray into the field; Madison Smartt Bell's novels on the Haitian Revolution are a case in point. This trend deserves serious study, especially since, in recent years, it has been supplemented by works like Edward Ball's *Slaves in the Family*, which links the contemporary white U.S. family not only with its slaveholding ancestors but with the families of the blacks they held in bondage. The current debates raging over slavery in the United States—regarding reparations, the relationship between Thomas Jefferson and Sally Hemings, Margaret Mitchell's estate's injunction halting the publication of Alice Randall's *The Wind Done Gone* (a parody of *Gone with the Wind* which was eventually published in 2001)— and the new controversies surrounding color prejudice and class divisions in the Caribbean (including a march in Puerto Rico commemorating Martin Luther King, Jr., and condemning race and color hierarchies) indicate that this hemisphere has yet to make peace with this aspect of its history.

One of the most fruitful directions for future research in this area would follow the contemporary narrative of slavery as it moves toward narratives of other cultural traumas and the possibility of New World liberation in the present. A brief reading of the transformation in Gayl Jones's oeuvre will illustrate the way in which the contemporary narrative of slavery has begun to open up to the world.

Jones's first novel, *Corregidora* (1975), is one of the most disturbing contemporary narratives of slavery. It depicts the oral tradition in an African American family of women as a tool of resistance against the slaveholding culture, but a tool that paralyzes the Corregidora women, fixing them in the past with the injunction to "make generations" who can bear witness to the evil that was perpetrated upon them. The purpose of future generations, in this novel, is solely to testify about the past, thus, the future is doubly foreclosed for the main character Ursa Corregidora (named for the slavemaster who was her great-grandfather and grandfather, not for her own father) when she is injured by her husband and learns that she cannot have children. The novel ends with the protagonist locked in a none-too-hopeful embrace with her ex-husband, recognizing that she has the power to castrate him as she imagines her grandmother may have attempted to castrate the master. The sense of claustrophobia created in the reader mirrors the protagonist's inability to escape from the locked box of the past, despite her attempts at freedom through blues performance.

Jones's most recent novel, *Mosquito* (1999), engages with slavery in a profoundly different way. While *Corregidora* gestures toward the hemispheric reach of slavery, since the master was a Portuguese slaveholder in Brazil, *Mosquito* links the Americas in a much more optimistic conjunction.

Mosquito is a postmodernist metafiction named for its main character and stream-of-consciousness narrator, whose full name is Sojourner Nadine Jane Johnson. An African American truck driver in the southwest United States, Mosquito primarily transports industrial and ecological detergents, until one day she finds herself transporting a pregnant Mexican immigrant woman. The novel details her growing involvement in the Sanctuary movement as she becomes a conductor on the "New Underground Railroad" (225). When Mosquito declares her knowledge of the entire Southwest and especially the roads of South Texas, one is immediately struck by how infrequently a woman's knowledge of geography and topography is invoked in the culture at large. Mosquito is virtually never represented within her domestic space; her truck, the road, and the cantina are the spaces she inhabits with the greatest degree of comfort. In fact, she has left domestic service for a new career as a trucker. She is clearly a new kind of African American heroine: a descendant of Pilate Dead from Morrison's *Song of Solomon*, a sister to Lauren Olamina of Octavia Butler's *Parable of the Sower* and Harlan Jane Eagleton from Jones's own previous novel *The Healing* (in fact, Mosquito is one of Eagleton's friends, in Jones's fictional universe), and a cousin to some of the women of Gloria Anzaldúa's *Borderlands/La Frontera*. Often, when female characters take to the road, tragedy results, but in this novel, the protagonist's mobility allows her to participate in a multiracial coalition dedicated to the permeability of borders of all kinds.

The idea of freedom is *Mosquito*'s overarching concern; meditating on the end of a difficult relationship with a man, Mosquito says to herself and her "listeners" [readers]:

> I gots to drive my truck. I gots to. Even if he don't think that's the essence of who I am or who I could be. 'Cause that's something I know I gots to do. It always makes me wonder why people, and ain't just mens, that always wants

to try to make you stop doing the very thing you gots to do. . . . I don't know why you gots to do it. Maybe it's the closest thing you come to to [*sic*] what freedom mean. Your own idea of freedom. And don't nobody want freedom for you. Not the true thing. And I ain't talking about license or decadence. I'm talking about freedom, the true thing. (112)

Mosquito focuses on textual as well as material liberation, especially through its sustained investigation of the analogy between the escape from U.S. slavery and the escape from contemporary oppressive governments (as well as the United States Immigration Service). The protagonist wonders about the possibility of

a true jazz story, where the peoples that listens can just enter the story and start telling it and adding things wherever they wants. The story would provide the jazz foundation, the subject, but they be improvising around that subject or them subjects and be composing they own jazz story. If it be a book, they be reading it and start telling it theyselves whiles they's reading. . . . anyplace in the novel they wants to integrate they own story or the stories of the peoples they knows, so they be reading and composing for theyselves, and writing in the margins and ain't just have to write in the margins, 'cause I ain't wanting my listeners to just be reserved to the margins, but they writing between the lines, and even between the words, and be adding they own adjectives here and there. . . . I ain't know if I wants them peoples to be changing names, though they can compose around the themes, but they could still bring they own multiple perspectives everywhere in that novel, and they own freedom. (93–94)

Here, Jones returns to one of the most powerful tropes from Frederick Douglass's 1845 *Narrative of the Life of Frederick Douglass, An American Slave* and utterly transforms it. In the arduous process of learning to write (Douglass had to improvise his own "pedagogy of the oppressed" since teaching a slave to write was forbidden by law in Maryland and virtually every other slave state), Douglass finds an old copybook in which the young Master Thomas has done his lessons. To practice his letters, he covertly writes between the lines of that copybook, an act which will prepare him to write one of the founding texts of African American literature, a text whose reason for being was the will to freedom. Moving beyond the idea of freedom as merely the absence of slavery, Jones is attempting "to tell a free story" (to borrow critic William Andrews's phrase) in the postmodern era, inviting readers to write between the lines and even between the words as they construct a truly democratic work of fiction. As readers we find ourselves asking, Is this novel we're reading Mosquito's jazz ideal? What could be more fitting than for the "free story" of contemporary black life to fuse jazz, Black English, Mexican Spanish and Spanglish, rap (U.S. and Caribbean), *Oprah,* the "Perfectability Baptist Church" (2) and the geography of the border?

Mosquito's status as a postmodernist novel challenges established definitions of postmodernity in fiction. Jameson identifies four major "constitutive features of the postmodern":

> a new depthlessness, which finds its prolongation both in contemporary "theory" and in a whole new culture of the image or the simulacrum; a consequent weakening of historicity, both in our relationship to public History and in the new forms of our private temporality . . . ; a whole new type of emotional ground tone . . . which can best be grasped by a return to older theories of the sublime; [and] the deep constitutive relationships of all this to a whole new technology, which is itself a figure for a whole new economic world system. (6)

As I noted in chapter 3, theorists of Latin American and Caribbean literature and culture have discussed the ways in which "local postmodernities" (Colás 267) may follow rules different from those pertaining to mainstream U.S. and European postmodernist culture, especially in dealing with history. The same may be true for what I call *black feminist postmodernism: Mosquito* shows neither the flattening of affect nor the crisis of historicity that Jameson identifies as properties of postmodernist texts, yet, in this novel and in *The Healing* (1998), Jones has clearly moved beyond the modernist aesthetic. Acutely aware of the "whole new economic world system" as it plays itself out along the border between Mexico and the United States, Jones has crafted a novel about the possibility of organizing resistance to that system across lines of race, class, gender, language, religion, and nationality. Jameson believes political art to be a near impossibility in the postmodern moment, yet this is a profoundly political novel. *Mosquito*'s most powerful political statement may be its focus upon the multiple subjectivities of three working-class women of color: Mosquito herself and her friends Delgadina, a Chicana bartender and organic intellectual, and Monkey Bread, who works as a housekeeper/personal assistant to a Hollywood star and is a member of the Daughters of Nzingha, a mysterious, eclectic empowerment group for women of African descent (or "descendants of the African Diaspora Holocaust" [427]). Throughout the novel, their identities are revealed not as essentialized but as fluid and continuously shaped by their political and social realities, demonstrating Stuart Hall's contention, which I use as the epigraph to this conclusion: "identities are the names we give to the different ways we are positioned by, and position ourselves within, the narratives of the past" (394). This most contemporary of contemporary narratives of slavery closes with the voice of a liberated and liberating African American speaking subject: the *griot* and prophet of the New World.

NOTES

Introduction: "The Middle Passage Never Guessed Its End"

The quotation "The middle passage never guessed its end" is from the poem "Laventille," by Derek Walcott.

1. In *The Oxford Companion to African American Literature*, Rushdy employs a much more expansive definition of "Neo-slave narrative" in his entry under that title. His second work on contemporary narratives of slavery, *Remembering Generations: Race and Family in Contemporary American Fiction* (2001), addresses many of the gaps in *Neo-slave Narratives* and, in effect, broadens the category in keeping with the *Oxford Companion* definition.

2. Like Beaulieu's and Mitchell's books, Venetria Patton's *Women in Chains: The Legacy of Slavery in Black Women's Fiction* (2000) focuses on African American women's narratives. However, Patton devotes just one chapter to contemporary works; her book primarily addresses nineteenth- and early twentieth-century literature.

3. Though George Handley's *Postslavery Literatures in the Americas* devotes only a chapter to contemporary narratives of slavery, his comparative analysis of works from the Anglophone and Hispanophone Americas is an important step in this direction.

4. As Marianne Hirsch indicates in *Family Frames*, she and the psychoanalyst Nadine Fresco appear to have derived this term independently. I am relying on Hirsch's articulation of postmemory.

5. Dominick LaCapra discusses this concept of traumatized "acting out" in *Representing the Holocaust*, and Hirsch cites his work in "Projected Memory," 16. The question I am taking up becomes even more difficult to address when violent, dehumanizing acts continue to be directed at black communities as a means of social control. In general, borrowing Hirsch's concept of postmemory, developed in response to the experiences of children of Holocaust survivors, entails several significant problems. In a U.S. context, the Holocaust is valorized as the ultimate cultural trauma, in which most Americans can see the country and its military as liberators of the oppressed. U.S. and Caribbean slavery has had a very different history as a cultural trauma. The violent debates in the United States over apologies and reparations for slavery attest to the fact that the nation is far from unanimous in the belief that slavery was responsible for lasting harm to post-Emancipation generations of African Americans. It is possible to voice the opinion that U.S. slavery placed contemporary African Americans in an economic and political situation far superior to the great majority of Africans without being summarily dismissed from intelligent public discourse. Such comments are certainly not relegated to

the margins of public dialogue as are Holocaust denials or claims that the Nazi death camps were simply labor camps with a very high mortality rate. In the Commonwealth Caribbean, the British colonial education system suppressed or minimized the history of slavery; movements for independence, like the Civil Rights Movement in the United States, made possible the unearthing and reconsideration of this history. Furthermore, New World slavery is often dismissed as ancient history, while the Holocaust is generally perceived as the preeminent modern genocide. These differences mean that the cultural field in which "postmemorial" art and literature about slavery are produced is deeply resistant to recognizing the lingering effects of slavery. Yet despite these significant differences between the status of the Holocaust and the status of New World slavery as cultural traumas, Hirsch's concept of postmemory remains a useful tool for understanding the position of black writers from the mid-1960s to the present.

6. In a later article, "Does Theory Play Well in the Classroom?" Christian makes an argument based more on African Americans' historical access to formal education than on cultural predisposition (245–47).

7. After I began using this term, I came across it in Gayl Jones's remarkable novel *Mosquito* (1999).

1. *Beloved*

1. In *Caliban's Reason*, Paget Henry argues, "The ethical dimensions of traditional West African philosophy are cosmogonic and communitarian in nature" (38). Because most slaves in the Americas came from West Africa, and because many Africanisms in North American and Caribbean culture appear to be derived from West African ethnic groups, I will be using the adjective "West African" to describe the cultural practices and beliefs the slaves brought with them to the Americas. I will also use "African" as a more general designation for those who survived the Middle Passage. While I am aware of the problems of homogenizing Africa into single entity, the similarities between West African ethnic cultures and the extent to which these cultures merged in the Americas make "West African culture" as legitimate a term as "Western civilization" for the present purposes.

2. Here I am attempting to sidestep the rich and long-standing debate about the nature—capitalist or pre-capitalist/feudal—of U.S. slavery. By the mid-nineteenth century, U.S. and New World slavery more generally exhibited significant capitalist features, and Morrison focuses upon these. Major works in this debate are Paul David et al., *Reckoning with Slavery;* Robert Fogel and Stanley Engerman, *Time on the Cross;* Eugene Genovese, *Roll, Jordan, Roll* and *The Political Economy of Slavery;* and Eric Williams, *Capitalism and Slavery* (full citations in bibliography). While this debate has not been resolved, it is no longer at the forefront of U.S. and Caribbean slave studies.

3. See "'Somebody Forgot to Tell Somebody Something': African-American Women's Historical Novels," by Barbara Christian, in *Wild Women in the Whirlwind: Afra-American Culture and the Contemporary Literary Renaissance*, ed. Joanne M. Braxton and Andrée Nicola McLaughlin (New Brunswick, N.J.: Rutgers University Press, 1990).

4. Mae Henderson's "Toni Morrison's *Beloved:* Re-Membering the Body as Historical Text" has been the most influential for my own interpretation. Henderson's assertion that "the act of remembering, for the unlettered slave, constitutes the act of constructing a private self" (73) serves as a foundation for my assertion that the ex-slave's self is constructed and expressed through musical improvisation.

5. See "The African Philosophical Heritage" in Paget Henry's *Caliban's Reason,*

Michael A. Gomez's *Exchanging Our Country Marks*, and John S. Mbiti's *African Religions and Philosophy* for extended discussions of these aspects of traditional African societies.

6. See Blassingame 22 and Levine 6.

7. Film scholar Mary Ann Doane notes this type of indirect interpellation in a discussion of Frantz Fanon's "The Fact of Blackness" (chap. 5 in *Black Skin, White Masks*). She writes,

> Fanon persistently returns to the imperative call—"Look, a Negro!"—uttered by a little white boy in a state of fascination and terror. The call is a somewhat perverse version of the Althusserian process of interpellation or hailing. Although it addresses and at the same time refuses to address the black directly (the second person pronoun is not used), the exclamation fixes the black person, producing a subjectivity which is fully aligned with a process of reification." (224)

Though I agree with Doane's argument about the intended effect of the call, one of my primary arguments in this chapter is that such sideways hailings, and the direct classic version of interpellation, do not inevitably produce "a subjectivity which is fully aligned with a process of reification." Sethe's resistance makes this clear.

8. See, for example, Sander Gilman's "Black Bodies, White Bodies: Toward an Iconography of Female Sexuality in Late Nineteenth-Century Art, Medicine, and Literature."

9. Months later, when Sethe kills her daughter, the physical sensation of needles in her scalp recurs; she thinks of the needles as the beaks of hummingbirds and she herself flies to put her children beyond reach of the whip, the bit, and the measuring tape. Finally, Sethe's "mistaken" attack on Mr. Bodwin is also attended by needles in the scalp and the sound of hummingbird wings. Though technically Sethe is mistaken as to the identity of the white man coming into her yard, there is a great deal of symbolic meaning in Mr. Bodwin's coming for one of her daughters. He's not coming to enslave Denver, but he is going to put her to work in domestic service. Her experience of labor may not differ significantly from that of many slaves.

10. Like many actual slaveholders, Garner has even implemented a money-free wage system through which Halle, by selling his extra labor, can purchase his mother's freedom.

11. See Marlon Riggs's film "Ethnic Notions" for an extended critique of objects such as these. As any number of recent controversies demonstrate, hatred of and fetishistic attachment to the black body have persisted into the twenty-first century.

12. Robert Farris Thompson's groundbreaking study *Flash of the Spirit* illuminates the artistic and philosophical connections between West Africa and Afro-America. He records the transformation of cultural philosophies from one context to the other.

13. This is one of the negative consequences of the primacy of the slave narratives; in them, personhood is mostly constructed in Western terms.

14. In a remarkable article entitled "Keys to the Ancestors' Chambers: An Approach to Teaching *Beloved*," Valorie Thomas shows how Morrison has drawn upon Yoruba and Kongo spiritual traditions throughout the novel. She argues, convincingly, that the main characters have characteristics of West African *orisha*, and that the graphics that introduce the novel's sections are related to ritual drawings from Kongolese tradition. This essay is the most extensive discussion of African influences in *Beloved* that I am aware of.

15. Nan and Sethe's mother are "shipmate" relatives, fictive kin whose source of connection is their experience of the Middle Passage. In a number of New World, African-descended cultures, these relationships were a very important source of identification and resistance for slaves (Price 27–28; Mullin 37–38).

16. Of African beliefs regarding death and remembrance, theologian John Mbiti

writes, "while the departed person is remembered by name, he is not really dead: he is alive, and such a person I would call the *living-dead*" (32). After death, Baby Suggs is among the "living-dead," remembered and called upon for emotional sustenance by both Sethe and Denver.

17. Beloved's return in the flesh is in itself an extended evocation of certain African belief systems. Beloved is a complex, contradictory character; she is both the daughter Sethe killed and the embodiment of the individual and communal dismemberment of African Americans. She is a catalyst of positive events, helping Sethe and Paul D to re-connect with their pasts, yet she also forces Paul D into an anguished re-assessment of his manhood and almost destroys Sethe. It is important to look at Beloved in the context of African spirituality because many enslaved Africans and their descendants retained concepts of reincarnation and the afterlife that account for the girl's return. It is striking how easily the African American community around 124 Bluestone accepts the fact that Beloved is the reincarnation of Sethe's dead child. Janey, the Bodwin's domestic servant, even knows what signs to ask for (lines in the palm of the hand) to determine if the girl is in fact a re-embodied spirit. As Morrison herself says, "[I]t was clear to me that it [Beloved's incarnation] was not at all a violation of African religion and philosophy; it's very easy for a son or a parent or a neighbor to appear in a child or in another person" (*Darling* 249). In representing Beloved as an actual human being, Morrison has registered the continued existence of two African traditional religious beliefs, one from the Yoruba and Igbo and one from the Akamba people of Kenya. In discussing the character Beloved, Carole Boyce Davies writes of "the legendary *abiku* children of Yoruba cosmology or the *ogbanje* in Igbo culture, who die and are reborn repeatedly to plague their mothers and are marked so that they can be identified when they return" (139). And according to Mbiti, among the Akamba people of Kenya, a child who dies before she is named is still an "object" belonging to the spirits; she has not been ritually separated from the world of the spirits and the ancestors (the living-dead) (Mbiti 156). Like Beloved, a child like this has a foot in both the human and the spirit worlds.

18. The antiphonal structure of Baby Suggs's ceremony is another element that connects it to West African musical traditions. Many scholars of African and African American music have commented on the use of antiphony and the tendency to incorporate body movements into musical performance in both traditions. See Olly Wilson's articles on these topics.

19. Title of a book of poems by Michael S. Harper.

20. See Thomas 93.

21. Baby Suggs's choice of color as the object of meditation deserves far greater elaboration than I am able to give it here.

22. A remarkable reversal of American social norms is subtly enacted throughout *Beloved*. Whiteness is consistently marked while blackness is represented as the standard human condition. To be black is to be among the people; to be white is to be set apart, marked. The word "white," attached to "man," "woman," "boy," or "girl," designates a range of subject positions all determined to a significant extent by their participation, direct or indirect, literal or psychological, in the subjugation of black people. Whites use blacks as a mirror in which they see themselves magnified; this magnification creates other distortions, visible and palpable to blacks but largely invisible to whites themselves. Morrison has spoken explicitly about the transformation of Europeans and Euro-Americans wrought by slavery: "Slavery broke the world in half, it broke it in every way. It broke Europe. It made them into something else, it made them slave masters, it made them crazy" ("Living Memory" 178).

23. Baby Suggs is reduced to/chooses the world of the seen over the unseen; she says to Stamp Paid, "What I know is what I see: a nigger woman hauling shoes" (179). This

is a direct rejection of her faith ("Faith is the substance of things hoped for, the evidence of things not seen.") and her call to preach.

24. The women come together at three o'clock on a Friday afternoon, the day and time that Christianity has established for the death of Christ. Beloved's death/unmaking is a sacrifice for the greater good of the community.

25. The metaphor of the concert is a particularly felicitous one in terms of my analysis. The European symphonic music to which Althusser alludes is typically performed as written; improvisation has little or no place in it. One can see how improvisation might serve as a useful model and trope for resistance to the repressive, capitalist system for which the concert is Althusser's metaphor.

26. Though I do not employ them here, Stuart Hall, in "The Problem of Ideology: Marxism Without Guarantees," and Satya Mohanty, in *Literary Theory and the Claims of History,* have produced thorough critical discussions of the importance and the shortcomings of Althusser's theory of interpellation.

27. Feminist theory has made clear the importance of physical coercion in the formation of female subjects under patriarchy. Catherine MacKinnon's work, in particular, addresses this point.

28. Homi Bhabha's acclaimed "Of Mimicry and Man" shows how the inevitable difference produced through mimicry deconstructs colonial discourse; however, he does not address the ways in which colonial or white-supremacist discourse is *deliberately* deconstructed through "signifying" and improvisatory revision.

29. African American music contains elements of both European and African music, combined into a new whole. At least two traditional forms are being improvised upon. Scholar Charles Keil writes, "The Afro-American tradition represents not only a variety of mixtures between European and African elements but a series of blendings within itself" (Keil 33).

2. Being, Race, and Gender

1. In his profoundly disturbing "Postscript" to "A Phenomenology of the Black Body," added to the original essay in 1993, Johnson catalogues the negative meanings that accrue to the black male body in contemporary culture and then delivers his quite remarkable conclusion about the social perceptions of black female bodies, saying,

> [I]t's important to point out that none of these cultural meanings cluster around the black *female* body. In an amazing and revolutionary feat of cultural reconstruction, contemporary black women have made dominant the profile of the female body as, first and foremost, *spiritual:* a communal-body of politically progressive, long-suffering women who are responsible, hard-working and compassionate, who support each other in all ways, protect and nurture their children and live meaningful lives without black male assistance. The black female body is, in fact, frequently offered to us as the *original* body of a humankind descended from a black Eve of Africa. Clearly, this profile owes much to both black cultural nationalism of the late 1960s . . . and to the embracing of feminism by many black women in the 1980s. Nevertheless, like the Negro Beast stereotype, the Ur-mother profile is a mythology that obscures and one-dimensionalizes our possibilities for experiencing each black person as individual. (120)

Clearly, Johnson believes that African American women have transcended the stereotypes of Mammy, Jezebel, and conjure woman that have dominated their representations for centuries, as well as the negative images of more recent vintage: welfare queen, crack mother, emasculating bitch. Johnson's argument can easily be refuted by reference to any number of contemporary cultural artifacts and situations; what's striking about his comments is that they betray an acute sympathy with black male victims of public calumny, but a complete inability to see black female victims of the same social processes. Among the attacks on the black male image that Johnson lists are "the sexual harassment charges against Clarence Thomas, who according to Anita Hill described himself as 'Long Dong Silver,'" "the sexist 'gangster' lyrics offered by Ice T and other rap artists," and "even . . . the popular novels of several black women authors during the decade of the 1980s" (120). He fails to note that the largely white and male Senate confirmed Clarence Thomas, who now holds one of the highest public offices in the country, that black women are the targets at whom Ice T and other misogynist rappers direct their venom, and that African American women writers of the 1970s and '80s were attempting to address the historical silencing and negative portrayals of black women, sometimes by black male writers. Johnson's inclusion of the lyrics of gangster rap in his catalogue of ills is especially strange, since he seems to be arguing that the primary injury created by these black men's descriptions of black women as 'bitches' and 'hos' is that it reflects badly on the perpetrators, and, by extension, upon other black men.

2. The transformation of Sophia Auld in Frederick Douglass's *Narrative* is one telling example of this phenomenon.

3. Husserl used this method of phenomenological inquiry. Because of the extent of Johnson's debt to Husserl, I'm looking at Johnson's anachronistic situations as fantasy variations played out for the purpose of arriving at "truths" not apparent in our everyday way of seeing. (Ihde 39–40)

4. In one of his characteristically clever and apt allusions, Johnson has Harriet reading "a volume by one M. Shelley, a recent tale of monstrosity and existential horror" (17) just before she's killed by Mingo. Like Frankenstein's monster, Mingo kills his creator's companion. However, Mingo doesn't kill for revenge; instead, he acts out his master's submerged hostility and preserves the master-slave, creator-creature dyad.

5. This ending recalls the final act of Aimé Césaire's *Une Tempête,* a revision of Shakespeare's *The Tempest* in which Prospero is unable to leave the island with Miranda and the other Italian characters. He's too caught up in his military and psychological conflict with Caliban to move back to Europe.

6. Of course, having placed Africans outside the realm of history, Hegel probably did not consider them eligible for the role of bondsman/slave in his scenario.

7. In other works, Johnson resolves the problem of the domineering female in different ways: sometimes the male protagonist is able to escape from her and sometimes she changes significantly, becoming much closer to the submissive feminine ideal.

8. Muther uses this phrase to describe Isadora Bailey in *Middle Passage,* but it is equally applicable to Harriet Bridgewater.

9. The narration of this event bears a strong resemblance to the "Trueblood episode" in Ralph Ellison's *Invisible Man;* it's another tale of sexual transgression told entirely from the point of view of the male perpetrator.

10. Because Andrew's mother is a white woman, he may be legally free from birth, if South Carolina, like most Southern states, ruled that the child shall follow the condition of the mother. This argument is not made in the novel; I read the need for a technically free character to escape from slavery as yet another one of Johnson's existential jokes.

11. As Keith Green, a graduate student in my seminar "History, Memory, and Subjectivity in Contemporary African American and Caribbean Literature" pointed out, this scene reads like a rape scene with the traditional gender roles reversed.

12. The paragraph ends, "It goes without saying that I had found in Noah Walters a friend; it was almost (I thought, stunned) as if I'd slept with *him* by proxy" (96). The homoeroticism of this passage is echoed in other places in the novel, as well as in *Middle Passage*. The intensity of male bonding in these works seems to lead almost inevitably toward images of sexual love between men.

13. Another disturbing feature of Andrew's first masquerade is that it depends upon his willingness to deliver another group of slaves to certain death in the mines. He saves only himself and Reb, and his representation of himself as an overseer/driver is guaranteed by the presence of the visibly black men he turns over to Noah Walters. Like many tricksters, Andrew not only "puts on ole Massa," his tricks also may have damaging effects on other slaves.

14. Retman does raise the question of Andrew's whiteness as a problem, arguing that "this union potentially colludes with the hegemonic valuation of whiteness and devaluation of blackness, implying that Andrew can only attain freedom if he, in essence, leaves behind the black community for a white wife and a 'white' persona." She also notes the horrifying moment when "Andrew is interpellated as a white buyer" (432) at the auction where he sees Minty for sale. Unfortunately, Retman sets these critiques aside and concludes with a positive interpretation of Johnson's argument for fluid subjectivities and the value of love "as a means of achieving a radically liberating subjectivity" (431).

15. The fact that Andrew/William often refers to Peggy this way (as Wife with a capital 'W'), underscores her function rather than her individual qualities.

16. The moment when Andrew sees Minty on the auction block owes a clear debt to Charles Chesnutt's short story "The Wife of His Youth."

17. Interestingly enough, Reb's daughter dies of pellagra, the same disease that kills Minty.

18. It is definitely possible that Andrew/William will follow the injunction to "live like a bourgeois, but write like a revolutionary." Johnson's characterization of Marx as a "householder" indicates that this status may be consistent with a radical critique of society and that perhaps the author intends us to read Andrew/William, the novel's other "householder," as a theorist/critic like Marx.

19. Vera Kutzinski arrives at a different conclusion in "Johnson Revises Johnson: *Oxherding Tale* and *The Autobiography of an Ex-Coloured Man.*"

3. *The Chosen Place, The Timeless People*

1. This, of course, is Eric Williams's argument in *Capitalism and Slavery.*

2. I have borrowed the term "semi-colonial" from Ernest Mandel, because it seems much more precise than "postcolonial."

3. Christine Levecq's "'We House and We Land': History and Radical Politics in Paule Marshall's *The Chosen Place, The Timeless People*" lucidly discusses the problems of tourism and "dependency" more generally.

4. Part of the brilliance of Marshall's critique is the way in which she demonstrates the connection between corporate and educational institutions, a connection that we need to bear in mind more and more as academics.

5. I will discuss this character at greater length later in the chapter.

6. Ironically, it is Merle's husband's enactment of just such a male prerogative that completely undoes her, but because of her profound guilt and shame about her sexual and financial relationship with her white female benefactor in London, it takes her years to condemn Ketu Kinbona for taking her child from her.

7. Critic VèVè Clark coined the term "diaspora literacy" in a piece published as "De-

veloping Diaspora Literacy and *Marasa* Consciousness." *Comparative American Identities: Race, Sex, and Nationality in the Modern Text,* ed. Hortense J. Spillers (New York: Routledge, 1991), 40–61. Abena Busia designates *Praisesong for the Widow* as a "diaspora novel" in her essay, "What Is Your Nation?: Reconnecting Africa and Her Diaspora through Paule Marshall's *Praisesong for the Widow,*" in *Changing Our Own Words: Essays on Criticism, Theory, and Writing by Black Women,* ed. Cheryl Wall (New Brunswick, NJ: Rutgers University Press, 1989), 196–211.

8. This is the title of Jamaica Kincaid's 1988 critique of First World tourism in Antigua.

4. Performance, Identity, and "Mulatto Aesthetics"

1. Though Roger Abrahams uses the spelling "Anansi," I, and the critics I cite, use the more common spelling "Anancy."

2. A revised version of this essay appears in Olaniyan's *Scars of Conquest/Masks of Resistance.* I quote from both in this chapter.

3. The critic Elaine Savory Fido has examined and critiqued Walcott's consistently negative representations of women in detail in "Value Judgements on Art and the Question of Macho Attitudes: The Case of Derek Walcott." She argues "that not only is the work of Derek Walcott, a deservedly celebrated poet, dramatist and theatre practitioner in the Caribbean, inclusive of strong prejudices about women but that these are often associated with weakening of power in his writing" (109).

4. I make this assumption because creating this kind of nickname is a widespread Afro-Caribbean and African American practice.

5. Bruce King, *Derek Walcott and West Indian Drama: "Not Only a Playwright But a Company": The Trinidad Theatre Workshop, 1959–1993* (New York: Clarendon-Oxford University Press, 1995) 82. In this remarkable book, King supplies a wealth of detail about the development and production of all of Walcott's plays. He notes that *Dream* was initially performed at the first Caribana Festival in Toronto, Canada, and that much of the play came out of improvisation with the actors. He writes,

> Walcott's plays at this time still used animal symbolism. . . . In *Dream* the animalization is in the symbolism and workshops were devoted to doing animal mannerisms which were later incorporated into the characterization. Errol Jones [who played Makak], for example, did workshop exercises with his body and voice imitating apes and lions, while Stanley Marshall [Moustique] tried to be a mosquito. (82)

6. Derek Walcott, "XIV" (from *Midsummer*), *Collected Poems, 1948–1984* (New York: Farrar, Straus and Giroux, 1986), 476.

7. In *Making Men,* critic Belinda Edmondson makes a different argument about the unrepresentability of the black woman in Caribbean "novels of revolution" by men. She writes,

> The desire of the novel of revolution to liberate the Caribbean space by remaking it, literally and figuratively, in the image of the Caribbean man is tied to its corresponding impulse to "erase" the symbolic body of the black woman. As a symbol of the slave past, the black woman represents a double threat. For Caribbean men, on one hand, she carries within her the ability to "name" her descendants, which is, as Spillers suggests, the ever-present discursive reminder of

the subjugated status of [black] Caribbean men to white European men. For European men, on the other hand, the black woman's ability to "race" the mulatto child in her own image was a direct assault on the cherished European ideal that male sperm was stronger than female, an idea that was the basis for European laws of inheritance. (107)

What Edmondson fails to consider is the fact that slave law in the United States and the Caribbean reversed European laws governing the status of children, declaring that the child would "follow the condition of the mother," not because of any challenge to the faulty biological consensus of the time, but to ensure that mulatto children would be enslaved and, after emancipation, would find it very difficult to make legal claims on their white fathers. Had Europeans of the time been correct about the greater strength of male sperm, and had they used this to determine the status of mixed-race children, this would have profoundly complicated the caste systems established under New World slavery.

8. The man of color's claims to women of color are also limited, to a lesser degree, by the claims of other men of color, to the extent that individual men of color have enough social power to threaten and impose sanctions upon black men who violate those claims.

9. See, in particular, Mary Prince's narrative and Caryl Phillips's 1991 novel of slavery, *Cambridge.* It is also interesting to note that contemporary U.S. novels of slavery, like Sherley Anne Williams's *Dessa Rose* and Charles Johnson's *Oxherding Tale,* register the female slaveowner's ability to exact sexual services from her male slaves.

10. Various other Caribbean writers have made different choices in representing slavery and colonialism, in part because of the work done by Lamming, Césaire, and others writing in the early period of decolonization. Paule Marshall, in *The Chosen Place, The Timeless People;* Michelle Cliff, in *Abeng,* and Peter Abrahams, in *The View from Coyaba,* have used actual stories of the Maroons and other slave rebels, or created slave rebels based on historical information to ground their texts in the past and to reflect upon present conditions. Caryl Phillips, in *Cambridge,* has borrowed a strategy from the slave narrative and used Equiano's narrative as the pre-text for his text, while also signifying on the construction of the Caribbean through European travel writing by creating the diary of an English woman who spends time on her father's plantation. One thing that these other choices reveal is that as historical work on the Caribbean brought to light more information about creolized Africans and their descendants, Caribbean writers incorporated this new history into their reconstructions of the past. Decolonization also allowed a re-valuation of oral history and culture, and the "nation languages," to use Brathwaite's term, gained greater legitimacy as literary languages.

11. In the context of this chapter, it is not possible to address the economic aspect of their task in any detail.

12. Furthermore, Lamming's view of Caliban contains an error that leads Lamming to despair of ever escaping from the framework imposed by Prospero's language. He writes,

Prospero has given Caliban Language; and with it an unstated history of consequences, an unknown history of future intentions. This gift of Language meant not English, in particular, but speech and concept as a way, a method, a necessary avenue towards areas of the self which could not be reached in any other way. It is this way, entirely Prospero's enterprise, which makes Caliban aware of possibilities. Therefore, all of Caliban's future—for future is the very name for possibilities—must derive from Prospero's experiment which is also his risk.

Provided there is no extraordinary departure which explodes all of Prospero's premises, then Caliban and his future now belong to Prospero. (*Pleasures of Exile* 109)

Of course, there *was* an "extraordinary departure," the process of creolization. For Lamming was wrong in asserting that Prospero gave Caliban Language as distinct from English. Prospero gave Caliban English and he made something else out of it, using his African tribal language as a base. The slave was not a *tabula rasa* on which any language could be written, creating a perfect image. Lamming has accepted at face value the slave's languageless state. Aimé Césaire, in his version of *The Tempest*, moves beyond Lamming in practice by giving Caliban a language and a worldview that pre-dated Prospero's arrival. But it is Edward Brathwaite's concept of nation languages—the Caribbean languages based on African tribal language structures and incorporating European vocabularies—that finally serves as a corrective to Lamming's despair. This concept of the nation languages as literary languages is articulated in *History of the Voice*. We can move from Caliban to his historical counterparts.

13. Fanon's *Peau Noire, Masques Blancs* was published in 1952; its English translation appeared in 1967, the same year as Walcott's *Dream*.

14. Mary Ann Doane, in *Femmes Fatales: Feminism, Film Theory, Psychoanalysis*, also discusses Fanon's unequal treatment of men and women of color. She writes,

How can one explain the vacillation of Fanon when confronted with the relations between race, psychopathology, the individual, and the social? One is tempted to see the vacillation as the effect of a certain conceptualization of sexual difference. The woman of color, Mayotte Capécia, no matter how white the color of her skin, becomes the exemplary representative of a blackness delineated as the inevitably impotent desire to be other. Jean Veneuse, on the other hand, does actually achieve otherness through his intense intellectual endeavors—he is only accidentally, "coincidentally" black. Given the fact that his pathological behavior is unrelentingly *individual*, according to Fanon, and whiteness confers upon the subject the "right" of individuality, Jean Veneuse has indeed attained a form of whiteness in Fanon's schema. The white mask is most perceptible as a mask in the case of the woman of color who seems more at home in the realm of mimicry. (220)

Doane's analysis clarifies Fanon's double movement here—his rejection of the idea that black men are inseparable from the biological, along with his reinscription of black women as representatives of the biological. This movement is similar to Charles Johnson's in *Oxherding Tale*, in which, I argue, black female characters embody blackness and slavery.

15. Furthermore, his dream-death is like the deaths of the animal characters of the tales in that it is not permanent.

16. In fact, Walcott is probably familiar with the folktale in both traditions, having grown up in St. Lucia and having later moved to Trinidad, islands whose colonial legacy from the French was overlaid by colonization by the British. This layering of colonial legacies is represented in the play when Corporal Lestrade, the representative of English law, orders Makak to stop speaking in French Creole. Another play of Walcott's, *Ti-Jean and His Brothers,* is based on the French Creole folktales about the title character.

17. In *Derek Walcott—Memory as Vision: Another Life,* Edward Baugh identifies Sidone more fully as Walcott's "great-aunt Sidone Wardrope" (11). Biographer Bruce King clar-

ifies her relationship to Walcott: she was the sister of Walcott's grandmother on his father's side (*Caribbean Life* 8).

18. African-Diaspora scholar VèVè Clark has called my attention to the fact that the Anancy stories were referred to as "Aunt Nancy" stories in the southern United States, a name change that emphasizes the importance of the often-female storyteller.

5. The Geography of the Apocalypse

1. I thank my colleague Anita Norich for calling my attention to the fact that the Hebrew Bible has 24 books.

2. In Greek mythology, Atreus was the father of Agamemnon and Menelaus. An enemy, Thyestes, laid a curse upon Atreus and his descendants which destroyed the family over several generations.

3. Because *Thereafter Johnnie*, like James Joyce's *Ulysses*, makes numerous references to the Homeric epics, it was tempting to imagine that Herron would represent the title character circumnavigating her chosen city, as Joyce does with Leopold Bloom. However, in my attempts to map the novel, I was not able to find any such pattern.

4. Pecola Breedlove from *The Bluest Eye* falls into this category, and the young Maya Angelou in her autobiography, *I Know Why the Caged Bird Sings*, does not speak for some time after the murder of her molester. Spillers notes that Matty Lou, the daughter whom Jim Trueblood impregnates in *Invisible Man*, never speaks.

5. This subheading, as well as the subheadings "Voyeurs or Walkers" and "On Ground Level, with Footsteps," come from de Certeau's *The Practice of Everyday Life.*

6. Pamela Scott and Antoinette J. Lee, *Buildings of the District of Columbia* (New York: Oxford University Press, 1993) 293–94.

7. Though Brenda Daly argues that John Christopher is named for John the Baptist in "Whose Daughter Is Johnnie? Revisionary Myth-making in Carolivia Herron's *Thereafter Johnnie*," *Callaloo* 18, no. 2 (1995): 476–77, the text systematically connects him with John the apostle. The museum artifact is clearly connected to the second John, and in the chapter "Atlantis" the John alluded to over and over again is Christ's "beloved disciple." Also, the continuous references to Revelations indicate that John of Patmos is the biblical figure Herron is interested in highlighting.

8. In a critical essay written for my graduate seminar "History, Memory, and Subjectivity in Contemporary African American and Caribbean Literature," Clare Counihan analyzes the silences in the passage where John Christopher encounters the chicken-pox vagabond as moments when the old man may have molested the boy. John Christopher does, after all, come down with chicken pox immediately after this encounter, implying that the old man touched him, though the physical contact between them is not narrated. The possibility of John Christopher's molestation as a boy provides a link between the victimization of black men and their subsequent victimization of black women, according to the novel's historical vision.

9. Webster would have been chagrined to learn that the ground on which the Washington Monument sits is not firm at all. The foundation was fortified before the monument was completed in the 1880s; nevertheless, the monument sinks approximately one quarter of an inch every thirty years.

10. The novel also contains a spatial reference to Frederick Douglass: Camille grows up in a house on Douglass Street. There is evidence that suggests that John Christopher may also have molested Patricia in this house. See pages 188 and 200. The novel is also calling our attention to relative importance, within the "official" city, of the monuments to Lincoln and Douglass.

11. Here I am borrowing from Judith Herman's *Father-Daughter Incest* (Cambridge, MA: Harvard University Press, 1981).

12. Patricia's death by drowning in the Potomac is yet another of *Thereafter Johnnie*'s references to William Wells Brown's *Clotel*, in which the enslaved, tragic-mulatta heroine commits suicide in the same fashion.

13. Though these thoughts are Patricia's, Johnnie is actually the speaker in this chapter. She recounts a number of incidents from Patricia's perspective.

14. In the chapter "Sestren," an encounter between Patricia and Eva raises this possibility. Patricia asks Eva "[W]ould it have been worse for you if Dad had slept with you instead of me?" Before responding, "Eva stares quietly into Patricia's face, stares and thinks and waits, her mind flinches stumbles and carries on obliterating an almost memory that thus loses its only chance to arise" (Herron 194). Then she answers, "No, Patricia, that wouldn't have been worse, I probably would have enjoyed sleeping with Daddy, but I don't know why" (195). Though Eva does not actually remember her father molesting her, it may be this experience that informs her sense that she would have enjoyed sleeping with John Christopher and drives her into the streets in pursuit of some sexual encounter that will allow her to forget the pain of her existence.

15. Camille, the green-eyed mother and cultivator of roses, is associated with traditionally masculine and feminine spaces. She takes schoolchildren (and Johnnie) on a tour of "[l]and and water forms of Washington, D.C." and teaches Johnnie "how to recognize the monuments to the three presidents: Washington has a pointed top, Jefferson has a round top, Lincoln has a flat top" (Herron 179). In this way, she is connected to the masculine architecture of the city. Yet she is unable to occupy the place of the voyeur, even when she wants to. When she has learned that her husband and daughter have had sex, her breathing becomes impaired and she thinks,

> [W]hy is the air pressing down on me so hard . . . I think I can fly through it, I bet I could, if only I had a chance to try, . . . if she [Cynthia Jane] would only stop the car a minute I could fly up and get some fresh air, and I could look down and find out what has happened since the beginning of time, I could see the Trojan war and the theft of Africans, and how they killed the Indians, I could see all the myths when they were born, and I could see all the way down here to the pit of hell, the annihilated, the deceived, the forsaken, the despicable, the wretched, injustice and sorrow and cruelty and despair and torture and lynching and murder and starvation and burning flesh and eyes put out and Eva raped I would see Eva raped and I would see my husband fucking our daughter, my husband fucking our daughter, my husband fucking our daughter. (Herron 95–96)

Camille desires a view not only panoramic but historically all-encompassing to help her through the "threshing of [her] soul" (94), but she is not able to achieve this all-powerful, disengaged perspective.

16. Daly, "Whose Daughter Is Johnnie?" 476–77; Elizabeth Breau, "Incest and Intertextuality in Carolivia Herron's *Thereafter Johnnie*," *African American Review* 31, no. 1 (1997): 101. In an elegant turn of phrase, Breau refers to the X as "this crucifix on which Patricia writhes, unable to control the feelings that course through her body."

17. It is tempting also to read the X in its specifically African American context, as the signatory mark of those whose illiteracy was enforced under slavery and as the symbolic last name adopted by members of the Nation of Islam to reject slavemasters' names, which many blacks carried into the post-slavery era.

18. The novel's interest in questions of love is highlighted by the presence of a character named Diotima; the classical bearer of this name is the itinerant mystic whose phi-

losophy of love Socrates recounts in Plato's *Symposium*. Plato, *Symposium*, trans. Robin
Waterfield (Oxford: Oxford University Press, 1994), 41, 85.

19. In "Whose Daughter Is Johnnie? Revisionary Myth-making in Carolivia Herron's
Thereafter Johnnie," Brenda Daly analyzes the novel in terms of Freudian/Lacanian psychoanalytic theory. She uses official Freudian interpretations, feminist critiques of
Freud, and the works of Lacanian feminists who have interpreted father-daughter incest as "a psycho-linguistic phenomenon" (475). Her questioning of the psychoanalytic
model as the primary or sole interpretive method to be used in an analysis of Herron's
representation of father-daughter incest is an important critical move. Yet Daly reads
Patricia's agency in psychoanalytic terms:

> Though one might argue that Patricia loses all possibility of agency through her
> father's sexual violation of her at the age of two . . . her pursuit of her father is
> obsessive and unmistakable. Patricia Snowdon behaves, in psychoanalytic terms,
> as an Electra figure, a daughter who desires her powerful father and, as a conse-
> quence, devalues and even hates her mother (479).

I do, in fact, want to argue that the possibilities of agency for Patricia have been significantly diminished and that her pursuit of her father is highly ambivalent.

While using psychoanalysis to account for Patricia's agency within the "adult" incestuous relationship between her and John Christopher, Daly also critiques psychoanalysis as a model for fully explaining incest in *Thereafter Johnnie*. Freudian/Lacanian
psychoanalysis falls short, in Daly's view, for two major reasons: first, because it treats incest primarily as fantasy and disregards fathers' desire for their daughters; and second,
because it does not adequately address the historical and mythic dimensions of the
novel. Daly concludes,

> [T]he novel itself appears to offer a historical/mythical explanation of the fa-
> ther's incestuous desires which, buried in John Christopher's childhood, are also
> psychological. Finally, although *Thereafter Johnnie* tells the story of father-daugh-
> ter incest, that narrative is framed by Johnnie's quest for a mother, a design that
> emphasizes how this plot has tragically divided mothers and daughters for cen-
> turies. (480–81)

The father-daughter incest plot, inscribed and re-inscribed through Herron's allusions
to and transformations of classical and biblical stories, is, for Daly, altered and transcended through the mother-daughter plot. She argues, "*Thereafter Johnnie* achieves this
transformation by its framing of the narrative, which shifts the mother-daughter plot,
or Johnnie's quest for origins, especially her maternal origins—from the background
to the foreground" (484). Johnnie's "othermother" (a term Daly borrows from Patricia
Hill Collins), the original Diotima, and the story-telling tribe of Diotima, one of whom
is narrating the story of Johnnie's family, are, in Daly's argument, the focus of the novel's
end.

> Within this complex time-frame [of *Thereafter Johnnie*], daughter Patricia repre-
> sents the present (already past) while Johnnie represents the future (already pres-
> ent), and Diotima's descendants represent the future of that future. The future,
> and survival, are located in warm Mexico, with othermother Diotima, whereas
> the past and death are located in the Arctic Cold, with the paternal Patricia. A
> surviving society, with an oral story-telling tradition, is founded by Diotima, a les-
> bian who bears the name of Plato's philosopher queen (486–87)

Daly goes on to argue that Herron's achievement is that she "neither submits to the patriarchal point of view nor fully contests it. Instead, she . . . 'dialogizes' it," creating a host of characters who tell similar stories from different points of view (487). None of these characters speaks in "the authoritative epic voice" (487). The democratic form and the focus on female characters in *Thereafter Johnnie* lead Daly to conclude that Herron, like Johnnie, is indebted to her black foremothers.

While Daly makes a number of important points in her discussion of psychoanalytic interpretations of incest and *Thereafter Johnnie*, she does not adequately analyze the issue of incest in the context of slavery in the United States. She touches upon slavery at several points in her essay, but she does not analyze the correspondence between incest in the black bourgeois family and incest between white slaveholders and their black female children. Thus, she is able to discuss the ways in which "the father's desire for his daughter has been denied and repressed in patriarchal discourses" (Daly 474), but she is not able to discuss the ways in which the white master's desire for his black female slaves (sometimes his daughters) has been similarly denied and repressed. Understanding the correspondence between these two scenarios is crucial to understanding of the full scope of the novel. In my view, Daly's failure to deal fully with the legacy of slavery leads her to misread Patricia's pursuit of her father and to ignore the incestuous nature of the master-slave sexual domination portrayed at the end of the novel. Finally, Daly's article attempts to avoid the essentially tragic nature of the novel and to recuperate the ending as the story of the beginning of "a new nation, a mother-country" (473).

20. Patricia's, Camille's, and Cynthia Jane's memories all support the fact that John Christopher molested Patricia as an infant. Herron has created a family constellation that closely matches the prototypical incestuous family described in current psychotherapeutic literature.

21. Daly notes the critiques of Freud's abandonment of his seduction theory, but fails to follow the implications of the original seduction theory and the ways in which they are played out in Herron's text. Jeffrey Masson's *The Assault on Truth: Freud's Suppression of the Seduction Theory* asserts that Freud renounced the seduction theory out of allegiance to Wilhelm Fliess, his friend and fellow doctor, and more generally out of allegiance to a masculine medical profession which simply would not accept male sexual abuse of female children as the primary cause of hysterical symptoms. Masson also notes that, while psychoanalysis took up the term "seduction" precisely because of its ambiguity, Freud was originally using this term as a euphemism for "a real sexual act forced on a young child who in no way desires it or encourages it. . . . an act of cruelty and violence which wounds the child in every aspect of her . . . being" (5). Patricia's reaction to having intercourse with her father can be interpreted as a hysterical seizure, a case that, except for the graphic way in which it is described, and the fact that it is sexual contact with the father himself that triggers the hysteria, could have come from the pages of Freud's early *Aetiology of Hysteria*. In that work, Freud declares, "Sexual experiences in childhood consisting in stimulation of the genitals, coitus-like acts, and so on, must therefore be recognized, in the last analysis, as being the traumas which lead to a hysterical reaction to events at puberty and to the development of hysterical symptoms" (Freud, Appendix B in Masson 275). Freud further argues that *"hysterical symptoms are derivatives of memories which are operating unconsciously"* (280); this certainly applies to Patricia, who only recovers her memory of being molested by her father when she has sex with him. She clearly fits the pattern Freud outlines of pubescent girls developing hysteria when an event in the present triggers their unconscious memories of molestation.

22. As I noted in a previous section of this chapter, one of the few weaknesses of Herron's novel is the starkness with which the comparison between white, slaveholding fa-

thers and black property-owning fathers is made. The novel pays lip service to the idea that black men are oppressed, but represents the sole black male character as having as much power as any white man. From the point of view of the abused child, there is little to distinguish one from the other, yet, at some level, the differences in their social power must be acknowledged. Herron does so only superficially.

23. Seventeen years previous, Patricia's pregnancy and her refusal to have an abortion almost sent John Christopher into cardiac arrest (214). While Brenda Daly sees Johnnie as the son Camille was unable to give John Christopher and interprets Patricia's creation of this fourth child as an act in which the daughter asserts her power within the family, John Christopher does not accept Johnnie as the son he never had; in fact, he is terrified of the child when he sees her as a baby and dies when he sees her as an adolescent.

24. The sexual promiscuity in women that often results from childhood sexual abuse is also represented and mythologized in *Thereafter Johnnie*. Of their subjects, Herman and Hirschman write, "One third (35 percent) of the women had periods in their lives when they were sexually promiscuous, by their own definition of the word. Many oscillated between periods of compulsive sexual activity and periods of asceticism and abstinence" (100). It is possible to read Eva, Patricia's younger sister, as an incest victim, and to see in her sexually loose behavior a response to a childhood instance of molestation like Patricia's. As mentioned in an earlier note, Eva may also have been molested by John Christopher.

25. Epigraph to *Thereafter Johnnie*.

26. Kandinsky, quoted in de Certeau, *The Practice of Everyday Life*, 110.

Conclusion

1. "Poet Laureate Rita Dove." Video interview with Bill Moyers. Princeton, N.J.: Films for the Humanities, 1994.

WORKS CITED

Abrahams, Roger D., ed. 1985. *Afro-American Folktales: Stories from Black Traditions in the New World*. New York: Pantheon.

Ahmad, Aijaz. 1987. "Jameson's Rhetoric of Otherness and the 'National Allegory.'" *Social Text* 17:3–25.

Alexander, M. Jacqui. 1994. "Not Just (Any) *Body* Can Be A Citizen: The Politics of Law, Sexuality and Postcoloniality in Trinidad and Tobago and the Bahamas." *Feminist Review* 48:5–23.

Althusser, Louis. 1971. "Ideology and Ideological State Apparatuses." *Lenin and Philosophy*. New York: Monthly Review Press.

Andrews, William L. 1988. *To Tell a Free Story: The First Century of Afro-American Autobiography, 1760–1865*. Urbana: University of Illinois Press.

Andrews, William L., Frances Smith Foster, and Trudier Harris, eds. 1997. *The Oxford Companion to African American Literature*. New York: Oxford University Press.

Angelou, Maya. 1969. *I Know Why the Caged Bird Sings*. New York: Bantam, 1980.

Anzaldúa, Gloria. 1987. *Borderlands/La Frontera: The New Mestiza*. San Francisco: Spinsters/Aunt Lute.

Aptheker, Herbert. 1943. *American Negro Slave Revolts*. New York: International Publishers, 1963.

Arnold, A. James. 1996. "Animal Tales, Historic Dispossession, and Creole Identity in the French West Indies." In *Monsters, Tricksters, and Sacred Cows: Animal Tales and American Identities*, edited by A. James Arnold, 255–68. Charlottesville: University Press of Virginia.

Baer, William, ed. 1996. *Conversations with Derek Walcott*. Jackson: University Press of Mississippi.

Bakhtin, M. M. 1986. *Speech Genres and Other Late Essays*. Translated by Vern W. McGee. Austin: University of Texas Press.

Baker, Houston A., Jr. 1984. *Blues, Ideology, and Afro-American Literature: A Vernacular Theory*. Chicago: University of Chicago Press, 1987.

Ball, Edward. 1998. *Slaves in the Family*. New York: Ballantine.

Baugh, Edward. 1978. *Derek Walcott, Memory as Vision: Another Life*. London: Longman.

Beaulieu, Elizabeth Ann. 1999. *Black Women Writers and the American Neo-Slave Narrative: Femininity Unfettered.* Wesport, Conn.: Greenwood Press.

Bechet, Sidney. 1960. *Treat It Gentle.* New York: Hill and Wang.

Bell, Bernard W.. 1987. *The Afro-American Novel and its Tradition.* Amherst: University of Massachusetts Press.

Benhabib, Seyla. 1996. "On Hegel, Women, and Irony." In *Feminist Interpretations of G. W. F. Hegel,* edited by Patricia Jagentowicz Mills, 25–43. University Park: Pennsylvania State University Press.

Benítez-Rojo, Antonio. 1992. *The Repeating Island: The Caribbean and the Postmodern Perspective.* Translated by James E. Maraniss. Durham, N.C.: Duke University Press.

Benjamin, Walter. 1968. *Illuminations.* Translated by Harry Zohn. New York: Schocken Books, 1969.

Bhabha, Homi K. 1984. "Of Mimicry and Man: The Ambivalence of Colonial Discourse." *October* 28:125–33.

Blassingame, John W. 1979. *The Slave Community: Plantation Life in the Antebellum South.* New York: Oxford University Press.

Bontemps, Arna. 1936. *Black Thunder—Gabriel's Revolt: Virginia, 1800.* Boston: Beacon Press, 1992.

Brathwaite, Edward. 1973. *The Arrivants: A New World Trilogy.* New York: Oxford University Press, 1992.

——. 1971. *The Development of Creole Society in Jamaica, 1770–1820.* Oxford: Clarendon Press.

Brathwaite, Edward Kamau. 1984. *History of the Voice: The Development of Nation Language in Anglophone Caribbean Poetry.* London: New Beacon.

Breau, Elizabeth. 1997. "Incest and Intertextuality in Carolivia Herron's *Thereafter Johnnie.*" *African American Review* 31.1:91–103.

Brown, William Wells. 1853. *Clotel, or, The President's Daughter.* New York: Carol Publishing Group, 1969.

Busia, Abena P. A. 1989. "What Is Your Nation?: Reconnecting Africa and Her Diaspora through Paule Marshall's *Praisesong for the Widow.*" In *Changing Our Own Words: Essays on Criticism, Theory, and Writing by Black Women,* edited by Cheryl Wall, 196–211. New Brunswick, N.J.: Rutgers University Press.

Butler, Octavia E. 1993. *Parable of the Sower.* New York: Warner Books, 2000.

Byrd, Rudolph P., ed. 1999. *I Call Myself an Artist: Writings by and about Charles Johnson.* Bloomington: Indiana University Press.

Carby, Hazel V. 1989. "Ideologies of Black Folk: The Historical Novel of Slavery." In *Slavery and the Literary Imagination,* edited by Deborah E. McDowell and Arnold Rampersad, 125–43. Baltimore: Johns Hopkins University Press.

Certeau, Michel de. 1988. *The Practice of Everyday Life.* Translated by Steven Rendall. Berkeley: University of California Press.

Césaire, Aimé. 1969. *A Tempest.* Translated by Richard Miller. New York: Ubu Repertory Theater Publications, 1985.

Chesnutt, Charles W. 1899. *The Wife of His Youth and Other Stories of the Color Line.* Ann Arbor: University of Michigan Press, 1998.

Christian, Barbara. 1996. "Does Theory Play Well in the Classroom?" In *Critical The-*

ory and the Teaching of Literature: Politics, Curriculum, Pedagogy, edited by James F. Slevin and Art Young, 241–57. Urbana, Ill.: National Council of Teachers of English.

———. 1991. "Epic Achievement." *Women's Review of Books* 9.1:6–7.

———. 1993. "Fixing Methodologies: *Beloved.*" *Cultural Critique* 24:5–15.

———. 1987. "The Race for Theory." In *The Nature and Context of Minority Discourse,* edited by Abdul R. JanMohamed and David Lloyd, 37–49. New York: Oxford University Press, 1990.

———. 1990. "'Somebody Forgot to Tell Somebody Something': African-American Women's Historical Novels." In *Wild Women in the Whirlwind: Afra-American Culture and the Contemporary Literary Renaissance,* edited by Joanne M. Braxton and Andrée Nicola McLaughlin, 326–41. New Brunswick, N.J.: Rutgers University Press.

Clark, VèVè A. 1991. "Developing Diaspora Literacy and *Marasa* Consciousness." In *Comparative American Identities: Race, Sex, and Nationality in the Modern Text,* edited by Hortense J. Spillers, 40–61. New York: Routledge.

Colás, Santiago. 1992. "The Third World in Jameson's *Postmodernism or The Cultural Logic of Late Capitalism.*" *Social Text* 31/32:258–70.

Crouch, Stanley. 1983. "Charles Johnson: Free at Last!" In *I Call Myself an Artist: Writings by and about Charles Johnson,* edited by Rudolph Byrd, 271–77. Bloomington: Indiana University Press, 1999.

D'Aguiar, Fred. 1994. *The Longest Memory.* London: Chatto and Windus.

Daly, Brenda O. 1995. "Whose Daughter Is Johnnie? Revisionary Myth-Making in Carolivia Herron's *Thereafter Johnnie.*" *Callaloo* 18.2:472–91.

David, Paul A., et al. 1976. *Reckoning with Slavery: A Critical Study in the Quantitative History of American Negro Slavery.* New York: Oxford University Press.

Davies, Carole Boyce. 1994. *Black Women, Writing and Identity: Migrations of the Subject.* New York: Routledge.

Davis, Angela Y. 1971. "The Black Woman's Role in the Community of Slaves." *The Black Scholar* 3.4:2–15.

De Groot, Silvia W. 1979. "The Bush Negro Chiefs Visit Africa: Diary of an Historic Trip." In *Maroon Societies: Rebel Slave Communities in the Americas,* edited by Richard Price, 389–98. Baltimore: Johns Hopkins University Press.

Diedrich, Maria, Henry Louis Gates Jr., and Carl Pederson, eds. 1999. *Black Imagination and the Middle Passage.* New York: Oxford University Press.

Doane, Mary Ann. 1991. *Femmes Fatales: Feminism, Film Theory, Psychoanalysis.* New York: Routledge.

Douglass, Frederick. 1845. *Narrative of the Life of Frederick Douglass, An American Slave, Written by Himself.* Edited by David W. Blight. Boston: Bedford, 1993.

Edmondson, Belinda. 1999. *Making Men: Gender, Literary Authority, and Women's Writing in Caribbean Narrative.* Durham: Duke University Press.

Elkins, Stanley M. 1959. *Slavery: A Problem in American Institutional and Intellectual Life.* New York: Universal Library–Grosset & Dunlap, 1963.

Ellison, Ralph. 1952. *Invisible Man.* New York: Vintage–Random House, 1995.

———. 1964. *Shadow and Act.* New York: Vintage-Random, 1972.

Eyerman, Ron. 2001. *Cultural Trauma: Slavery and the Formation of African American Identity.* Cambridge: Cambridge University Press.

Fanon, Frantz. 1967. *Black Skin, White Masks.* Translated by Charles Lam Markmann. New York: Grove Press, 1982.

Fido, Elaine Savory. 1986. "Value Judgements on Art and the Question of Macho Attitudes: The Case of Derek Walcott." *Journal of Commonwealth Literature* 21.1: 109–19.

Foucault, Michel. 1980. "Questions on Geography." In *Power/Knowledge: Selected Interviews and Other Writings, 1972–1977.* Translated by Colin Gordon, Leo Marshall, John Mepham, Kate Soper. Edited by Colin Gordon, 63–77. New York: Pantheon.

Freud, Sigmund. 1896. "Aetiology of Hysteria." Translated by James Strachey. Reprinted in *The Assault on Truth: Freud's Suppression of the Seduction Theory,* by Jeffrey Moussaieff Masson, 259–90. New York: Penguin, 1985.

Gaines, Ernest J. 1971. *The Autobiography of Miss Jane Pittman.* New York: Bantam, 1972.

Gates, Henry Louis, Jr. 1988. *The Signifying Monkey: A Theory of African-American Literary Criticism.* New York: Oxford University Press.

——. 1991. Jacket copy for *Thereafter Johnnie. Thereafter Johnnie.* New York: Random House.

Genovese, Eugene D. 1965. *The Political Economy of Slavery: Studies in the Economy and Society of the Old South.* New York: Pantheon.

——. 1974. *Roll, Jordan, Roll: The World the Slaves Made.* New York: Pantheon.

Gikandi, Simon. 1992. *Writing in Limbo: Modernism and Caribbean Literature.* Ithaca, N.Y.: Cornell University Press.

Gilman, Sander L. 1986. "Black Bodies, White Bodies: Toward an Iconography of Female Sexuality in Late Nineteenth-Century Art, Medicine, and Literature." In *"Race," Writing, and Difference,* edited by Henry Louis Gates Jr., 223–61. Chicago: University of Chicago Press.

Gilroy, Paul. 1993. *The Black Atlantic: Modernity and Double Consciousness.* Cambridge: Harvard University Press.

Glissant, Edouard. 1989. *Caribbean Discourse: Selected Essays.* Translated by J. Michael Dash. Charlottesville: University Press of Virgina, 1992.

Goldberg, Jonathan. 1996. "The History That Will Be." In *Premodern Sexualities,* edited by Louise Fradenburg and Carla Freccero, 1–21. New York: Routledge.

Gomez, Michael A. 1998. *Exchanging Our Country Marks: The Transformation of African Identities in the Colonial and Antebellum South.* Chapel Hill: University of North Carolina Press.

Gordon, Lewis, ed. 1997. *Existence in Black: An Anthology of Black Existential Philosophy.* New York: Routledge.

Haley, Alex. 1976. *Roots.* New York: Doubleday.

Hall, Stuart. 1994. "Cultural Identity and Diaspora." In *Colonial Discourse and Post-Colonial Theory: A Reader,* edited by Patrick Williams and Laura Chrisman, 392–403. New York: Columbia University Press.

——. 1986. "The Problem of Ideology: Marxism Without Guarantees." In *Stuart Hall: Critical Dialogues in Cultural Studies,* edited by David Morley and Kuan-Hsing Chen, 25–46. London: Routledge, 1996.

Handley, George B. 2000. *Postslavery Literatures in the Americas: Family Portraits in Black and White.* Charlottesville: University Press of Virginia.

Hartman, Saidiya V. 1997. *Scenes of Subjection: Terror, Slavery and Self-Making in Nineteenth-Century America.* New York: Oxford University Press.

Hayward, Jennifer. 1991. "Something to Serve: Constructs of the Feminine in Charles Johnson's *Oxherding Tale.*" *Black American Literature Forum* 25.4:689–703.

Hegel, G. W. F. *Phenomenology of Spirit.* Translated by A. V. Miller. Oxford: Oxford University Press, 1977.

Henderson, Mae G. 1991. "Toni Morrison's *Beloved:* Re-Membering the Body as Historical Text." In *Comparative American Identities: Race, Sex, and Nationality in the Modern Text,* edited by Hortense J. Spillers, 62–86. New York: Routledge.

Henry, Paget. 2000. *Caliban's Reason: Introducing Afro-Caribbean Philosophy.* New York: Routledge.

Herman, Judith Lewis, with Lisa Hirschman. 1981. *Father-Daughter Incest.* Cambridge: Harvard University Press.

Herron, Carolivia. 1991. *Thereafter Johnnie.* New York: Random House.

Hill, Errol. 1972. *The Trinidad Carnival: Mandate for a National Theatre.* Austin: University of Texas Press.

Hirsch, Marianne. 1997. *Family Frames: Photography, Narrative, and Postmemory.* Cambridge: Harvard University Press.

———. 1999. "Projected Memory: Holocaust Photographs in Personal and Public Fantasy." In *Acts of Memory: Cultural Recall in the Present,* edited by Mieke Bal, Jonathan Crewe, and Leo Spitzer, 3–23. Hanover, N.H.: University Press of New England.

Hobbes, Thomas. 1651. *Leviathan.* Edited by Richard E. Flathman and David Johnston. New York: W. W. Norton, 1997.

Ihde, Don. 1986. *Experimental Phenomenology: An Introduction.* Albany: State University of New York Press.

Jacobs, Harriet A. 1861. *Incidents in the Life of a Slave Girl, Written By Herself.* Cambridge: Harvard University Press, 1987.

James, C. L. R. 1938. *The Black Jacobins: Toussaint L'Ouverture and the San Domingo Revolution.* New York: Vintage–Random House, 1989.

Jameson, Fredric. 1991. *Postmodernism, or, The Cultural Logic of Late Capitalism.* Durham, N.C.: Duke University Press, 1995.

———. 1986. "Third-World Literature in the Era of Multinational Capitalism." *Social Text* 15:65–88.

Johnson, Charles. 1988. *Being and Race: Black Writing Since 1970.* Bloomington: Indiana University Press.

———. 1998. *Dreamer.* New York: Scribner-Simon & Schuster, 1999.

———. 1974. *Faith and the Good Thing.* New York: Viking Press.

———. 1990. *Middle Passage.* New York: Plume-Penguin, 1991.

———. 1982. *Oxherding Tale.* New York: Grove Press, 1984.

———. 1975–76, 1993. "A Phenomenology of the Black Body." In *I Call Myself an Artist: Writings by and about Charles Johnson,* edited by Rudolph Byrd, 109–22. Bloomington: Indiana University Press, 1999.

———. 1994. *The Sorcerer's Apprentice: Tales and Conjurations.* New York: Plume-Penguin.

Johnson, James Weldon. 1927. *The Autobiography of an Ex-Coloured Man.* New York: Vintage-Random, 1989.

Johnson, Walter. 1999. *Soul by Soul: Life Inside the Antebellum Slave Market.* Cambridge: Harvard University Press.

Jones, Gayl. 1975. *Corregidora.* Boston: Beacon Press, 1986.

——. 1998. *The Healing.* Boston: Beacon Press.

——. 1999. *Mosquito.* Boston: Beacon Press.

Jones, LeRoi. 1963. *Blues People: Negro Music in White America.* New York: Morrow-Quill.

Keil, Charles. 1966. *Urban Blues.* Chicago: University of Chicago Press.

Kincaid, Jamaica. 1988. *A Small Place.* New York: Plume-Penguin, 1989.

King, Bruce. 2000. *Derek Walcott: A Caribbean Life.* New York: Oxford University Press.

——. 1995. *Derek Walcott and West Indian Drama.* Oxford: Clarendon Press.

Knight, Franklin W. 1978. *The Caribbean: The Genesis of a Fragmented Nationalism.* New York: Oxford University Press, 1990.

Kutzinski, Vera. 1999. "Johnson Revises Johnson: *Oxherding Tale* and *The Autobiography of an Ex-Coloured Man.*" In *I Call Myself an Artist: Writings by and about Charles Johnson,* edited by Rudolph Byrd, 279–87. Bloomington: Indiana University Press.

Lamming, George. 1970. *In the Castle of My Skin.* New York: Schocken Books, 1983.

——. 1960. *The Pleasures of Exile.* Ann Arbor: University of Michigan Press, 1992.

Levecq, Christine. 1994. "'We House and We Land': History and Radical Politics in Paule Marshall's *The Chosen Place, The Timeless People.*" In *Liminal Postmodernisms: The Postmodern, the (Post-)Colonial, and the (Post-) Feminist,* edited by Theo D'haen and Hans Bertens, 161–87. Amsterdam: Rodopi.

Levine, Lawrence. 1977. *Black Culture and Black Consciousness: Afro-American Folk Thought from Slavery to Freedom.* New York: Oxford University Press.

Lipsitz, George. 1998. *The Possessive Investment in Whiteness: How White People Profit From Identity Politics.* Philadelphia: Temple University Press.

Little, Jonathan. 1997. *Charles Johnson's Spiritual Imagination.* Columbia: University of Missouri Press.

Lowe, Lisa. 1994. "Unfaithful to the Original: The Subject of *Dictée.*" In *Writing Self, Writing Nation: A Collection of Essays on Dictée by Theresa Hak Kyung Cha,* edited by Elaine H. Kim and Norma Alarcón, 35–69. Berkeley: Third Woman Press.

Mandel, Ernest. 1972. *Late Capitalism.* Translated by Joris De Bres. London: NLB, 1975.

Marshall, Paule. 1969. *The Chosen Place, the Timeless People.* New York: Vintage-Random, 1992.

——. 1983. *Praisesong for the Widow.* New York: Plume-Penguin.

——. 1995. "'Re-creating Ourselves All Over the World.' A Conversation with Paule Marshall." By 'Molara Ogundipe-Leslie. In *Moving Beyond Boundaries: Volume 2—Black Women's Diasporas,* edited by Carole Boyce Davies, 19–26. London: Pluto Press.

Marx, Karl. "The Communist Manifesto." *The Marx-Engels Reader,* edited by Robert C. Tucker, 331–62. New York: W. W. Norton, 1972.

Massey, Doreen. 1994. *Space, Place, and Gender.* Minneapolis: University of Minnesota Press.

Masson, Jeffrey Moussaieff. 1984. *The Assault on Truth: Freud's Suppression of the Seduction Theory.* New York: Penguin, 1985.

Mbiti, John S. 1970. *African Religions and Philosophy.* New York: Anchor-Doubleday.

McDowell, Deborah E., and Arnold Rampersad, eds. 1989. *Slavery and the Literary Imagination.* Baltimore: Johns Hopkins University Press.

Miller, Errol. 1989. "Educational Development in Independent Jamaica." In *Jamaica in Independence,* edited by Rex Nettleford, 205–28. Kingston: Heinemann.

Mitchell, Angelyn. 2002. *The Freedom to Remember: Narrative, Slavery, and Gender in Contemporary Black Women's Fiction.* New Brunswick: Rutgers University Press.

Mohanty, Satya P. 1997. *Literary Theory and the Claims of History: Postmodernism, Objectivity, Multicultural Politics.* Ithaca: Cornell University Press.

Morrison, Toni. 1987. *Beloved.* New York: Knopf.

——. 1970. *The Bluest Eye.* New York: Plume–Penguin, 1994.

——. 1988. "In the Realm of Responsibility: A Conversation with Toni Morrison." In *Conversations with Toni Morrison,* edited by Danille Taylor-Guthrie, 246–54. Jackson: University Press of Mississippi, 1994.

——. 1993. "Living Memory: A Meeting with Toni Morrison." In *Small Acts: Thoughts on the Politics of Black Cultures,* by Paul Gilroy, 175–82. London: Serpent's Tail.

——. 1992. *Playing in the Dark: Whiteness and the Literary Imagination.* New York: Vintage-Random.

——. 1990. "The Site of Memory." In *Out There: Marginalization and Contemporary Cultures,* edited by Russell Ferguson, Martha Gever, Trinh T. Minh-ha, and Cornel West, 299–305. New York: New Museum of Contemporary Art, and Cambridge: MIT Press.

——. 1977. *Song of Solomon.* New York: Plume, 1987.

Moyers, Bill. 1994. "Poet Laureate Rita Dove." Video interview. Princeton: Films for the Humanities.

Mullin, Michael. 1992. *Africa in America: Slave Acculturation and Resistance in the American South and the British Caribbean, 1736–1831.* Urbana: University of Illinois Press.

Muther, Elizabeth. 1996. "Isadora at Sea: Misogyny as Comic Capital in Charles Johnson's *Middle Passage.*" *African American Review* 30.4:649–58.

Nixon, Rob. 1987. "Caribbean and African Appropriations of *The Tempest.*" *Critical Inquiry* 13:557–78.

Olaniyan, Tejumola. 1993. "Corporeal/Discursive Bodies and the Subject: *Dream on Monkey Mountain* and the Poetics of Identity." In *Imagination, Emblems and Expressions: Essays on Latin American, Caribbean, and Continental Culture and Identity,* edited by Helen Ryan-Ranson, 155–72. Bowling Green, Ohio: Bowling Green State University Popular Press.

——. 1995. *Scars of Conquest/Masks of Resistance: The Invention of Cultural Identities in African, African-American, and Caribbean Drama.* New York: Oxford University Press.

Painter, Nell Irvin. 1995. "Soul Murder and Slavery: Toward a Fully Loaded Cost Accounting." In *U.S. History as Women's History: New Feminist Essays,* edited by Linda K. Kerber, Alice Kessler-Harris, and Kathryn Kish Sklar, 125–46. Chapel Hill: University of North Carolina Press.

Patterson, Orlando. 1982. *Slavery and Social Death: A Comparative Study.* Cambridge: Harvard University Press.

——. 1967. *The Sociology of Slavery: An Analysis of the Origins, Development and Structure of Negro Slave Society in Jamaica.* Rutherford, N.J.: Fairleigh Dickinson University Press, 1975.

Patton, Venetria K. 2000. *Women in Chains: The Legacy of Slavery in Black Women's Fiction.* Albany: State University of New York Press.

Phillips, Caryl. 1991. *Cambridge.* New York: Vintage-Random House, 1993.

Plato. *Symposium.* Translated by Robin Waterfield. Oxford: Oxford University Press, 1994.

——. "Timaeus." Translated by Benjamin Jowett. In *The Collected Dialogues of Plato,* edited by Edith Hamilton and Huntington Cairns, 1151–211. Princeton: Princeton University Press, 1982.

Poynting, Jeremy. 1996. "From Ancestral to Creole: Humans and Animals in a West Indian Scale of Values." In *Monsters, Tricksters, and Sacred Cows: Animal Tales and American Identities,* edited by A. James Arnold, 204–29. Charlottesville: University Press of Virginia.

Price, Richard, ed. 1979. *Maroon Societies: Rebel Slave Communities in the Americas.* Baltimore: Johns Hopkins University Press.

Randall, Alice. 2001. *The Wind Done Gone.* Boston: Houghton Mifflin.

Retman, Sonnet. "'Nothing was Lost in the Masquerade': The Protean Performance of Genre and Identity in Charles Johnson's *Oxherding Tale.*" *African American Review* 33.3:417–37.

Richards, Sandra. 1995. "Writing the Absent Potential: Drama, Performance, and the Canon of African-American Literature." In *Performativity and Performance,* edited by Andrew Parker and Eve Kosofsky Sedgwick. New York: Routledge.

Riggs, Marlon. 1986. "Ethnic Notions: Black People in White Minds." San Francisco: California Newsreel. Produced in association with KQED.

Rose, Gillian. 1993. *Feminism and Geography: The Limits of Geographical Knowledge.* Minneapolis: University of Minnesota Press.

Rushdy, Ashraf H. A. 1999. *Neo-Slave Narratives: Studies in the Social Logic of a Literary Form.* New York: Oxford University Press.

——. 2001. *Remembering Generations.* Chapel Hill: University of North Carolina Press.

Ryan, Michael. 1995. *Secret Life: An Autobiography.* New York: Pantheon.

Scarry, Elaine. 1985. *The Body in Pain: The Making and Unmaking of the World.* New York: Oxford University Press.

Scott, Dennis. 1985. *An Echo in the Bone.* In *Plays for Today,* edited by Errol Hill, 73–137. Kingston: Longman.

Scott, Pamela, and Antoinette J. Lee. 1993. *Buildings of the District of Columbia.* New York: Oxford University Press.

Shakespeare, William. 1623. *The Tempest,* edited by Stephen Orgel. New York: Clarendon-Oxford University Press, 1987.

Smith, Paul. 1988. *Discerning the Subject.* Minneapolis: University of Minnesota Press.

Smith, Valerie. 1993. "'Circling the Subject': History and Narrative in *Beloved.*" In

Toni Morrison: Critical Perspectives Past and Present, edited by Henry Louis Gates Jr., and K. A. Appiah, 342–55. New York: Amistad.

———. 1987. *Self-Discovery and Authority in Afro-American Narrative.* Cambridge: Harvard University Press.

Spillers, Hortense J. 1993. "Black, White, and in Color, or Learning How to Paint: Toward an Intramural Protocol of Reading." In *New Historical Literary Study: Essays on Reproducing Texts, Representing History,* edited by Jeffrey N. Cox and Larry J. Reynolds, 267–91. Princeton: Princeton University Press.

———. 1985. *"Chosen Place, Timeless People:* Some Figurations on the New World." In *Conjuring: Black Women, Fiction, and Literary Tradition,* edited by Marjorie Pryse and Hortense J. Spillers, 151–75. Bloomington: Indiana University Press.

———. 1987. "Mama's Baby, Papa's Maybe: An American Grammar Book." *Diacritics* 17.2:65–81.

———. 1989. "'The Permanent Obliquity of an In(pha)llibly Straight': In the Time of the Daughters and the Fathers." In *Changing Our Own Words: Essays on Criticism, Theory, and Writing by Black Women,* edited by Cheryl A. Wall, 127–49. New Brunswick, N.J.: Rutgers University Press.

Styron, William. 1966. *The Confessions of Nat Turner.* New York: Random House, 1967.

Taylor, Patrick. 1989. *The Narrative of Liberation: Perspectives on Afro-Caribbean Literature, Popular Culture, and Politics.* Ithaca, N.Y.: Cornell University Press.

Taylor-Guthrie, Danille, ed. 1994. *Conversations with Toni Morrison.* Jackson: University Press of Mississippi.

Thomas, Valorie. 1994. "Keys to the Ancestors' Chambers: An Approach to Teaching *Beloved.*" *Reading Between the Black and White Keys: Deep Crossings in African Diaspora Studies. Proceedings of the St. Clair Drake Graduate Cultural Studies Forum,* edited by VèVè Clark, 81–102. Berkeley: University of California Department of African American Studies.

Thompson, Robert Farris. 1983. *Flash of the Spirit: African and Afro-American Art and Philosophy.* New York: Random House.

Walcott, Derek. 1996. "Animals, Elemental Tales, and the Theater." In *Monsters, Tricksters, and Sacred Cows: Animal Tales and American Identities,* edited by A. James Arnold, 269–77. Charlottesville: University Press of Virginia.

———. 1986. *Collected Poems, 1948–1984.* New York: Noonday–Farrar, Straus and Giroux.

———. 1970. "Dream on Monkey Mountain." In *Dream on Monkey Mountain and Other Plays,* 207–326. New York: Noonday Press.

———. 1993. "The Figure of Crusoe." In *Critical Perspectives on Derek Walcott,* edited by Robert D. Hamner, 33–40. Washington, D.C.: Three Continents Press.

———. 1971. "Man of the Theatre." In *Conversations with Derek Walcott,* edited by William Baer, 17–20. Jackson: University Press of Mississippi, 1996.

———. 1977. "Reflections Before and After Carnival: An Interview with Derek Walcott." In *Conversations with Derek Walcott,* edited by William Baer, 34–49. Jackson: University Press of Mississippi, 1996.

Walker, David. 1829. *David Walker's Appeal, In Four Articles; Together with a Preamble, to the Coloured Citizens of the World, But in Particular, and very Expressly, to those of the United States of America.* New York: Hill and Wang, 1996.

Walker, Margaret. 1966. *Jubilee*. New York: Bantam Books. 1967.

———. 1972. *How I Wrote Jubilee*. Chicago: Third World Press.

Williams, Eric. 1944. *Capitalism and Slavery*. Chapel Hill: University of North Carolina Press, 1994.

Williams, Patricia J. 1991. *The Alchemy of Race and Rights*. Cambridge: Harvard University Press.

Williams, Sherley Anne. 1986. *Dessa Rose*. New York: Quill–William Morrow, 1999.

Wilson, Olly W. 1985. "The Association of Movement and Music as a Manifestation of a Black Conceptual Approach to Music Making." In *More Than Dancing: Essays on Afro-American Music and Musicians,* edited by Irene V. Jackson, 9–24. Westport, Conn.: Greenwood Press.

———. 1974. "The Significance of the Relationship Between Afro-American and West African Music." *The Black Perspective in Music* 2.1:3–22.

Wynter, Sylvia. 1990. "Beyond Miranda's Meanings: Un/silencing the 'Demonic Ground' of Caliban's 'Woman'." In *Out of the Kumbla: Caribbean Women and Literature,* edited by Carole Boyce Davies and Elaine Savory Fido, 355–72. Trenton, N.J.: Africa World Press.

INDEX

ABOUT THE AUTHOR

Arlene R. Keizer is Associate Professor of English and African American Studies at the University of Michigan, Ann Arbor.